Globalization, Communication and Transnational Civil Society

INTERNATIONAL ASSOCIATION FOR MASS COMMUNICATION RESEARCH

This series consists of books arising from the intellectual work of IAMCR sections, working groups, and committees. Books address themes relevant to IAMCR interests; make a major contribution to the theory, research, practice and/or policy literature; are international in scope; and represent a diversity of perspectives. Book proposals are submitted through formally constituted IAMCR sections, working groups, and committees.

Globalization, Communication and Transnational Civil Society

edited by
Sandra Braman
University of Illinois-Champaign
Annabelle Sreberny-Mohammadi
University of Leicester

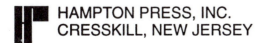
HAMPTON PRESS, INC.
CRESSKILL, NEW JERSEY

Printed in the United States of America

Library of Congress Cataloging-in-Publication Data

Globalization, communication, and transnational civil society / edited by
   Sandra Braman, Annabelle Sreberny-Mohammadi.
      p. cm. -- (IAMCR book series)
   Includes bibliographical references and index.
   ISBN 1-57273-020-X. -- ISBN 1-57273-021-8 (pbk.)
   1. Communication, international. 2. Communication and culture.
I. Braman, Sandra. II. Sreberny-Mohammadi, Annabelle. III. Series.
P96.I5G57   1996
302.23--dc20   96-22694
                                                         CIP

Hampton Press, Inc.
23 Broadway
Cresskill, NJ 07626

Contents

AUG 2 8 1996

Series Preface

The International Association for Mass Communication Research (IAMCR) launched in early 1994 a new book series. The series intends to make the distinctive and innovative approaches of the IAMCR in communication theory and research methodology more widely available to the general field of communication. It aims to identify new theoretical approaches and to develop the series as a forum for defining and debating these approaches. The series will enable the Sections of the IAMCR to plan collaborative research projects of high quality. It also provides a forum for publication of research by scholars now emerging in parts of the world where there is not a very strong academic publication base in communication. Through this a wider range of thought is made accessible to the international community of communication scholars. The new series should give the IAMCR a more visible public profile and will expand its academic activities beyond the annual scientific conferences.

The international context of the IAMCR creates special opportunities for the series. Established in 1957, the IAMCR has grown into an organization with more than 2,000 members in 70 countries. It entertains close liaisons with a number of intergovernmental organizations such as Unesco, the World Intellectual Property Organization (WIPO), and the Council of Europe. Associate Members of the IAMCR include the major regional organizations in the field of communication research and such professional bodies as the International Federation of Journalists.

Much of the Association's intellectual work is conducted by its twelve sections. These cover the areas of Documentation and Information Systems, History, Law, Sociology and Social Psychology, Political Communication, International Communication, Political Economy, Communication Technology Policy, Gender and

Communication, Local Radio and TV, Media Education, and Professional Education. IAMCR also contributes to conferences, seminars and hearings held by other international organizations through research reports and position papers.

The present series has a long history and a special context. It originated in many years of discussions about the type of publications activity the IAMCR should engage in. The IAMCR is the largest international organization in the field of communication research and from its early history in the 1950s there have been initiatives for a variety of publications. In the 1960s the Association was involved with the publication of the periodical *Gazette* and issued a "Bulletin" and a "Letter from the President." When *Gazette* and the IAMCR parted ways, the Bulletin and Presidential Letter continued and the latter was for a long time the IAMCR's main regular forum of exchange. At various occasions in the past years the proceedings of the scientific conferences were published as monographs. In the 1970s the discussion about an academic journal edited by the IAMCR was reactivated but for a variety of reasons it was decided in 1974 that the IAMCR would not undertake the publication of its own journal. In 1986 it was decided to explore the feasibility of a series of occasional papers in which work by IAMCR members was published. In 1989 one of the IAMCR governing bodies (the International Council) appointed a Publications Committee that was to investigate possibilities with regard to journals, occasional papers, newsletters and books. The Committee was mandated to begin the publication of a regular Newsletter.

One of the items on my presidential agenda between 1990 and 1994 was to get the book series going. Thanks to the committee members, and in particular to Brenda Dervin and Robert White, this worked.

The first two books of the series originated from the IAMCR conference that was held in Dublin, Ireland, in 1993. The editors of the present volume, Sandra Braman and Annabelle Sreberny-Mohammadi, deserve special credit for their outstanding editorial work and the effort to put together a remarkable book that reflects the scope and academic quality of work done by members of the IAMCR.

Given the precarious state of academic budgets both individually and institutionally and the large volumes of publications in our field, one may question and wisdom of our endeavor. My main motive to wholeheartedly support it is the conviction that the IAMCR represents a unique blend of research resources and experiences. I am confident that the series can mobilize unique talents in the field of communication research and thus make a difference worth a place on bookshelves around the world.

Cees J. Hamelink
President, IAMCR, 1990-1994
Amsterdam, March 1994

Globalization, Communication and Transnational Civil Society: Introduction

Annabelle Sreberny-Mohammadi
University of Leicester

The terminology of the "global" and globalization" quickly became the new buzzwords of the 1990s. Advertising campaigns promoted telecommunications and banking as global companies providing global services; but now haircare products also include global ingredients, new cuisine smells of global spices, and clothing reflects global colors. Social theory has also awoken to the theoretical challenges posed by the real-world dynamics of globalization, although there is little agreement within the mass of new literature on the topic as to the precise antecedents, impact or scope of the process; indeed, if it is one process or many. Yet there is widespread recognition of the considerable role played by communications structures and information networks in establishing the new global environment. This volume is one of the first to take that focus as its central concern and to examine the part that media and cultural products play within a globalized environment.

Many of the concerns and issues around globalization have been current in the fields of international communication and communication and development for a very long time. A considerable body of work over the past 25 years has focused on the increasingly transnation-

1

al spread of the media and taken up issues related to that spread; issues around the diffusion of technologies and their impact; issues relating to the flows of cultural products, from news to television entertainment to electronic data; and issues of impact, on economic and political development processes, on social attitudes and cultural practices, and on audience habits and tastes.

The International Association for Mass Communication Research (IAMCR) is the major international association for scholars and researchers in the field of mass communication. Recognized for many years as an NGO affiliated with UNESCO, that branch of the United Nations system that deals with cultural and communications issues, IAMCR has fostered research and policy-oriented discussions about the international flows and effects of media technologies, institutions, and products over the past three decades. It played a particularly significant role in promoting the New World Information and Communication Order (NWICO) debate and academic research around NWICO-related issues in the late 1970s-1980s, and continues to be at the forefront in facilitating critical debate and promoting comparative research in many aspects of international communication.

It is thus fitting that this early volume in the series emanating from such an international organization should be a volume on globalization and the media. While for some there is an element of dejá vu when concerns about the nature and impact of international communications are put forward as new; but at the very least we should be pleased that the media and communications-related issues have finally been allotted a more central place in contemporary social theory and analysis.

The challenge of globalization is two-fold: first is the need to recognize and understand the real changes in the world, especially but not solely the implications of global media diffusion; the second is to develop adequate theoretical tools to conceptualize the dynamics of globalization. Simply put, globalization implies both actual changes in the real world as well as a new theoretical conception of that world. This volume tries in varied ways to look at both these dimensions and their interconnection, with a particular focus on dimensions of media and cultural policy. What new theoretical questions and empirical challenges do the debates around globalization bring to the study of the media? Whose discourse does it represent, what are its vantage points, what does it allow to be spoken, and what does it silence?

CONTENTS OF THIS VOLUME

This volume is mainly drawn from papers presented at the IAMCR conference in Dublin in July, 1993.[1] The book is divided into two sections: the first contains broadly conceptual pieces, while the second section contains a variety of pertinent case studies. Instead of introducing each chapter in order, I have chosen to set out some of the major lines of contemporary theorizing on globalization and to locate the book's chapters within those debates.

THEORIZING GLOBALIZATION:
A MOVEMENT ACROSS THE DISCIPLINES

The terms of the theories, and thus the debates in international communication, have shifted considerably over the post-World War II period. In the early 1960s, the rhetoric of modernization and development dominated much research work and was adopted by UNESCO in its policy recommendations for developing nations, particularly in the area of communications and development. Later, the paradigms of media and cultural imperialism, linked to broader critiques of Third World development such as dependency theory, tended to dominate the critical research agendas of the 1970s-1980s, challenging the modernization paradigm. The emergent struggle around and demands for a New International Economic Order and a New World Information and Communication Order (NWICO) were articulated in innumerable meetings of UNESCO, the Non-Aligned Movement, and other international fora. These led to the withdrawal in 1984-1985 of the United States, the United Kingdom, and Singapore from UNESCO, which they have still not rejoined, despite the increased use since 1989 of other elements of the UN system as key supports for a very different New World Order.

    The discourses of globalization, growing out of broad social and political theory, yet often recognizing the key global roles of communications technologies and mediated culture (Giddens, 1990; Harvey, 1989), indicate yet another phase of orientation. Globalization is one of those awkward adverbial nouns that have proliferated in English, signifying process. Globalization "suggests that political, economic and social activity is *becoming* worldwide in scope" (Held, 1991, p. 203; emphasis added). Thus, to some extent the critique that globalization is not total,

---

[1]The paper by Paula Saukko was delivered to the seminar on communication systems, Institute of Communications Research, University of Illinois, Champaign, December 1993.

that not everything, everyone, or indeed every nation is caught up in its dynamics, essentially misses the conceptual point—that central tendencies of modern societies have a pronounced global reach.

There is an infelicity in the English terms we can use: *global* refers to the globe, itself a form of representation; *earth* seems too naturalized, decultured. *World* seems to conjure up the possibility of other worlds (Robertson, 1992) and also suggests a too simple singularity, whereas *the global* almost always conjures up issues of the level of analysis, including its polar term, *the local*. The conceptual confusion reflects a lack of agreement as well as the limits of our visualizations: Is the global the perimeter, or the outside skin of the world, the container of difference, all surface? Or is it three-dimensional, not so much power geometry (Massey, 1991) as power geology, with many different levels of interaction and identification?

Although many earlier social scientific theories have posited various kinds of global linkages, these have been in the main single-factor models based on traditional academic disciplines. Classic international relations theory has typically worked with a conceptual framework centered on a political system of sovereign nation-states and concerned itself predominantly with interstate relations. Such a model is challenged by the rise of supranational organizations like NATO, the European Community (EC), and the World Bank; by the dynamics of multilateral diplomacy; by the growth of international law and its mechanisms of adjudication; by the rise of new social movements that transcend national boundaries; by the proliferation of nongovernmental organizations that operate at a transnational level, often involving participants from many countries; and by varied global economic and cultural influences that impact on the political system (Held, 1991). The very notion of geopolitical sovereignty clearly demarcated by territory is threatened, and the internal/external boundary of the state has become blurred (Dalby, 1994; McGrew, 1992; Walker, 1993). International relations theorizing, and political theory more generally, is trying to cope with possible new world orders and new political actors, moving from an older model of international society to a newer model of global society that is less state-centric and recognizes the complexity of new actors and issues (Falk, 1987; Lipschutz, 1992; Peterson, 1992).

Models of political economy, such as dependency theory and world systems theory (Wallerstein, 1974), usefully examined the globalization of capitalism, the rise of transnational corporations, and the related global division of labor and global movements of capital. Yet, they seemed to suffer a kind of sclerosis as global dynamics proffered intercapitalist rivalries, too many cores, and unclear peripheries for these models to operate coherently. Also, whereas political economy theories drew together two major skeins of interaction, the dynamics of "cultural

interaction" were bracketed, a lacuna Wallerstein (1991, 1992) has recognized and tried to rectify in his recent work (see also King, 1991),
although it could be argued that his model is still fundamentally an econ-
omistic base-superstructure model in which culture is a mere by-product
of the capitalistic world economy.

GLOBAL MONEY, MEDIA, AND MOVEMENTS

Much of the original locus of images and discourses of globalization
came from capitalistic marketing strategies, based on the transnationalization of capital. The political economy of global media usefully maps
the process of conglomeratization of giants such as Time-Warner and
Reuters, the rise of the new mogul empires such as Finivest and News
International, Matsushita, and Sony, and the corporate strategies of
global cultural production. Yet, it is also clear that some of the most
interesting questions center not on the facts of these global production
and marketing strategies, but on their meaning and effects.

Such concerns are now debated by anthropologists, among others, with opposing positions emerging. Hannerz makes culture the central focus of analysis, arguing that

> cultural interconnections increasingly reach across the world. More
> then ever, there is a global ecumene. The entities we routinely call
> cultures are becoming more like subcultures within this wider entity,
> with all that this suggests in terms of fuzzy boundaries and more or
> less arbitrary delimitation of analytical units. (1992, p. 218)

Hannerz argues that understanding of this fact of globalization is now the
central task of a "macroanthropology of culture" (p. 218). Yet to talk of
increased interaction is not the same as showing similarity of meaning, a
basic assumption of a culture, and Hannerz seems to lose sight of the
evident localization and reclaiming of specific identity formations at the
present time. Appadurai's analysis (1990) tends toward chaos and disjuncture, while Hannerz looks toward a singular, perhaps homogenous,
global culture. Friedman (1994) tries to develop a model that acknowl-
edges both tendencies are occurring in the global arena: "first, a localization of the global system and the consequent multiplication of local projects and localizing strategies; and secondly, a simultaneous globalization
of political institutions, class associations and common media of representation" (p. 211). In this volume, Braman (Chapter 1) also takes up the
task of exploring "interpenetrated globalization" in which the global and
the local are mutually constitutive and indeed are only thinkable together.

GLOBALIZATION THEORY AS MULTIDIMENSIONAL

The new challenge, most compelling after 1989 and the new world disorder, is how to conceptualize the multifaceted interacting global dimensions of change. The need for interdisciplinary or, at the very least, multidimensional analysis is apparent, and the voluminous literature on globalization over the past decade is evidence of both the need and the difficulty of satisfying that need.

Giddens (1990) connects global processes to modernity, arguing that "modernity is inherently globalizing" (p. 63). He presents four key elements of modernity, each of which has a globalizing thrust: the rise of the nation-state system, the emergence of military blocs, the development of capitalistic world markets, and the rise of global infrastructures of communications. This model is an advance on earlier conceptualizations because of its multidimensional analysis; but it tends to omit analysis of the impacts of these dimensions on each other. There is no single, clear carrier of modernity, but a sort of additive process, a skein of interacting elements, none of which is privileged, but which together constitute the barely controllable "juggernaut of modernity" (p. 139). It is pertinent to note, however, that Luhmann suggests an antithetical proposition: that modernity is not inherently globalizing but rather a tendency developed merely as a result of weak obstacles to its growth (Beyer, 1994). In these emergent global conditions, Giddens (1990) argues, like Harvey (1989), that social relations are stretched in new forms of time-space distantiation. These create a complex interplay between "local involvements (circumstances of co-presence) and interaction across distance (the connection of presence and absence)" (p. 64). Thus, Giddens defines *globalization* as "the intensification of worldwide social relations which link distant localities in such a way that local happenings are shaped by events occurring many miles away and vice versa" (p. 64). Posing a dialectic of interaction between the global and the local or the intersection of presence and absence as the hallmarks of globalization are ways of avoiding the construction of globalization as yet another evolutionary and teleological narrative. Such a dialectic is perhaps most clearly evident in global media dynamics, bringing events in once remote places into our homes and thus making them in some ways familiar. Thus, whereas the dynamic elements of this model of globalization originate in the industrialized world, there is no simple one-way diffusion out from the West to the rest, but multiple, complex sets of interactions (albeit Giddens leaves the empirical examples for others to flesh out).

Older models of modernization (Inkeles, 1974; Lerner, 1958) also stressed the psychosocial impacts of the diffusion of "modern ways of life" from the West, offering a significant focus on the microlevel practices of modernity that would repay reinvestigation into their resonances with current concerns, albeit these were couched in a simple, triumphalist vision of the diffusion of Western values and ways of life. They offered few tools for theorizing the resistances and the dynamics of retraditionalization that the encounter with the West often provoked, nor could they account for the development of antimodernist tendencies inside the West. Both tendencies are most vivid globally in the current appeal of various religious fundamentalisms at odds with Western popular culture (Ahmed & Donnan, 1994).

Appadurai (1990) also offers a multidimensional model of the emerging global cultural ecumene. Using the metaphor of a landscape, a usefully blurred, imprecise, but evocative image, Appadurai traces out five fluid "scapes" of global interaction: (a) the ethnoscape of mobile populations, including refugees and diaspora communities, migrant workers, students, and business people; (b) the technoscape of diffusion and adoption of mechanical and informational technologies; (c) the financescape of global capital; (d) the mediascape, which includes not only the global spread of media channels, but the images these carry; and (e) the ideoscape of political discourses such as democracy and rights. For Appadurai, no single scape is privileged over the others, and their interactions create disjunctures and differences. The visual imagery conjures up geological platelets bumping and grinding into each other; even if stacked vertically, the lowest is not the most fundamental in determining the shape of the others. Waterman (1993), in a similar conception, proffers the image of global interactions as a set of overhead transparencies, each of which can be moved to create new densities and qualities of color. Appadurai describes the key problem of today's global interactions as the tensions and disjunctures between cultural homogenization and cultural heterogenization, echoing the still ongoing debate in international communications between the media imperialism/cultural imperialism perspectives on the one hand (Hamelink, 1994; Schiller, 1991) and what might be called a global cultural studies orientation on the other (Lull, 1991; Morley, 1992).

Robertson (1990) also proffers a multidimensional process of globalization developing over the past century based on a general acceptance of the nation-state structure; the increase in international organizations and agencies, including the UN system and its NGO network; the spread of media technologies; the standardization of world time; the growth of global competitions and prizes; and the increasing acceptance of shared notions of citizenship, rights, and concepts of humanity. However, Robertson's (1992) concern is more directed toward the singularity and autonomy of the process of globalization, particularly the idea of and the lived experience of the world as a "single place" (p. 60). Thus, whereas Robertson is interested in the historical processes that have compressed the world, his analytic focus centers more on the set of questions entailed in "the intensification of consciousness of the world as a whole" (p. 8), including the spread of "globe-oriented ideologies" (p. 79); in short, the cultural-political dimensions of globalization.

EXPERIENCING THE WORLD AS A SINGLE PLACE

Many theorists of globalization are concerned with mapping the world as a single system (Worsely, 1984), a single place (Robertson, 1992), or a single world society (Albrow & King, 1990) in which there are no longer any others (Giddens, 1991). What can these ideas mean? On the one hand, there is evidence of increasing popular awareness of our global connectedness and concern for the consequences of actions for others, including others far away. Real-time coverage of the big news stories of the day, broadcast by global channels such as CNN and BBC World television, do reach an audience across the world, creating a sense of a shared "now" of information flow, a sense of cohabiting the planet at the same time. There are no others in the sense that even the most "remote" of groups has been studied, documented, televised; often the distancing media discourse stresses both a time element, "backward" as well as spatial element, "over there" rather than here (Walker, 1991). Yet at the same time, the shifting global ethnoscape brings about new discourses, both of self-identification and of prejudice, and in Britain this means that "others" live next door, attend "our" schools, vote in "our" local elections. Racist discourse, tighter immigration law, "back to Christian basics" all serve to redefine and reinvent otherness. There are no others while at the same time the others are everywhere.

This constant tension of homogenization and heterogenization implies that identity formation is a key issue in globalization (Friedman, 1994). It also raises questions about the world as a "single place." Although there is evidence for the widespread acceptance of the idea of a singularity of the global, the world as a single place, it is also evident that the content of that idea is extremely varied. For example, the global networks of competing religious faiths both inhabit and envision different worlds from each other and from secular networks. They live in the world differently and would fashion it differently, making the mere fact that they all operate with "global imaginaries," have global pretensions, a rather weak similarity in the face of so much difference. The extreme case, as Featherstone has noted, is that a unified global culture is impossible because that would mean an "outside to the globe, a sphere of global threat" (1990, p. 11). Tomlinson (Chapter 3) takes up the phenomenology of globalization, the way it is actually experienced in ordinary lives.

He plays out the experiential issues of globalization alluded to by both Giddens and Robertson. In essence, most people continue to lead local lives, whereas the phenomenal worlds that we inhabit have become global. The media are key players in this development, bringing the world into our homes. Thus, global media modernity seems to undermine the sequestering of modern experience through the public representation of both public and private phenomena (Thompson, 1995).

GLOBALIZATION AND A TRANSNATIONAL CIVIL SOCIETY

Attempts to analyze the dynamics of globalization, its relation to modernity or postmodernity, its universalism or essential Westernization, often become—implicitly or explicitly—envisionings of global futures. Many authors clearly try to explore the political potentials of a project of globalization. So I now turn briefly to the other core construct of the book, the arguments around the public sphere and its apparent or possible growth into a transnational civil society (Lipschutz, 1992). The return toward political issues and concerns in the mid-1990s is quite marked in social theory in general, and in media studies in particular. The popular Third World revolutions of the late 1970s (Iran, Nicaragua, the Phillipines), the collapse of the Soviet Union and the spread of "velvet revolutions" across Eastern Europe since 1989, and the pressures for democratization in the South, have triggered important new lines of research work. Some have focused on the dynamics of political mobilization in repressive state formations and the role of the media as oppositional spaces within such structures, often indicating various forms of international communication that have played significant roles in the mobilization (e.g., Sreberny-Mohammadi & Mohammadi, 1994).

The long-awaited translation of Habermas's (1962) work on the public sphere into English in 1989 has also brought a revival of interest in the concept; the public sphere being that space of social life determined neither by market nor by the state in which the formation and reformation of public opinion through open debate is deemed possible (Calhoun, 1992; Robbins, 1993). This theorizing presses in different directions. Some ask, if the public sphere was or still is essentially bourgeois, then where is the proletarian public sphere (Hansen, 1993)? If it is male, then where is the feminist (Fraser, 1992)? If it is not singular, then can there be multiple alternate public spheres (Downing, 1988)? If it is White, what about the Black public sphere ("On thinking," 1994)? If it is no longer nationally defined, then how does an international—global—sphere emerge (Garnham, 1992)? Many ask about the nature of the contribution of the media to its maintenance (Dahlgren, 1991), yet few deal with the question of whether a global mediated public sphere can be the harbinger of political democracy. That is, in situations in which there is (as yet?) no civil society, can transnational news media, exile publishing, and the Internet really help in the creation of such a space? The over-optimistic arguments in international communications sometimes seem to suggest that mere electronic linkages herald a new millennium of global political participation. The implications of new technologies, however, raise significant public policy issues. The U.S. government, ostensibly concerned with public security and secrecy, is seeking to control encryption of information on the Net as one example of what seems to be a potential for restriction of democratic rights.

"Rights" returns us to one of the most basic concerns of political philosophy and communications: the tension between the collectivity and the individual as the original locus of rights. Venturelli (Chapter 5) appropriately asks once again what the philosophical basis is of our conceptions of rights. She uses arguments from Aristotle to Arendt to challenge the prepolitical notion of the individual that much rights discourse is based on and reasserts the primacy of the political sphere based on justice and active citizenship as the necessary foundation for the enjoyment of all other rights. It is reasonable to ask how public is the public sphere and how civil is civil society? There are many fundamental questions to be asked about the nature and shape of "publicness" in an electronic media-saturated environment. Public is often counterposed to private, a polarity in which the latter pole has been considered less socially significant in many societies, with profound implications as to gender and as to the nature of what is defined as political activity. But public also means transparency, availability, with historically the co-presence of the public being the partial guarantee of these qualities (Giddens, 1992; Thompson, 1994, 1995). Media help to structure publicness.

There is an apparent paradox that although modernity seems to increasingly sequester experience, electronic media make a wide range of issues, including the traditionally "private," the legitimate domain of public inquiry (think of the *Oprah Winfrey Show*, the *News of the World*). However, the conditions in which that information is received are predominantly "private"—in socially and spatially divided audiences—and the possibilities of response by the public have been highly circumscribed in short "points of view" presentations or radio talk shows. Thompson (1994) talks of the need for a "reinvention of publicness" (p. 425) and there are indications of new television genres of audience participation, not only (to use some current recent examples from Britain) through the questioning of experts (*Question Time*), or discussion with them (*Central Weekend Live*), but with the audience as the agonistic members themselves, as in the *People's Parliament*, a show in which 100 "ordinary" people debated some of the crucial issues of the day.

Such programming is popular (Sreberny-Mohammadi, 1994b), and could be cynically seen as pseudo-participatory circuses, merely attempts to improve ratings. But it also seems to indicate a contemporary search for new forms of mediated publicness and political debate ("Lean democracy," 1994), which may be of particular significance for women and minorities not traditionally included in older forms of publicness. In Western industrial democracies there are still considerable difficulties in gaining access to the public sphere and constructing truly participatory and authentic forms of participation.

At the same time as the apparent crisis of politics at the national level, there is a significant call to rethink civil society at the transnational level. Sakamoto (1991), in the context of an argument about the need to deepen democracy into the heart of civil society, argues that as issues such as peace, development, the environment, and human rights assume a global character, only the globalization of democracy can provide a solution. This means "the creation of a global perspective and values in the depths of people's hearts and minds, establishing the idea of a global civil society. . . . In a word, democracy can be deepened only if it is globalized; and it can be globalized only if it is deepened" (p. 122). Sakamoto's focus is mainly at the level of a growing public consciousness of globalization, tending to echo Robertson's concerns, whereas the mechanisms for transformation of national identifications and political rights into something global remain vague in the extreme. Indeed, Walker (1991) argues that, "to ask what democracy could possibly be in relation to 'the people' in general or to structures of global power is to engage with the great silences of contemporary political discourse" (p. 247).

Yet some are trying to develop these discourses. Arato (1994) suggests analysis of the articulation between local and global civil participation, noting that:

> many of the most important civil society organizations are now global in nature . . . similarly all genuine civil publics are today of an international character. . . . We need to study the relationships of global associations and publics to local societies and cultures as well as to both national states and international governmental organizations. (p. 45)

Hamelink (1994) has usefully elaborated the common category of international nongovernmental organizations (INGOs) into professional and public interest groupings (PINGOs), business interest groupings (BINGOs), and intergovernmental organizations, IGOs, that constitute the range of internationally oriented but nonstate actors and their influence on the politics of world communication. Held (1991) suggests a federated structure of democratic states and civil societies and a new international democratic assembly to replace the old UN state-controlled structure. Garnham (1992) forcefully suggests that the only possible response to global market forces is an equally strong political response and a media system to match, a universal public sphere in which common interests can be recognized and acted on. All acknowledge that these remain incomplete projects, far from actuality. The new imagining of such possibilities is a necessary part of the prefiguring that might lead toward their development; hence, the considerable attention to normative theory across the social sciences.

There is a growing political and ethical groundswell supportive of the idea of global citizenship, as in the contributions to the volume appropriately entitled *Global Visions* (Brecher, 1993) and a growing body of literature that focuses on the political possibilities of or in globalization: of extrastate politics, movements of international solidarity, or the growth in popular participation, alternative media, and grassroots democracy. Waterman's (Chapter 2) contribution in this volume is centrally located in the new multidimensional theorizing about globalization and new social movements, adding yet more elements—including the growth of an international feminist movement and ecological activism—to the previously mentioned models. He appropriately reminds us that there have been other, historical, constructions of internationalism, including labor internationalism, often based on the rigidities and lacunae of the "nationalist" project. He proposes that globalization is not only a useful analytic construct, but is becoming an active political theory with its own project of global solidarity, an argument that is implicit in other contributions. Waterman both elaborates the concrete manifestations of some strands of global political solidarity and shows how contemporary media can be effectively used to build popular social movements.

The Internet, with its guestimated 60 million users, is as of yet the largest public global conversation (*Guardian*, February 25, 1995). Topics include the prurient and the political, the religious and the racist, an open space for progressive groups and nondemocratic ideas alike. These forms of computer-mediated communication may support new forms of publicness, with their ecumenism of access once in the system with the public posting of information and in the public nature of the dialogue in which one can listen as well as speak. Both identity politics, the gay and lesbian movements, for example, and issue politics, like environmentalism, use the Net as well as a variety of older media forms and social spaces to articulate their concerns and to indicate the possibilities for emergent global solidarities and competing global publics and public fora. Again, it remains unclear whether our dialogical entanglements in the Net can lead to the adoption of new ideas and identities or persuade us to somatic involvement in political action in specific locales.

Tomlinson (Chapter 3) remains appropriately skeptical about the reality of a "global public sphere," wondering what collective memories can sustain it and what political structures can facilitate it. Yet, the discussions on the restructuring of the UN with a new pattern of national representation and perhaps a military force of its own; the emergence of a whole layer of international organizations making global policy on a huge range of issues; the growth in international legal conventions on the acceptance of human rights concerns; membership in international organizations such as Friends of the Earth, Amnesty International, etc., are all indications of the development of transnational thinking—even vision—that seem set to strengthen in the future and that are reinforced by the articulation of new imaginings (Brecher, 1993).

The contradictions at present, again both real and discursive, are palpable. On the one hand, it can be argued that it is the dynamics of postindustrialism and postmodernity that have brought global issues to the fore, and thus it is impossible to resurrect the project of modernity at the moment of its demise. Others would argue that globalization is the outcome of modernity, a global civil society would be its apogee, and that even those most often identified with alternative positions at heart espouse modernist values (Said, 1995). These intractable issues cut across contemporary debate. This volume shows how various theorists and researchers concerned with issues around media industries and popular culture approach these problems. The variety of arguments in the book is typical of the more general state of affairs.

MEDIA, SECULARISM, AND RELIGION

One of the key issues of the post-Cold War era is the reassertion of religious identities: As the secular political ideologies were peeled away like the top layers of an onion, the primordial identifications of religious community were once again revealed. Religious ritual, imagery, and morality fill the void of postmodern ethical relativity and secular despair (Turner, 1994). Global religious identifications, often centered on specific religious places, merely reinforce the brevity of the history of national affiliations. Such developments once again challenge all teleologically loaded paradigms and the neat progressivism of both modernization theory and classical Marxism, requiring more open-ended models.

Shinar (Chapter 4) is concerned with constructing just such a model. He tries to identify the key elements present in processes of change and to map the various scenarios of change that specific mixes of these elements could produce. Building on the work of Victor Turner, Shinar identifies a trio of elements productive of change: root paradigms (myths, religious beliefs, etc.), transformative agents, and formulative efforts. The particular combination and balance of these elements can lead to different scenarios of social change. The model also usefully suggests a recursive dynamic of change and stasis, the dialectic of history, rather than a linear movement of progress so beloved by both conservative and radical theorists of modernity.

Bar-Haim (Chapter 6) talks about media charisma, suggesting that the popular perception that the media (television) are connected to the "center of society" or, increasingly, the center of the globe, endows the media with a kind of secular sacredness and role of moral arbiter, taking over a traditionally religious function. Furthermore, with the decline of ritual in a secular world, cultural experience is increasingly mediated and consequently flattened, whereas the fictionalizing of the social does not lead to understanding, but the promotion of bias and stereotypes.

MEDIA, "THE OTHERS," AND MORALITY

What we do not seem to know enough about is how audiences around the world react to mediated images of others. In the West, do images of remote suffering, for example, merely reinforce Western stereotypes about African "primitiveness?" Or can such images mobilize sympathy, humanitarian sensibilities, and useful social action? This is an area of much essay writing but insufficient empirical investigation. There is thus a lurking danger of globalization becoming a new totalization that provides a new master narrative. Instead, in a postcolonial world, one central issue remains: how to embrace a different development in contexts that are already deeply structured and irrevocably altered by the forms of modernity. Difference within globalization is the challenge. What about "others" do we learn from electronic media? Are the "others" always spoken for, or can they speak for themselves? Clearly such questions are not radically new; indeed, the field of international communication has grown around attempts to answer such questions. But there are important shifts of emphasis away from the simple structural model of media effects toward the dynamics of meaning making and media as promoters or blockers of cross-cultural understandings, including a better, deeper understanding of self-identity and the consequences for action of mediated information about others.

There are also the issues of how global audiences can respond to mediated content. Some international feminist critics have argued that one of the consequences of globalization has been to shut down the public arena of response, displacing even the weak politics of protesting to the national media structure, be it state-run or public service, to the amorphous dislocated and invisible structures of global media conglomerates (see Sreberny-Mohammadi, 1994a). Although on the one hand, global media production is increasingly dominated by transnational media conglomerates, on the other hand, there is greater possibility for global audiences to become producers, through the enormous spread of small/alternative/participatory media projects, many of which are run by women. In the variety of minority media, exile media, and religious media, many are not nation-centric but write diverse global trajectories through geographically dispersed yet communities. Thus, Appadurai (1993) talks of the emergence of transnations. Increasingly, the colonies not only write but video back.

NEWS, PUBLIC OPINION, AND TRANSNATIONAL SENSIBILITIES

At a time when news images of Rwanda threaten to reinforce Western stereotypes of the Third World, even as they mobilize charitable sympathy, we badly need more studies of such mediated power geometry, to use Massey's (1991, 1993) evocative phrase. Globalization for whom? Who cares about whom? What is the outcome of such "care"? There are many complex ways that audiences can react to the global events and peoples who now enter their living rooms almost uninvited. In the industrialized world, perhaps there is a mobilization of sympathy, donations to charity, that raise some fascinating questions. What is it about some issues that mobilizes sympathy? Does the international charity structure merely reinforce the worst colonial stereotypes of the White West as the saviors of starving Black Africa, or is it humanitarian action of the noblest sort? Does charity let governments off the hook as they decrease aid allocations? Can the fragmented mode of international news presentation be transcended, and should it be part of the ethical responsibilities of the media to indeed suggest actions that might be taken as a follow-up to (inter)national news coverage, indicating how local acts might impinge on the global? Or is charity itself to be seen as an individualized, decontextualized act, that builds no form of solidarity, neither with other givers, nor with those to whom one gives. In fact, is it the antithesis of solidarity?

Serra's chapter (Chapter 10) is an example of the detailed empirical work that needs to be done to answer some of these questions by disentangling the complex sets of relations among political institutions, NGOs, media structures, and public opinion in the mediation of social issues and the possibilities of the development of a transnational public sphere. She presents a fascinating case study of mediated local-global dynamics, examining how the media mobilization of international public opinion helped effect local initiatives to deal with a very specific problem, the issue of the killing of street children in Brazil. She offers a detailed analysis of the intricate dynamics between local lobbyists and international organizations such as Amnesty, and national and international channels of communication, to create a movement in support of the street children. This is the kind of innovative empirical study that helps put flesh on the overly theoretical skeleton of globalization.

Giffard's (Chapter 9) focus is on another story that happens to have a Brazilian location, the international coverage of the UN Conference on Environment and Development held in Rio in 1992. The conference raised many issues that require positive, cooperative, sometimes truly global solutions. Giffard's analysis shows, however, that despite the huge volume of news material provided by the news agencies, the emphasis was on the underlying conflicts about issues rather than about cooperation, and the views of a few rich nations and their spokespeople, rather than the views of the developing world, were reported.

Saukko's (Chapter 11) work examines the manner in which national media constructed an alternative environmental movement, Orange, in Finland. Although the movement itself made a variety of local, national, and international linkages in its political analysis and activity, and explored positive alternative modes of living, including an egalitarian "genderscape," the only frame that the media used was a negative one of opposition, ignoring the global ramifications of the group's activities. The central implication here seems to be that the media cannot readily place or frame activities with a global outlook, but rather try to contain them within a narrower frame of reference, which has consequences for the way in which new social movements act in regard to media coverage.

Thus, the chapters by Serra (Chapter 10), Giffard (Chapter 9), and Saukko (Chapter 11) once again raise questions about the role of news coverage and news agendas in relation to key issues that could be the basis of an emergent global civil society, the type and range of sources used by the media, and the interplay among media interests, political interests, and grassroots activists.

NATIONAL POLICYMAKING IN A GLOBAL CULTURAL ECUMENE

In the discussions about the dialectics of the global and the local, there is often a tendency to omit the level of the national. Yet currently, the resurgence of nationalist movements and struggles about the cultural definitions of states haunts one part of Europe, just as another part takes steps to construct not only a regional juridical and regulatory structure, but indeed a regional identity. It is still in the main at the national level that contests about control and regulation of the media are waged and

broader cultural policies are formulated. Indeed, media and cultural policy are vital counters in the definition of national identity.

Language is a contested arena in such policymaking, with many
multicultural states facing competing claims about language use. Van den
Buelk and Van Poecke (Chapter 7) explore the complex and dynamic relationships between public service media, concepts of national cultural identity, and language policy in Belgium and Switzerland. They compare the
very different language policies of Flemish and German-Swiss public service broadcasters in what they describe as modern and postmodern periods. Essentially, they argue that the increasingly globalized, market-driven
media environment of the last 15 years has eroded national audiovisual
space, and they trace the effects this has on media language policy
through increased linguistic variation and a weakening attempt to teach
the "correct" language. Again, models of the global media market are usefully anchored to very detailed and specific changes in national cultural
environments, looking specifically at language policy and usage, issues all
too often disregarded in media analysis.

THE GLOBAL IMPACT OF NONLINGUISTIC MEDIA FORMS

Another form of communication that is also marginalized in media analysis, or consigned to a narrow popular culture focus, is music. Despite
strong national and regional variations in musical form, instrumentation,
and rhythm, music appears to be one of the most approachable of
human languages. For many open to listening, difference is not a barrier
but an exciting addition and challenge, calling up emotional and somatic
responses and cross-cultural connectivity, moving us in more ways than
one, and clearly demonstrating a global reach, from the broad popularity
of Western pop music to the interest in "world music" in the West. Negus
(Chapter 8) challenges the logocentrism of much work in international
communication and in shifting our attention to what he evocatively calls
"the music of the public spheres," by suggesting that there is more in the
study of international musical flows and practices than meets the ears.
He analyzes how music escapes the commercial control of producers
and flows over the borders of states. He also makes the important and
often overlooked point that music, as a form of nonrational communication, has the potential to mobilize affective ties, which could be an even
stronger foundation than instrumental calculation of shared interest for a
transnational, transcultural public sphere.

DEFINING THE LOCAL

If defining globalization is difficult, at least theoretical energy is spent on the problem. But how local is local? It is a question that has received little definition in current theorizing. Is the local smaller and more parochial than the regional? Is the local the urban unit in which many live, with their civic structures, spending allocations, and city pride? Or is it a subunit of that, for example, a borough in London with its mayor and council and respon-sibility for the administration of educational and housing matters, among others? Or is the local a "ward" of a larger electoral unit within which a subset of the politicized population, like the Labour Party in Britain, orga-nizes? Or is it a street or a block organization as in some U.S. cities? Or is local as precise as a particular apartment building, in New York, for exam-ple, with so many units that it can compete in numbers and density with many (global) villages? Or is the pub on the corner the English local? Or is it merely me and my family in our house? Given the range of local civic patterns and administrative units, and the diversity of social formations with which it is possible to identify, the range of possible phenomena that can comprise the local is extremely large, making it perhaps surprisingly the pole that needs most conceptual and empirical attention, and suggest-ing that there may be many levels of localness with which people can identity and in which they can act. Perhaps the stronger the patterns of affiliation and activity at the local level, the better the basis and the stronger the need for developing means for participating at a global level. Braman (Chapter 1) in this volume further unpacks the *local*, offering fasci-nating distinctions between *local, locus, location*, and *locale*, where the lat-ter is an historic identification, rather than any "real" spatial attribute.

Among the contributors, both Tomlinson (Chapter 3) and Bar-Haim (Chapter 6) directly question the emergence of a single "global cul-ture" and stress the importance of local culture as the interpretative frame of reference through which "global culture" has to pass. Thus, even if certain cultural products do have a global spread, that does not at all imply that the meaning of that product is the same everywhere.

Some of the biggest challenges facing a transnational civil soci-ety center on issues of access and democratic procedures. For many analysts, freedom is not a protection for community, but a requirement in it. Community and the individuals who comprise it are in a reciprocal rela-tion to one another, mutually constituted, a process that requires the community to be substatively democratic. Thus Glasser (1991) argues that "Community life . . . is not what democracy brings about but what democracy is" (p. 244) and politics is not what the state and its officials do but what private people do in their capacity as citizens to cultivate those forms of communal life in which dialogue and mutual concern are part of everyday life. If one criterion of civil society is a sense of involvement with the affairs of other, unknown, nonkin citizens, then what kinds of process-es can we distinguish as evidence of the emergence of a global civil soci-ety? A transnational civil society seems to be the confluence of both polit-ical and communicative or cultural processes. Sakamoto (1991) exhorts us to "express our full humanity by identifying ourselves as citizens of the globe" (p. 127). Yet what kinds of symbols and what kinds of structures can support that citizenship? Considerable hope rides on the develop-ment of global communications infrastructures that can facilitate the activ-ities of NGOs, grassroots popular movements, issue-based global soli-darities, and a great deal of contemporary theorizing that pushes the poli-tics of identity and community out of place into space (Keith & Pile, 1994). Yet it is not clear that these represent anything more than "virtual commu-nities" (Reingold, 1994), and it is probably more productive to think of these as multiple new forms of deterritorialized collectivities than as com-prising a single transnational public sphere.

CONCLUSION

Although there are precedents across the social sciences for transnation-al theorizing, what these new, contending, and often extremely abstract notions of globalization suggest is a Kuhnian paradigmatic challenge across the social sciences toward reconceptualizing nation-bounded models of social dynamics and change. Some of these emergent notions add multidimensionality, disjuncture as well as conjuncture, and further undermine simplistic, triumphalist, or even critical models of unidirectional Eurocentric influence out to the rest of the world. Indeed, the current eco-nomic difficulties of Western economies, faced with structural unemploy-ment, deskilling, and an aging infrastructure shows the impact of shifts in global capital that are not readily controllable by states alone. Thus, in some sense, we are all faced with a radically new environment in which it is not clear what the appropriate resources, skills, and policies are for col-lective survival in a truly globalized "risk" environment (Beck, 1992).

The range of issues thus opened up by theorizing on globalization and the transnational public sphere is extensive and exciting. Minimally, two things seem evident. First, none of the social sciences can ever quite be the same again, with singular national sociologies and politics chal-lenged both by substructures of identity and interest as well as by supra-national affiliations and linkages. Second, attempts to clarify the scope and meaning of culture, to identify and understand the new forms of identity, and to study the role of the media as sites of production of meaning and as disseminators of particular kinds of cultural products, will remain central to developing the analysis of the processes of globalization.

1

Interpenetrated Globalization: Scaling, Power, and the Public Sphere

Sandra Braman
University of Illinois at Urbana-Champaign

Globalization is both cause and effect of other social processes, but several problems make its analysis difficult:

- Although few deny the reality of globalization, there is little agreement about what it is; diverse conceptualizations are often undistinguished in the literature.
- "Globalization" is one pole; an understanding of the other, "localization," is also necessary in order to fully understand either. Primary, secondary, and tertiary localization and relocalization processes are of particular importance today.
- We approach questions of globalization with research tools and concepts inherited from the study of other units of analysis and processes, although the particular qualities of globalization/localization issues appear to demand the use of new methodological and conceptual approaches. This methodological problem has been highlighted by those sociologists who are arguing that their field should turn its focus from the individual and the state to the globe as the fundamental unit of analysis (e.g., Archer, 1991; Bergesen, 1980).

21

There have been two types of theories of globalization: Some look from the perspective of the whole to the parts, understanding phenomena and processes that appear below the global level, such as nation-states, to arise out of and in response to global processes. Others look from the perspective of the parts towards the whole, arguing, for example, that the global system has emerged out of interactions among nation-states.

We are less accustomed to discussing theories of localization, but they do exist both in themselves and as embedded within discussions of other matters. As we struggle to understand today's social, cultural, political, economic, and ecological turbulence—and think through the implications of localization—a third way of conceptualizing globalizaton and localization processes appears: The relationship between the parts and the whole may be understood as mutually constitutive, what we can call *interpenetrated globalization*. The concept of interpenetration draws attention to the fact that the global never exists except in the local—and today there is no local that is not infected by the global. Although the term *interdependence* refers to mutual interactions among different actors and processes (Rosenau, 1984, used the term *cascading interdependence* to refer to the multiplying mutual dependencies of nation-states), *interpenetration* refers to ways in which different actors and processes have become a part of each other.

Today the process of identity formation at the individual level is problematized in much the same way that the identity of the nation-state is problematized, and the resolution of one—either one—necessarily involves at least some attention to the other; thus, renewed attention to the nature of citizenship. Conditions of interpenetration make the identification of social units and their mapping onto discourse arenas such as the public sphere even more difficult. The real public sphere is the interface between particularistic cultural communities and subcommunities. Thus the emergence of a genuine transnational public sphere is possible only when three different types of processes scale together: self-organizing social processes, communication processes (including both infrastructure and the social organization of communication), and the processes of power.

Technological development has affected and continues to affect the scaling of each of these three types of processes with outcomes that are still unclear. Across society, conditions are turbulent and increasingly chaotic. Contemporary difficulties in locating and participating in the public sphere derive from shifting scales within each type of process and our consequent inability to bring the three process scales into harmonization. Further articulation of concepts of globalization and localization should contribute to our ability to analyze the shifting scales of social processes in this environment and to create, maintain, and participate in a genuine public sphere.

A review of the key features of the now ubiquitous global Net may be useful: It is the single largest machine in human history. It is geodesic and fractal (Huber, 1987) in structure, meaning there is redundancy in paths, the organization of its use need not be hierarchical, and organizational questions reemerge at each level of the structures of the communication, political, and social systems. It is, relative to historical experience, vast in capacity. Access to the Net is clearly demarked along socioeconomic, educational, cultural, gender, and geographic lines. The Net has made possible qualitatively new types of organizational, and therefore social, forms. It is intelligent, and the intelligence is dispersed and in the hands of users. The Net is coming to be understood as both a source of knowledge and of innovation in itself. It can diagnose its own problems and write its own software. The Net is getting bigger, and faster, and smarter, all the time.

THEORIES OF GLOBALIZATION

Discussion about globalization has historically been linked to utopian views of communication systems, first appearing with the invention of the telegraph: Morse's comments to the U.S.Congress pleading for financial support in 1838 already talked about a global village. A first peak of excitement about globalization attended the opening of the first international cable in the middle of the 19th century, and, indeed, globalization is an identifying characteristic of the first stage of the information society (Braman, 1994). Vail, the first president of AT&T, and Carty, his innovative engineer, both envisioned a global communication system and the globalization of social, political, and cultural processes that would accompany the development of this system, as did radio's Tesla (who foresaw the portable radio as early as 1904), television's Sarnoff, and others.

Garnier (1987) argues that it was also over the course of the 19th century that the distinction between what he calls "world" and "local" technologies developed. As he describes it, world technologies involve large-scale production, high technology, research and development (R&D) and capital intensive products and processes, and association with the largest organizations. Local technologies, on the other hand, are geared to limited groups of populations or regions, are aimed at satisfying specific local needs, employ local factors of production, often contain small-scale production, are often labor-intensive, and are associated with small firms. Today, he notes, we see this distinction blurred as computers permit high-level technologies to be used in the production of small scale production adapted to specific local needs.

Featherstone (1990) offers a five-phase history of globalization that includes: (a) a germinal phase from the early 15th through the mid-18th century in Europe, during which national communities began to grow and concepts of the individual and humanity emerged; (b) an incipient phase, mainly in Europe from the mid-18th through the late 19th centuries, during which the conceptions of international relations and a standardized citizenry developed. There was a sharp increase in the number of international conventions and agencies concerned with international and transnational regulation and communication, and non-European societies began to be "admitted" to international society; (c) a take-off phase from the 1870s to the mid-1920s, during which global conceptions were increasingly offered as standards for the acceptability of national societies, there was a very sharp increase in the number and speed of global communications, and global competitions, such as the Olympics and the Nobel prizes—as well as World War I—developed; (d) a struggle-for-hegemony phase from the early 1920s through the mid-1960s during which conflicts over fundamental ways of organizing society became global, the possibility of global extinction became focused by the atomic bomb, and the United Nations was formed; and (e) our current uncertainty phase, beginning in the 1960s and displaying crisis tendencies in the early 1990s.

The current phase is characterized by the heightening of global consciousness and inclusion of developing countries into global society, a great increase in the number of global institutions and movements, the spread of multiculturalism and polyethnicity, an increasing fluidity in the international system, growth of interest in world civil society and world citizenship, consolidation of the global media system, and a problematization of concepts of the individual as gender, ethnic, and racial considerations enter our thinking. It was in the 1960s that a global consciousness reached the mass level, spurred by mass media experiences and stimulated by the first photographs of Earth from space. The 1960s also saw the first studies of the world as a whole in international relations, although it was not until the 1980s that globalization per se became a significant subject of study within academia.

The notion of globalization has also historically been linked to notions of universalism, reaching, as Featherstone (1990) notes, its fullest fruition in the work of Durkheim, who argued that the only thing that will be shared as societies expand and increase in complexity and degree of social and cultural differentiation is our humanity. It is this relationship with universalism that leads to the connection between globalization and postmodernism. Friedman (1988) points out that because modernist identity depended on expanding horizons, perception of a "closed" global system would not surprisingly lead to a crisis for modernity. Robins (1991) understands postmodern geography to be about forging new relationships between the global and the local. Jameson (1991) goes so far as to draw a connection between global processes and post-modernism in architecture, noting that the latter movement, one of the first of the now dozens of "posties," appeared first in buildings built by transnational corporations.

Globalization: From the Whole to the Parts

The most influential and explicit approach to globalization is probably that offered by Immanuel Wallerstein (1979, 1984), whose world system theory sees a global whole out of which the entities that identify themselves as states have emerged, and by which the characteristics of states are deter-mined. Commodity chains run from periphery to core and form the world division of labor that sustains capital and its growth. Culture (Wallerstein, 1990) is the current arena in which global struggles are being fought.

Two streams of research in the Wallerstein tradition are today co-extant. One group of scholars works from the premise that the econo-my continues to work the way it always has. Examples of this type of work include Dixon's (1985) analysis of trade patterns as indicative of the persistence of the world system, Modelski's (1979) mapping of long economic cycles onto processes at the nation-state level, and Zolberg's (1980, 1991) struggles with issues raised by transformations of the glob-al market. Analyses of national niches and development of policy in pur-suit of a niche fall here. Others start from the premise that the global economy has qualitatively changed as a result of the informatization process; Lash and Urry (1987) provide a quintessential example.

Wallerstein is, of course, speaking of capital as the driving force in the globalization process. Many explorations of globalization are analyses of the dynamics of capital accumulation within specific indus-tries. Pearce and Singh (1992) look at the international system of research, building on a stream of work that has explored differences and similarities across research cultures within different nation-states. Kobrak and Luey (1992) look at the internationalization of the publishing industry. Kloppenburg (1988) brilliantly describes the globalization process as it has been applied to the genetic information of plants. Calls for a New World Information Order (NWIO) from the developing world since the early 1970s is another type of acknowledgment of the global-ized nature of the communication system from the perspective of those in the periphery (Richstad & Anderson, 1981).

Although these and other industries share in their participation in the capital accumulation process, they also significantly differ along dimensions identified by the particular features of each set of activities. Thus, for example, it is not only economic issues (Coulmas, 1992) that brought English to the point of being the dominant language globally, but English as a language also has the largest vocabulary of any and is remarkable in its adaptability.

The cultural imperialism argument, which understands the diffusion of cultural products as globalizing exercises of particular nation-states, is such an analysis of the dynamics of capital accumulation within specific industries that focuses on the negative effects, including the destruction of local cultures and values and homogenization of cultural forms. Over the past decade we have become more sensitive to the varieties of meanings that the same cultural forms have within different settings (Marcus, 1994), however, raising questions about how homogeneous in meaning and function even forms that share surface characteristics may be. Another set of challenges to notions of cultural imperialism comes from the very globalization of cultural industries themselves. Whereas we still speak as if Hollywood films dominate the world, those films today are often produced by non-U.S. companies, financed by non-U.S. interests, and made outside of the United States, using technical crews and actors who are not from the United States. In this situation, whose culture is being exported from where (Wasser, 1995)? Enzensberger (1974, 1992), one of the first to write about the commodification of the cultural industries, goes further, denying any homogeneity at all:

> Market towns in Lower Bavaria, villages in the Eifel Hills, small towns in Holstein are populated by figures no one could have dreamed of only thirty years ago. For example, golf-playing butchers, wives imported from Thailand, counter-intelligence agents with allotments, Turkish mullahs, women chemists in Nicaragua committees, vagrants driving Mercedes, autonomists with organic gardens, weapons-collecting tax officials, peacock-breeding smallholders, militant lesbians, Tamil ice-cream sellers, classical scholars in commodity futures trading, mercenaries on home leave, extremist animal-rights activists, cocaine dealers with solariums, dominas with clients in top management, computer freaks commuting between California and nature reserves in Hesse, carpenters who supply golden doors to Saudi Arabia, art forgers, Karl May researchers, body-guards, jazz experts, euthanasists and porno producers. (1974, p. 179)

Globalization: From the Parts to the Whole

From the perspective of sociology, political science, international relations—and the practice of most working policymakers—the parts come before the whole. In theory as well as in practice, this is to some degree pragmatically driven. A policymaker for a particular nation-state has responsibility for making decisions from the perspective of the part as it relates to the whole.

In this view, nation-states are the original elements, and global processes have grown out of interactions among states. Characteristics of states exist prior to and are independent of their global participation. The concreteness of the sense in which this has historically been understood is demonstrated in the origin of the word *international*, coined by Jeremy Bentham in 1789 to describe that branch of law that had been going under the term *law of nations*.

In communications, the work of Deutsch (1968) and Pool, Inose, Taksaki, and Hurwitz (1984), who examine communicative interactions between nation-states, lies in this vein. Similarly, literature on development communication, from Lerner and Schramm (1967) through recent work on participatory development (e.g., Rahman, 1993; White, Nair, & Ashcroft, 1994), works from this position. Indeed, almost all of the work in communications and cultural studies aside from those areas that explicitly deal with the problem of globalization can be said to work from the perspective of the parts to the whole.

One weakness of this approach in understanding contemporary conditions is that its lens on the exercise of power is the nation-state, with other agents, such as corporations, understood through their relations with the state and so forth. This lens is no longer appropriate in an environment in which transnational corporate actors are in many cases more significant to the exercise of power than are nation-states, and in which the institutional aspects of a global civil society, the NGO (nongovernmental organization) movement, similarly exhibits efforts to exercise power globally.

LOCALIZATION

Interest in the local emerged in the 1980s in response to the experience of globalization: the local became visible as a resistance, as the source of particularities and variety, and as the ground of meaning for individuals and communities. Inspired by Ong's (1982) distinction between primary and secondary orality, we can now distinguish among primary, secondary, and tertiary locality. Identifying just what is meant by the local—its bounds in any particular circumstances—is now, however, problematic, and this is the problem of scale.

Reassertion of the Local

Interest in the local emerged across a range of social science disciplines in the 1980s as the accelerating experience of globalization forced a confrontation with the limits of globalizing processes as well. The development of the Net itself has provided manifestations of the "problem" of the local. Rakow (1991) argues that technological development has been so socially costly because it has been conceptualized from the perspective of the technology, not of the particularities of specific locales. In one detailed case study, for example, she found the telephone company set up local and long-distance service in such a way that the geographically close communities that were tightly linked socially through the spread of extended families whose members continued to interact in multiple ways were set up with long distance service so that every family call had an additional charge, whereas the service that was provided to what the phone company saw as local linked communities that had historically no social, cultural, or economic relationships. Pepper and Brotman (1987), looking across the development of multiple telecommunication systems, describe the local as a problem because it is a "bottleneck." The desire of specific locales to resist some types of broadcast content considered locally, culturally, and politically undesirable has certainly driven and continues to drive much debate over broadcasting policy around the world. Researchers looking at the diffusion of technologies and ideas describe some of this resistance as "adaptation" (Rogers, 1983).

The local also emerges as the source of particularities and difference. To some degree this understanding has long been embedded in our economic theory. Adam Smith long ago argued that the unique characteristics of particular nation-states comprised the comparative advantage of each. It is the comparative advantage that provides a niche for each country within the global economy, and the differences between the types of comparative advantage that drive economic exchange, making international trade central to the functioning of the economy. One stream of research looks at specific locales in terms of their niche characteristics from this perspectives, while another stream of research looks at the impact of cultural imperialism on specific locales (e.g., Marcus, 1994). These two sets of explorations are not in the end distinct, for even the cultural differences that result from local particularities are commodifiable in themselves. The explosion of tourism vividly demonstrates the commodity value of local difference in today's global culture (Leong, 1989).

In communication research, the Silverstone and Hirsch (1992) work identifying the home as an important site for ethnographic research seeking to understand the influence of communication technologies shifts effects research to the local. Interest in the local as a source of difference perhaps reaches its ultimate point in the work of those who focus on the body itself (e.g., Classen, 1993; Featherstone, Hepworth, & Turner, 1991; Taussig, 1993). From a technological perspective, Huber (1987), emphasizing the dispersion of intelligence throughout the Net and into the hands of users, and identifies local-level nodes as the first and most critical pieces of a vertically integrated net. (Huber also usefully argues that we ought to be treating time and space as equals, and therefore think about "chrono-communication," which shifts information across time, as well as "tele-communication," which shifts information across space.)

Perhaps most importantly, the local has reasserted itself as the source of meaning for individuals and communities. For the individual, the local—beginning with the home and then extending outward through the community—provides the coherence that makes sense out of the world and permits the story of daily life to unfold. Already in 1945, economist Hayek acknowledged that there is very important knowledge that is not scientific in the sense of knowledge of general rules, what he called "knowledge of the particular circumstances of time and place" (p. 521), which is significant economically. Hayek extends the notion of comparative advantage to the individual level. Today there is increasing interest, particularly among those interested in the nature of organizations, in the relationship between local knowledge and general knowledge (e.g., Jensen & Meckling, 1991). Geertz (1983) profoundly and influentially explored the significance of local knowledge for our understanding of the world. U.S. constitutional scholar Carter (1985) bought Geertz's argument and claims that only local knowledge can answer questions of justice. Mattelart and Cesta (1985) similarly argue that local information is critical to the formation of community identity.

Entrikin (1991) brilliantly works through what he calls the empirical-theoretical, normative, epistemological, and causal significance of the local. Although Entrikin works from a geographer's perspective, he ultimately points toward the methodological implications of an appreciation of the local for research methods used throughout the social sciences, thus expanding on, and therefore making more useful, the Geertzian (1983) point. Indeed, it appears to be confrontation with the local that is stimulating much of the debate over research methods that has colored the social sciences over the last few years.

Primary, Secondary, and Tertiary Locality

The differences between primary, secondary, and tertiary locality are chronological, cultural, and conceptual. Chronologically, movement from traditional to modern to postmodern culture has given us a shift in experience from primary to secondary to tertiary locality. Culturally, there is a shift from understanding the local in its material forms as constituting culture, to understanding it as a reference point, to experiencing the local as conceptual and, to some degree, willed. Conceptually, our understanding of the local has moved from an identification of the local with physical place, to seeing it as culturally defined, to understanding it, again, as a willed construct. The movement from primary to secondary to tertiary locality is thus a movement through what we may call the prereal, through the real, to the hyperreal.

Primary locality refers to the equation of the local with the world that is generally understood to be a feature of traditional societies. In most cultures there is an orientation toward place that understands it as the conjuncture of geographic, material, and social forces as they come together in the creation of a home—within the household, the community, the landscape, and within a spiritual universe.

Secondary locality refers to the renewed sense of appreciation for the local that is characteristic of high modernity. It has manifested itself in recent decades in a renewed interest in various dimensions of folk culture, very much extending Ong's (1982) notion of secondary orality. It is secondary locality that drives tourism economically—we go to see the local over there, what is different about it. This type of locality reaches its extreme expression in the revival of cultural difference as the motive force for political change, as in Bosnia.

Tertiary locality is that which is emerging out of the postmodern condition. (Apparently Thomas Wolfe was wrong—we go home again and again and again.) We are still engaged in the effort to understand the nature of locality in today's environment. Although many of our most significant institutional lives now exist in cyberspace (meaning, existing within the Net most significantly), as in the global financial industry, as we begin to reach the height of the diffusion curve and Net participation becomes a mass experience, there is an increasing sense of the local as the conjunction of those Net conversations in which one takes part. Virtual communities—those that exist through electronic connections rather than through geographic clumping—are more and more experienced as the most important, the most "real," of the communities in which one lives. For those whose identities are "grounded" in cyberspace, the linkage between the local and the material world has become completely broken.

If we understand the concept of the *prereal* to refer to social conditions that are epistemologically grounded in the spiritual world, as in traditional societies, the *real* to refer to social conditions that are epistemologically grounded in the empirical, and the *hyperreal* to refer to, in Baudrillard's (1983) sense, social conditions that are epistemologically grounded in the symbolic, then we can also understand the movement from primary to secondary to tertiary locality as being simultaneously the movement from the prereal through the real to the hyperreal.

Bounding the Local

Defining just what is meant, in any particular place, by the local is problematic in several ways. There are different dimensions along which the
question is raised; for this reason, it is useful to distinguish among different senses of the local conceptually. The term *local* can be used to refer
to geographic definitions; *locus* refers to a site of human agency; *locale*
refers to the cultural and historical aspects of a geographic site that
results in each unique construct of the local; and *location* to the material
features of a place that are reproducible elsewhere, as in a movie location.[1] Here I have been moving among these four types of meanings.
Distinguishing among them, however, makes visible some interesting
things. Forgacs (1992), for example, fascinatingly describes the tightly
drawn cultural aspects of the local in Italy as a reason for the relative
openness of Italians to cultural influences from other places. Because
the next village over was historically considered "foreign," foreignness
was in a sense always more familiar. In Brazil, there is a temporal
dimension to the local—how long something was done locally is a significant element of determining whether something is a local product for
international trade purposes (Brazil, 1988). Bruce Chatwin's *The
Songlines* (1987), a popular but well-done report of the migratory, communal, and aural orientation towards place found among aboriginal
Australian peoples, provides an example of construction of the local
through travel and through a sharing of songs and stories with other
groups in a traditional society.

   As the human population and urbanization processes have
grown, we have lost clear spatial boundaries to our communities. In
today's environment, the *local*, the *locale*, and *locus*, and the *location*
may each define the local differently. Different perceptions of the local
overlap and conflict. What is to be understood as the local often differs
according even to what type of social process is being discussed: local
politics may refer to a town, local communication systems to a state, and
local economy to a region.

   For general economic purposes, the city has emerged as the
meaningful pole of the local relative to the global, whereas most political
power continues to reside in the nation-state. It is for this reason that the
rhetoric about empowering peoples and communities by dispersing decision-making responsibilities to the local level is today profoundly disem-
powering. The Sony/counterculture admonition to "Think globally, act
locally" is a guarantee that one's actions will be largely ineffective. The
opposite, "Think locally, act globally," is a far more powerful approach.

---

[1]Thanks to Andrew Blau for this concept of location.

A last problem in defining the local is increasingly troublesome for working policymakers, and that is understanding even where a transaction that takes place through the Net actually takes place. One of the biggest problems in discussing the possibility of incorporating trade in services under the GATT (General Agreement on Tariffs and Trade) has been trying to figure out where foreign direct investment takes place. In the case, for example, of international data processing activities, where is the transaction: At the site of the consumer? Where does the processing takes place? At the base location (if any) of the seller?

INTERPENETRATED GLOBALIZATION

Several types of approaches focus on ways in which multiple organizational modes, types of social processes, and levels and identities of agency make interpenetration of units of analysis and of processes the most salient characteristics of globalization.

All religions are imbued with practices that link the concrete particularities of daily life to the universal (Eliade, 1959; Tuan, 1977). From this perspective, the local *is* the global. It is important to retain this category in our analyses of contemporary affairs, for the sacred impulse is still the human impulse and continues to drive far more human activity than is generally recognized. Systems that refuse to acknowledge and incorporate the sacred find themselves repressing a type of energy that historically has always insisted on reemerging, often in social movements with tremendous political energy; today we see this in the rise of religious fundamentalism.

The Gaia approach, which looks at the planet as one ecology, one system, of which social systems are but one part, can also be understood as a way of thinking about interpenetrated globalization. From this perspective, the local and the global are comprised of multiply interacting systems. This perspective has grown in power since the 1960s, when we first saw pictures of Earth as a whole from space, and the environmental movement drew public attention to interrelations among species. It is precisely around issues like the environment that we are seeing the beginnings of the emergence of a global civil society.

Ohmae (1990) describes today's decentered operations as requiring a genuine "equidistance of perspective," demanding treatment of all strategic markets in the same way and with the same attention as the home market. This "decentering" within the corporate world is what makes it possible for transnational corporations (TNCs) to evade the constraints of any particular nation-state. From the defense perspective, decenteredness is an advantage. Recently envisioned defense programs would be staffed by intelligent weapons free to roam space at will, rather than being tied, like all earlier weapons, to particular geographic places.[2] Cultural effects of the decentering of space are explored in theoretical broad brush by thinkers such as Baudrillard (1983) and Virilio (1986), and by those under their influence such as Kroker (1992) and Poster (1990).

Research into the concrete effects of interpenetrated globalization has just begun, notably in work by Silverstone and Hirsch (1993) that analyzes the effects of the use of information technologies within the home. (Note that this research, in order to approach interpenetrated globalization, begins with the local; it is much informed by the work of de Certeau, 1984, Silverstone & Hirsch, 1993, and LeFebvre, 1991). Garnier's (1987) vision of the blurring of the distinction between global and local technologies offers a "concrete" example of what interpenetrated globalization looks like in practice and as expressed in technologies.

Ulrich Beck (1992) discusses interpenetrated globalization in his analysis of the "risk society." With this phrase Beck refers to the effects on society of the extension of causal chains to such lengths and complexity that effects of actions are often so distant in time (as in genetic mutation), place (beyond national borders), or perceptibility (today's surveillance technologies are not sensible to the human body) that we no longer have any way of understanding causal relations. In this situation we can no longer assign accountability. The appeal of nonrational causal explanations grows. Because causal factors are so widespread and interpenetrated, there is no way of affecting them without changing the nature of the entire social system. In this environment, access to knowledge increases in value. Beck argues for calculations of long-term risk as a mode of economic analysis to include with the types of cost-benefit analysis of short-term consequences in prevalent use today.

Again providing a "concrete" example of interpenetrated globalization, it is the environmental arguments that are considered today the strongest arguments for justifying intervention into the internal affairs of a nation-state. Such intervention can take place through the practice of extraterritoriality (the attempted application of the laws of one nation-state within the territory of another). Another form in which it can take place is via decisions of international decision-making bodies such as the United Nations. This linkage suggests that one might adhere to the Gaia thesis and to the concept of interpenetrated globalization simultaneously, understanding the latter as a more articulated version of the former as it works out in the interplay of a few social systems and processes.

---

[2]See Braman, 1991, for a discussion of problematic consequences of this approach to national security.

It is also possible to view the state as a locus of power within and dependent on the multiple types of information flows within the Net environment. Because this interdependence is the definitional characteristic of the network state (Braman, 1995), it can be said to have not arisen either from the part up or from the whole down approach, but has emerged at the conjunction of multiple social forces. From this perspective, transnational corporations, too, are loci of power that have articulated themselves within global network conditions.

THE PUBLIC SPHERE

If we understand the public sphere to be the interface between particularistic communities and subcommunities, the globalization and localization processes discussed here have an influence upon the public sphere in these ways:

First, we can understand the public sphere as emerging when (and where) the three types of processes scale together: self-organizing social processes,[3] communication processes (including both infrastructural and social processes), and the exercise of power. Today all of these processes are Net dependent and, quite differently from historical circumstance, none has any inherent scale. Thus decisions today about how to scale each, and therefore about how they interact with each other, can be deliberate, self-conscious, and, hopefully, self-reflexive. When the scales of the three types of processes do not come together, we become incapable of identifying the public sphere functionally.

Second, although the literature has been dominated by treatment of the public sphere as if it emerges only one at a time, today we recognize that there are multiple, overlapping and interpenetrated public spheres. These spheres relate to each other in different ways: They may be co-extant at the same level of the social structure, as in the Poland of three public spheres in the late 1980s described by Jakubowicz (1990); they may be ranked in tiers (Dahlgren, 1991); they may be distinguished by the size of the social unit involved, from the nuclear family to the globe (Morley, 1993); or they may be ranked by the medium through which the public conversation takes place (as Giroux, 1992, for example, describes textbooks as a public sphere). Garnham (1990) sees the public sphere as a network of media, educational, knowledge, and opinion-forming institutions within civil society, whose operation is conducive to the emergence

---

[3]The beginnings of an approach to telecommunications policy based on using self-organizing systems theory as a normative guide are articulated in Braman (1994).

of public opinion as a political power, a view that includes the mass media within the public sphere. Furthermore, notions of an international or global public sphere (Gurevitch, Levy, & Roeh, 1991; Hallin & Mancini, 1991; Hjvarvard, 1993) also incorporate the sense of multiple interpenetrated public spheres.

Third, the use of new information technologies has significantly shifted the conditions under which the public sphere may emerge. Technological development has changed the nature of traditional forms of instrumental, structural, and symbolic (consensual) power and brought the newly emerged (or newly visible) form of transnational power to dominance. As a consequence of the availability of new forms of power under conditions to some degree different from those determining access to traditional forms of power, as well as of the recognition of forms of power not previously acknowledged within the power literature (such as the socialization power of mothers in the home), new players have entered the arena, and some of the negotiating rules have changed (Braman, 1995). The shift of scale offered by new technologies gives a momentary surge of energy to the social system of a kind that classically can result in a reconfiguration of the system. Anthony Rutkowski (1994) put it more directly in his electronic mail signature block: "The Internet is the revolution."

Fourth, although clearly the nature of the nation-state and of state power have changed, the state does remain a player. Jakubowicz (1990) reminds us of the real ability of the state to control the conditions in which a public sphere must function in his analysis of the public sphere(s) in Poland. In Latin America the state was critically important to the creation and sustenance of the public sphere because it provided a bulwark against incursion by international forces and was in control of the communications infrastructure as critical to the functioning of the public sphere. Mattelart and Mattelart (1990) note that the state is also a communicator within the public sphere and record an extraordinary growth in Brazilian state spending on advertising and image management during times of crisis, as well as ongoing efforts to participate in mass culture.

Finally, with acceptance of the notion of multiple interpenetrated public spheres come the additional analytical problems of examining interactions among power spheres at the same and disparate levels of the social structure. Hobbes's fixation on Galileo (Held, 1989) suggests a heliocentric model of the public sphere. Others see the public sphere as a more flexible environment, in which identities themselves are formed (Calhoun, 1991). For Dahlgren (1991), the public sphere is also a vision with the capability of motivating political struggle.

CONCLUSIONS

Under such conditions, perhaps the search and desire for a public sphere are futile. Silverstone and Hirsch (1990) suggest that the formation of the public sphere in this environment may be random, and Enzensberger (1992) that meaningful action is possible only at the individual level today.

Hal Himmelstein (personal communication, 1985) used to teach working-class students at Brooklyn College television production by having them produce three pieces in sequence, by Beckett, Brecht, and Shakespeare: Beckett for "I can't go on, I'll go on"; Brecht for a reason to go on; and Shakespeare for the fullness of the world once they got there. In his classic discussion of the public sphere, Negt and Kluge (1978/1993) suggests we return to Brecht's radio theory, which he considers one of the most important things ever written about the media. Brecht saw radio as epoch making and wanted to reveal the conditions under which radio could be made into a productive process for changing relationships among people. Although he knew that it was possible that radio would continue as a medium of distribution—in which case the task is to publicly expose those in power—Brecht really wanted to transform radio into an autonomous production process that would put people in touch with each other, generating mass culture independent of any monopolies of the ruling class.

It is in this context that Rutkowski's comment is pertinent, for today the Internet genuinely—at least for the moment—offers autonomous production processes for those with the ability to surf it. The Net in fact may offer the opportunity for creation of a public sphere or public spheres genuinely outside of the bounds of any single nation-state or organizational entity.

Now comes the more difficult task. For if our identities as individuals, local communities, and societies are no longer driven by geographic and material imperatives, communicative communities, or stable domains of power relations, any public sphere will come into being only with deliberate, self-conscious, and self-reflexive effort.

Our motive force has shifted. Although historically it had always been the practice to define power outward from the individual entity that is the source of agency, today the question is how, within a globalized process environment, to define a meaningful and effective locus of power. Because the public sphere is where civil society congregates, it is the place in which civil society recognizes itself as such, drawing system bounds. Because this is no longer `naturally' defined by genetics, geography, culture, or social organization, it must be decided on other grounds.

2

*A New World View: Globalization, Civil Society, and Solidarity**

Peter Waterman
Institute of Social Studies, The Hague

INTRODUCTION: A NEWLY IMAGINABLE COMMUNITY

There are at least three major historical traditions of internationalism: those of religious universalism, bourgeois/liberal cosmopolitanism, and labor/socialist internationalism. One could even add to these a distinct radical-democratic tradition (anti-authoritarian) as well as a Third Worldist one (anti-imperialist). It should be possible to propose a new kind of international community from within any of these traditions. If I do so from within the labor/socialist one, this is in no way to prioritize it or even to defend it. The past prioritization is one reason for its demise. A defense would imply concealing the problematic nature of socialist and labor internationalism, even in its late 19-century heyday, and denying the significance of current global change and new understandings offered of such.

*The arguments presented here were first tried out at a seminar at the Institute of Social Studies in The Hague and at a panel involving Anthony Giddens, at the International Association for Mass Communication Research conference in Dublin, both in June 1993. I am grateful to participants in both events for their reactions. I am also grateful to the editors of this book for their pertinent comments on both form and content.

What I rather wish to do is to confront the old labor and socialist tradition with the new world and conceptual (dis)orders. Such a confrontation is intended to be beneficial for all. Union members have proven themselves less internationalistic than the largely middle-class supporters of the new social movements. Showing the relevance of a new kind of internationalism to the provincial proletariat is more of a challenge than arguing it for the metropolitan middle class. Finally, it cannot be denied that there is a certain ironic pleasure to be had in speaking of socialism and the working class at a time in which even many progressive and cosmopolitan intellectuals consider socialism dead, class irrelevant, and internationalism a Eurocentric, totalizing, and repressive discourse![1]

From a base within this tradition, I argue that a specific understanding of globalization, and a critical and committed attitude toward it, could today—for the first time in history—make "internationalism" both an attractive utopia and an effective politic. I do the following: critique internationalization/internationalism discourse; sketch an understanding of globalization and look at the relationship between globalization and social movements; consider the meaning of global civil society; propose "global solidarity" as a successor to "internationalism;" and look at its implications for posttraditional internationalists.

INTERNATIONALIZATION AND INTERNATIONALISM AS PARTICULAR AND PARTIAL

I first settle accounts with the old internationalizations and internationalisms. "Internationalization," in either the liberal or socialist understanding, implies universalization and is accompanied by a related political/ethical universalism. In both cases, the internationalization and internationalism have meant Westernization. These are, thus, particularistic universalisms in which Western Enlightenment theories, models, aspirations, and utopias are offered down, or imposed on, the rest of the world. These are also partial universalisms, insofar as they prioritize or marginalize particular social structures, processes, and social movements. They fail, finally, to come to terms with traditionalisms or particularisms, including those they themselves provoke. Hall (1992) sees the matter as follows:

> Both liberalism and Marxism, in their different ways, implied that the attachment to the local and the particular would gradually give way to the more universalistic and cosmopolitan or international values

---

[1]Many possibly unfamiliar assumptions are made here. For relevant argumentation, see Waterman (1988, 1989).

and identities; that nationalism and ethnicity were archaic forms of attachment—the sorts of thing which would be "melted away" by the revolutionising force of modernity. According to these "metanarratives" of modernity, the irrational attachments to the local and the particular, to tradition and roots, to national myths and "imagined communities" would gradually be replaced by more rational and universalistic identities. Yet globalization seems to be producing neither simply the triumph of "the global" nor the persistence, in its old nationalistic form, of "the local". The displacements or distractions of globalization turn out to be more varied and more contradictory than either its protagonists or opponents suggest. However, this also suggests that, though powered in many ways by the West, globalization may turn out to be part of that slow and uneven but continuing story of the de-centring of the West. (p. 314)

There is another serious common limitation to the old discourses. Both Liberal and Marxist concepts of internationalization are two-dimensional. They depend on a planar understanding of space—of space as place—with the privileged place being that of the nation-state or blocs of states (Giddens, 1990). Yet the nation-state (actually, the state-defined nation, the *state-nation*) is an historically recent phenomenon; it ties rights and community to territory and rests finally on the use of violence against external and internal enemies. The nation-state evidently has continuing appeal and success in capturing the popular imagination and even mobilizing it for (self-)destructive war. But the primacy of the nation-state as against more local and more particular, or more general and nonterritorial, identities, communities, and values (e.g., democracy, pluralism) has always been tenuous and is increasingly in question.

In both the liberal and Marxist traditions, nation-state and society are considered as more or less synonymous and provide the essential parameters for sociology. For both, "international relations" tends to mean interstate relations. These traditions are not only unable to deal with globalization, but are also of decreasing value in explaining the particular terrain or relation they have abstracted for study. There is a multiplicity of social relations—beneath borders, within borders, across borders, without borders. We need a view of the nature of the world that allows us to understand these.

Internationalism, in both the 19th and 20th centuries, subordinated itself to a world of nation-states. For both liberal and socialist internationalisms, the projected future was one in which the breaching of borders, the occupation or merging of territories, would lead to the surpassing of the significant differences (that is "traditionalism" or "particularism") previously marking and distinguishing such places. But such territorial internationalization/internationalism has occurred only in the most contradictory or perverse ways.

For example, both the League of Nations and the United Nations were conceived as *inter-nation-state* organizations. Both attempts at surpassing national rivalries functioned simultaneously to reinforce and reify state-nationalism. Clinching evidence of the existence of a state—one licensed internationally to kill in its own defense—is UN recognition. This fundamental ambiguity of our suprastate order is today being revealed in ever more dramatic form as the UN tries to reconcile the universality of peace, human rights, and ecological concern with the particularity of the territorially based nation-state.

To take another example, the left, pertinently dubbed by Bauman (1986) "the counter-culture of modernity," made its own heroic effort at surpassing nationalism with the October Revolution of 1917, which created the Union of Soviet Socialist Republics. The name, it is worth remembering, means "union of socialist republican councils." Unlike the United States, this title made reference to neither states nor sites. It was an attempt to create a political form at once postimperial, postcapitalistic, postnationalistic, and post-parliamentarian. It was intended to be open to any who wished to join and any who wished to leave. It was, however, rapidly bent to the logics of international capitalism, the nation-state, and interstate relations. Those peoples that attempted to leave the USSR were repressed with extreme violence, and it was only by such violence that peoples were joined or allied to it. The Soviet Union was experienced by its multiplicity of peoples, and its foreign dependents, as imperial, state-capitalistic, chauvinistic and anti-democratic. In the most bitter and tragic of ironies, it now finds itself in the historical dustbin to which it had consigned both the world capitalistic economy and the bourgeois nation-state.

TOWARDS A CRITICAL AND COMMITTED GLOBALIZATION THEORY

A critical and socially committed globalization theory can, I think, surpass the traditional world-views of right or left: the spread of Western civilization, imperialism, development, dependency, interdependence, and globalism. It can do this without necessarily denying or ignoring such continuing processes as these may connote. I use "critical and committed" here in the tradition of Marx's *Critique of Political Economy* (Marx, 1904); in other words, as a rejection of an alienating social relationship, as a criticism of given understanding, and as an address to emancipation.

When I say that such a theory need not, or should not, deny or ignore the processes that other discourses attempt to explain, I mean that we should not, for example, reject imperialism discourse while abundant evidence of imperialism still exists (e.g., the Gulf War, drainage of capital from the poorest parts of the world). Critical globalization theory should, thus, rather be understood as both a new map and as a transparent overlay through which old structures, processes, and discourses are still visible. Although "imperialism" can still be used in relationship to the Western-led war against Iraq, it hardly explains widespread Third World complicity with this war, and even less can it lead us—as left anti-imperialist tradition led some—to identify with Iraqi state-nationalism. And although it is hardly logical to use Three Worlds discourse when the Second World has imploded, the common-sense understanding of "Third World" can be accepted, provided one has at hand an overlay with more explanatory and emancipatory value.

The concept of globalization I am working toward recognizes the limits of Western internationalization projects and universalisms. Exported (r)evolutions increasingly boomerang (George, 1992). Major "Northern" cities, states, and societies reveal "Southern" traits (see Davis, 1992, on Lima, Beirut, and Mexico City as showing Los Angeles its possible future). African Americans in the United States suffer the same quality of life as the people of Trinidad. Northern states lose the integration and control that previously permitted them to (believe they did or could) control the world, or even that they can fully control their own multiethnic or multireligious backyards (Forbes, 1993). Consider, here, Quebec in Canada, and then North American Indians within Quebec.

According to the new understanding I propose, the external invests the internal, the local redefines the global.[2] Thus, the global ecological movement discovered the rubber-tapper, rural organizer, unionist, socialist, and ecologist Chico Mendes (1992). In turn, his struggles, and his death in struggle, in a tiny isolated Amazonian community, informs the global ecological movement with a sense of how ecological struggles are life-and-death ones in a more than cosmic sense. He also provides the world with a new kind of working-class hero, one who is much more than a worker and a socialist. It is now a local hero that "is something to be,"[3] and local heroes (and heroines) can today be global also.[4]

---

[2]This is in contradiction with the vision of Vandana Shiva (1993). She presents local/global as a binary and Manichean division, the first invested with virtue and the second with vice. This reverses rather than surpasses the logic of the globalists she wishes to undermine.

[3]The reference is to John Lennon's song, which tells us that "a working-class hero is something to be" and how difficult it is to be one.

[4]Thus, in early 1992, an international human rights conference called by the Dutch development-funding agency, NOVIB, was renamed to honor Maria-Elena Moyano, the popular feminist Deputy Mayor of Lima's largest squatter settlement. Moyano had been recently assassinated and then dismembered by the authoritarian and militaristic Maoists of Peru's Shining Path movement. But the

RADICAL MODERNITY AS A COMPLEX,
GLOBALIZED, HIGH-RISK, INFORMATION CAPITALISM

Synthesizing arguments from Beck (1992), Giddens (1990), Melucci (1989), Poster (1984, 1990), and Walsh (1992), I refer to our contemporary period as one of *high* or *radical* modernity, characterized further as that of a *complex, globalized, high-risk, information capitalism.* Globalization (unlike imperialism, development, or dependency) must be understood as multidetermined: by the market, surveillance, militarization, industrialism, patriarchy, technocracy, informatism, racism, and so on. Table 2.1, which is based on but varies from the model originally offered by Giddens (1990), presents the matter schematically. Line A indicates the continuation of capitalism and its dominant ideology as one of the defining characteristics of modernity. Line B suggests the continuing connection with industrialization and ecological despoliation, legitimized by the ideology of consumption. Line C reveals the connection with administration and surveillance, both nationally and internationally. Line D shows the military connection. Line E suggests the increasing role of computers and electronic information and culture—both a cause and effect of the globalization of capital. Line F argues the crucial role of gender and sexuality, of their commoditization (by capital) and manipulation (by administrators and technical experts, operating via state or interstate agencies). Line G (and hypothetically, lines H-Z) are left open, to allow for others to argue for additional structures, processes, movements, and alternatives. Such a complex model of modernity and globalization is best appreciated in contrast with those fixated solely on capital, imperialism, state, or modernity. None of the latter would seem to allow for the variety of movements we find in Column 3, or, if they did, would rank and prioritize them according to a specific contradiction (or discourse, in the case of some discourse-fixated theorists).

Although insisting on the increasing interdependency of the indicated institutions, processes, or ideologies, I find it impossible not to recognize the priority of capital and state. By such prioritizing, I mean that I see these as the most dynamic and powerful sources or forces, even if increasingly dependent on the others. But recognizing the *priority* here of (transnational) capitalism and (inter-)statism does not necessarily entail the *primacy* of ant-capitalistic, anti-imperialistic, or anti-statist contradictions or struggles. Capital and state do not necessarily today confront

General Secretary of NOVIB, in opening the conference, also mentioned Chico Mendes and Shankar Guha Nyogi, the equally recently assassinated leader of a highly innovatory movement based on the tribal mine laborers of the Chatisgarh region in India. Video makes it possible for us to know about such local leaders. International electronic mail is already helping to keep people like them alive and free.

Table 2.1. Globalization—Its Discontents, Movements, and Alternatives.

	1. Institutional & Ideological Aspects of High Capitalist Modernity	2. Dimensions of Contemporary Globalization	3. Social Movements: Global, National, and Local	4. Alternative Global Civilization
A	capitalism (possessive individualism)	world capital extraction and concentration/	labor socialist	socialized economic organization
B	industrialization (industrialism and consumerism)	ecological despoliation	ecological and consumer	system of planetary care
C	administration and surveillance (bureaucracy)	hegemonic interstate regimes	democratic, human, civil, and social rights	coordinated multilevel world order
D	military (militarism)	world military/police repression, control, and espionage	peace, conflict- resolution, pacifist	transcendence of war via disarmament competition
E	computerization of information and culture (technocracy)	informatization of crucial global relations and culture	democratization and pluralization of information and culture	accessible and diverse information images, forms
F	gender/sexual commoditization and manipulation (patriarchy)	global gender/sexual family commoditization and programming	women's feminist, sexual rights	egalitarian and sexually pluralistic
G	. . .	. . .	. . .	. . . .

local, national, regional, or global communities in such direct and overt ways as in the 19th century—with the factory, the prison, the gun, and the flag. Studying and engaging in emancipatory global movements will tell us where, when, and for whom a contradiction has primacy.

THE CHANGING NATURE OF GLOBALIZED CAPITAL

Global capital still confronts labor globally. The rapidity of change in waged work, in its relative growth or decline, in its nature, in its separation by labor markets, in the balance and distribution of such (nationally, regionally, and globally), and in the nature of its product, requires us to radically rethink labor movement strategies.

Following Allen (1992), I argue that key to the contemporary transformation of the global capitalist economy and waged work is the leading role played by knowledge and information. Information technology, both as used in production and as product, is connected with a reduction in the total demand for labor; a shift in control within the labor process from the machine operator to the technician; a shift from economies of scale (mass production) to those of scope (e.g., batch production for "niche" markets) and from production to services; a decentralization of production (while retaining central managerial or financial control), and a networking of relations between such central controllers. Some would argue that this will lead to a new polarization (a) within national labor forces (skilled, secure, white, male versus unskilled, part-time/temporary, non-White, female), and (b) between an informatized North and an industrial (or at least partly industrial) South. Such images might suggest the necessity for (but not necessarily the possibility of) a new kind of class-like alliance nationally and internationally. But, in line with my earlier argument, I am inclined to see this process as simultaneously undermining an identity based on labor and creating the basis for new cross-class social movements, questioning the continuing subordination within and enslavement by work, the nature of products, the ethic of competition, consumerism, growth, and so on.

Allen (1992) raises two interesting questions here, one relating to the increasing interpenetration of development and underdevelopment, the other the implications of unevenness in a world in which cities or national economies increasingly become interchangeable sites for production, finance, and services:

> Alongside the financial and commercial practices of New York and London, for example, we find the sweatshops and outworking practices that are more often associated with Third World economies. Yet they are not opposing developments and nor are they unrelated. There is no simple equation of finance with post-industrialism and the informal practices often undertaken by a migrant workforce with pre-industrialism. On the contrary, they are part and parcel of the same global economic forces which are eroding the identity of the West as the "Rest", as it were, move to the centres of the modern world. (p. 202)

Furthermore:

If national economies increasingly become "sites" across which international forces flow, with some parts of a country passed over by the new growth dynamics, then the new uneven global order will very likely be characterized by more than one line of economic direction [division?—PW] within and between countries. (p. 202)

THE DECENTERING OF CAPITALIST POWER

Globalization means that internationally dominating power decreasingly resides in a unified territorial site (e.g., a state, a bloc) or in a single privileged subject (e.g., the international bourgeoisie), depends on a primary determinant (e.g., military/strategic), or lies at a primary level (e.g., the state-national). Rarely now do we see these four elements coinciding, as might have been the case during the Pax Britannica (up to 1914) or Pax Americana (after 1945). During the war against Iraq we saw the operation of a complex division of labor:

> The Gulf War coalition pooled different kinds of power possessed by different entities. The United States provided military equipment and trained personnel. Some Arab countries provided base areas. The emirs, the Japanese, and the Germans provided cash. The Security Council, dominated by the major powers, provided legitimation for the entire effort. While the war drew on nationalist sentiment in the United States and some other countries, its coalition model actually reflected the inability of the United States or any other single nation to function as a hegemonic power on its own. (Brecher, 1993, pp. 5-6)

One could go further, pointing out how the United States provided the (dis)information, and how ex-Communist and even erstwhile "non-aligned" countries of the Third World—oil dependent, with uncertain frontiers and predatory neighbors—enthusiastically joined the crusade. An understanding of globalization helps us understand these attempts to (re)create hegemonic blocs for the preservation of "world order." This does not, of course, mean that we can continue to understand world order as primarily a matter of relations between homogenous states or blocs. We need a more complex view, one that allows both for the increased intensity or complexity of relations between time and place and for the ambiguity of space as place.

THE CHANGING INTER-RELATIONSHIP OF SPACE AND TIME

Critical globalization theory requires a multidimensional understanding of space, a simultaneous process of "space-time scope/stretch" and "space-time intensity/deepening" (see Giddens, 1990; Harvey, 1989; McGrew, 1992) This passage from Giddens (1990) suggests both aspects:

> In pre-modern societies, space and place largely coincide, since the spatial dimensions of social life are, for most of the population, and in most respects, dominated by "presence"—localized activities. The advent of modernity increasingly tears space away from place by fostering relations between "absent" others, locationally distant from any given situation of face-to-face interaction. In conditions of modernity. . . locales are thoroughly penetrated by and shaped in terms of social influences quite distant from them. (p. 19)

Social relations in each locale are increasingly (if differentially) impacted by distant processes or events. Differentiation of involvement and impact is also notable between classes, ethnic groups, and genders. As Massey (1991) has pointed out, in the processes of globalization some groups have more initiative, whereas others receive, and yet others are imprisoned by, space-time stretching or intensification. There are, she suggests, three groupings: (a) those who are in charge of time-space compression and able to get the most advantage from it—corporate investors, film distributors and currency dealers, the jetsetters and e-mailers; (b) those who have both contributed in one sense but are imprisoned in another—slum dwellers of Rio, who may be a source of both global football and global music but may never have been to downtown Rio (nor, it occurs to me, to the 1992 UNCED global ecology conference held there); and (c) a group on the fringe of the first category, including those Western academics and journalists "who write most about it" (p. 26).

Massey's third category—which needs to include many "Southern" intellectuals, "Westernized" or not—is important for several reasons, First, it enables us to see that theories of space-time compression are not ineffable emanations of social science, but reflections or expressions of people occupying specific subject positions. Second, it enables those in such positions (including myself) to relate their experiences or ideas to those of the second category, which is what Massey herself is evidently attempting to do. And third, it helps us to understand how it is that whereas some classes, ethnic/religious groups, gender/sexual categories might welcome globalization as liberating, others seek to resist it, and yet others to surpass it.

We also need to recognize the complexity of time and the increasing centrality of what Rifkin (1987) calls "time wars." The shift from natural time (sun, moon, seasons) to the clock and from the clock to the computer has been accompanied by a distancing of humanity and society from nature and by the increasing power and reach of those who literally control time. Rifkin's time wars are class, gender and imperial ones that lead to "time pyramids" for the wealthy and "time ghettos" for the poor (p. 190). At the top of today's computerized global time pyramids are, of course, the multinational companies:

> The computer is their method of communication, their timepiece, their manager, and their forecaster. The multinationals take their power with them wherever they go. It resides deep inside the microworld of silicon chips and electronic circuits that guard the data and information used to programme the temporal affairs of local communities—and whole continents. (p. 189)

The increasing global hegemony of computer-defined and computer-controlled time increases, with dramatically increased urgency, the necessity for the democratization of place and space to be accompanied by "the democratization of time" (p. 219). Fast is no more beautiful than big.

Recognition of the increased scope and intensity of space-time relations, of an increasingly interdependent global sociality, makes, I think, simplistic traditional notions of the social world and its transformation increasingly archaic. Class, economic, and technological determinism; territorial nationalism as primary political identity; political-revolutionism or insurrectionism and global apocalypticism have all been part of the stock in trade of the left. They can even be found combined—if uneasily—in the doctrines of the last Maoist Communist Parties, such as the Communist Party of the Philippines or Peru's Shining Path. A growing awareness of global complexity and interdependence would allow these notions to be left to reactionary, conservative, or authoritarian ideologues. The new social movements, which both continue and break with the classical left, are beginning to point out more complex answers to our growing global concerns.

NEW GLOBAL SOCIAL MOVEMENTS, OR NEW SOCIAL MOVEMENTS AS GLOBAL

Globalization spreads the effects of capitalist development to everywhere and everybody (and, as feminists point out, to every body). It sharpens the combinations, unevennesses, ambiguities, and contradictions of high modernity. It gives rise to democratic and pluralistic social movements that point to the possibility of meaningfully postmodern—that is, postcapitalist, postmilitarist, postindustrial—global alternatives. (This thought is nicely expressed in the feminist postcard that declares "I will be a postfeminist in postpatriarchy.") We are now considering Columns 3 and 4 of Table 2.1, again extending the argument of Giddens (1990). If, previously, ideas of an alternative world order found expression in the writings of individual authors, or a particular movement from a particular world area (the West), they are beginning to find broader collective political expression. Introducing such a collection, which includes writings from a wide range of new and old social movements, ideological traditions, and world areas, Brecher (1993) argues for an ecological worldview:

> Such an "ecological" approach starts from a conception of the indi-
> vidual as a member of many groups—kinship, ethnic, religious, polit-
> ical, etc.—whose boundaries do not generally coincide and no one
> of which can be regarded as sovereign over the others. . . . Such an
> approach . . . recognizes the current reality of multiple overlapping
> transnational power networks. It envisions a multi-level system of
> regulation cutting across the boundaries of existing nation-states to
> control the transnational forces that actually shape today's world.
> (pp. 7-8)

Previously, emancipatory movements operated with worldviews in which the enemy was seen (or allied enemies were seen) as homogenous, or homologous, as omnipresent, and as more or less omnipotent (for such socialist discourse on "capitalism", see Gibson-Graham, 1993). The enemy also, of course, personified evil. The movement represented itself as the naturally, supernaturally, or socially and historically ordained alternative, as well as the personification of virtue. The new worldview offered by Brecher and others is deeply subversive of such a model. It is consistent, however, with the structure, strategy, and activity of the new pluralistic global movements, active at many social levels, in many social spaces, assuming overlapping areas of activity with others, and expecting to be involved in dialogue with them.

Globalization, of course, not only provokes democratic, pluralist, and forward-looking movements. It also gives rise to authoritarian, militaristic, and apocalyptical ones (religious and secular, right and left) attempting to deny, repulse, or escape a globalized capitalist modernity. We may here again refer to Peru's Shining Path. This movement is both a result of Peru's peripheralization from the latest phases of capitalist globalization and an attempt to isolate it even further. Its contradictory logic, ethical double standards, and political hypocrisies are striking. Shining Path assassinates Peruvian proletarians in the name of a proletarian revolution rejected by Peruvian proletarians. It is part of a "proletarian internationalist" network, consisting of the customary middle-class intellectuals, alienated from their national societies and self-isolated from the local masses. While blowing up the dying body of an assassinated popular feminist leader and denouncing Amnesty International for its bourgeois hypocrisy, Shining Path appeals to world public opinion (actually the more naive, ignorant, or romantic part of its socialist and left-liberal middle classes) to defend the human rights of its authoritarian leader.[5] Inhuman, irrational, archaic, and grotesque as such movements may seem, they cannot be either dismissed, repressed, or simply named and tamed as "fundamentalist," "fascist," "racist," or "totalitarian" (see Pieterse, 1994, on Western discourse on "fundamentalism"). Such labels may be necessary to trigger an initial response from the relevant public. But insofar as they seem to be increasingly provoked precisely by our complex, informatized, and globalized capitalism, these movements rather require those threatened by them to take action globally against the global conditions that provoke them.

A COMPLEX GLOBAL ORDER REQUIRES COMPLEX GLOBAL ALTERNATIVES

The identification here of global problems rather than universal enemies requires us to formulate and develop viable, convincing, attractive, and enjoyable global solutions. The word *enjoyable* is crucial here. Insofar as we recognize how state-nationalism and globalized capital capitalize (literally and figuratively) on enjoyment, those seeking to surpass capitalism must shrug off their fear or hatred of pleasure, sensuality, lust, and individual consumption (for the latter, see Ehrenreich, 1990). The notion of a worldwide Maoist Cultural Revolution will attract few—especially among people who have been already subjected to such puritanical authoritarianism and its accompanying hypocrisies.

Other leftist traditions, such as the undialectical reform or revolution opposition, must be abandoned. Incremental global reformism from within and radical global "alternativism" from without imply nonapocalyptic global strategies and a mutually educative dialectic for civilizing and transforming the world. Insofar as conservatives and traditionalists may be concerned with preserving the ecology, local cultures, and traditional structures from the careless destructuring or restructuring impact of

---

[5]The national and international activities of Shining Path were debated in the left and liberal press in the United States and United Kingdom in 1992-93. For a sample, see the correspondence pages of *NACLA Report on the Americas* (1993a, 1993b, 1993c).

globalized capitalism—and insofar as they are prepared to dialogue with us—we should not set ourselves up in principle against them either.

If we reject (r)evolutionary historical schemas, then we can extend globally the notion Calderon (1988) has applied to Latin America, of living in "mixed times." Such a notion undermines the binary oppositions of Traditional-Modern and Modern-Postmodern, reminding us that we live in an historical world, not just a sociological or linguistic universe. Realistic global utopias will then represent not negations of either "premodernity" or "modernity," but selective rejections and rearticulations—implying the necessary contribution also of those living under, rediscovering, or valuing precapitalistic civilizations and cultures. It is within such a framework that we can best understand why it is that the "premodern" Yanomani Indians in the Brazilian Amazon speak to "postmodern" movements in "modern" North America or Western Europe. How much, and in what ways, such nonhegemonic classes, groups, and forces speak to each other across times, spaces, and places is also crucial. I now consider this matter.

INFORMATION CAPITALISM AS AN EMINENTLY DISPUTABLE TERRAIN

There is considerable agreement on "the central importance of knowledge and information" (Allen, 1992, p. 182) in the current transformation of capitalism globally, even if the question of what the transition is to remains unclear or disputed. The growing centrality to social processes of the "mode of information" (Poster, 1984, p. 1990)—of data, ideas, values, images, theories, and cultures—makes it both possible and necessary for life-asserting or emancipatory movements to operate on these terrains. Here they can reveal, as Amnesty International does, what is globally concealed, or suggest, as Friends of the Earth might, new meanings for what is globally revealed (Melucci, 1989). A global information capitalism would seem to provide far more favorable terrains for emancipatory movements than those of an internationalized industrial capitalism (industry, polity, nation, battlefield). It has proven extremely difficult to radically democratize these old terrains.

Typically, in the past, it has been the terrain that has dominated the movement. This has tended to be the case even when new social movements enter the traditional spaces; witness the rise and fall of Green parties in parliamentary elections. As long as these spaces have public legitimacy we cannot ignore them. But the power of the new movements, locally, nationally, and internationally, lies rather in their new ideas, values, and organizational principles—the latter revealing at least an implicit understanding of the potential of the latest communication technologies. For one thing, they have highlighted networking as a relational principle—a reinstatement of the oldest and most commonplace relationship and an extension of it from the local to the global.

The new global solidarity movements are, in large part, "communication internationalisms". Communication is here increasingly understood not simply as a neutral means to an organizationally defined end, but as a means-end bearing complex with contradictory values that have to be understood and opted for or against. The new global movements are thus making increasing use of computer-mediated communications (Frederick, 1992a; Stefanik, 1993). But this process is not without its own contradictions. The slow transformation of one "organizational internationalism" into such a communication internationalism can be observed in the case of the international labor movement (Waterman, 1992).

Traditionally, the labor movement and socialist theorists have tended to see communication instrumentally, as a more or less neutral means to a mobilizing, organizing, and controlling end. Socialists have thus also tended to swing between wild optimism and black pessimism, depending on whether the latest means of communication (press, film, radio, video) appeared to favor labor or capital. Labor movements and socialist parties still overvalue the hierarchical organization. The recent development of international labor communication by computer has resulted in large part from enthusiastic and imaginative initiatives by the "alternative" international labor service centers coupled with a slow and cautious response from the traditional international union organizations. As the two forces interact and converge, they reveal problems facing the project as a whole. As with the new internationalisms more generally, it becomes increasingly necessary to research, theorize, or strategize— and to dialogue with other internationalist communicators—if the new projects are not to reproduce dominant international relations and communications practices.

FROM CULTURAL GLOBALIZATION TO AN ALTERNATIVE GLOBAL CULTURE

I now consider culture more specifically, in terms of a common language, commonly understood symbols and meanings, and shared aesthetic pleasures. There have been, and are, different ways in which a global culture has been conceived, proposed, or even organized and imposed. At one time, for example, it might have been seen as represented by the single worldwide Catholic faith, Rome, the Pope, Latin, a shared architecture, symbols, dogma, or rituals. In the 19th century, the *Communist Manifesto* spoke of the disappearance of national narrow-mindedness and the appearance of a "world literature" developed out of national and local ones (Marx & Engels, 1935). Such a literature, understood in Marxist terms, is, 150 years later, commonplace. Consider the way contemporary Chile and China have been brought to English paperback readers by Allende's *Of Love and Shadows* (1987) and Chang's *Wild Swans* (1991).

However, this is culture for the literate, literature-reading public and is brought to them courtesy of an increasingly globalized capitalist publishing industry. It can hardly be itself isolated from the more general electronic information, media, and advertising conglomerates into which publishing is increasingly integrated (see Table 2.1, Line E). World culture, thus, also includes Donald Duck (Dorfman & Mattelart, 1975), McDonalds, and Cable News Network (MacTV?). This brave new world of multinationalized culture has often been understood by the Left in terms of North American cultural imperialism, commercializing, homogenizing, and destroying local culture (Petras, 1993). Such a model can hardly account for the commercial production and international distribution of the filmed version of Allende's *House of the Spirits*, or the TV one of Chang's *Wild Swans*. And, if it does allow for them, it can hardly take an interest in their possibly subversive, emancipatory, empathy-creating, or inspirational impact.

Featherstone (1990), on the other hand, has argued that the existence of a unified global culture (on the nation-state model) is actually impossible, because:

> to contemplate this on the global level means imaginatively to construct an "outside" to the globe, a sphere of global threat captured only in the pages and footage of science fiction accounts of space invaders, inter-planetary and inter-galactic wars. In addition the transnational cosmopolitan intellectuals (serving which masters we might ask?) would have a long way to go to re-discover, formulate and agree upon global equivalents to the *ethnie*. (p. 11)

There are various ways in which the matter might be reconceived. In the first place, one can imagine a culture or subcultures that are not primarily territorial, or not necessarily linguistic, in nature (e.g., Islamic, socialist, female, or feminist). In the second place, one can recognize the "outside global threat" *intra*terrestrially, as science fiction increasingly becomes science fact. What of the somewhat pathetic "transnational cosmopolitan intellectuals," with no master to serve, no ethnie for reference? Given the increasing centrality of knowledge and information to a globalized modernity, it is not necessary to assume that its bearers serve masters (or, if feminists, mistresses). Some thinkers even see the knowledge class or elites as themselves the new masters of the universe (Frankel, 1987). I could imagine Featherstone's "transnational cosmopolitan intellectuals" in a cultural avant garde model (not the same as Lenin's vangardist one), hypothetically involved in a democratic dialogue or dialectic with mass communities of territory, interest, affinity, with these, again hypothetically, becoming globally aware.

Do intellectuals, in any case, need an *ethnie* or even a language? Only, perhaps, if one conceives them on the model of Featherstone, as those operating primarily through the (untranslatable?) written or spoken word. There are other "intellectuals," such as those educated and aware artists whose stock-in-trade is global synthesis and syncretism, and who are also involved in the complex and contradictory process of creating various kinds of global communities, whose efforts can hardly be understood in terms of "cultural imperialism". This is evident in the case of popular music, as when Reebee Garofalo (1992) not only shows rock as a medium for democratic mass movements cross-nationally, from London to Rio and Peking, but as a music of global awareness or protest, from the Band Aid Concert to the Mandela one. The same point is made by Rubén Martínez (1992) about Mexican *rocanrol*. Martínez, a Los Angeles-based journalist and poet, experiences a new transnational culture in ways that touch—if tangentially—on traditional religious, liberal, or socialist thought and values:

> Weaned on a blend of cultures, languages and ideologies (Anglo/Latino, Spanish/English, individualist/collectivist), I have lived both in the North and the South over my twenty-nine years, trying to be South in the South, North in the North, South in the North and North in the South. Now, I stand at the centre—watching history whirl around me as my own history fissures. . . . I cannot tell whether what I see is a beginning or an end. My quest for a true centre, for a cultural, political and romantic home, is stripped of direction. . . . One can spy on multilingual store signs in New York or Los Angeles . . . listen to the rhythms of every culture and time on the airwaves, but the fires of nationalism still rage, and in the cities of the United States, Blacks and Koreans and Latinos and Anglos live in anything but a multicultural paradise. As for myself, it is all too often that I yearn for the Other even when I am with the Other: nowhere do I feel complete. . . .With the walls coming down, it may be possible that I'll be able to see beyond the ruins. Gaze upon the other side and see the others—clearly. . . .It has been, it is...a search for a one that is much more than two. Because, wherever I am now, I must be much more than two. I must be North and South in the North and the South. (pp. 3-5)

So, even if we are obliged to recognize that we are still living more in a global theater than in a global civilization (Anderson, 1990), the issue is not without hope. But can the theater become a civilization?

CIVILIZING GLOBAL SOCIETY: AN ALTERNATIVE WORLD ORDER
THE PROBLEMATIC CREATION OF A NONCAPITALIST,
NONHIERARCHICAL GLOBAL ORDER

Globalization implies the growing centrality of the supra- or nonterritorial level of global institutions and instances, and therefore the possibility and necessity for the development of a global civil society. This means a non-capitalist/nonstate, or anticompetitive/antihierarchical, sphere for democratic efforts, within and without the multiple existing global terrains. There is increasing discussion here, some relating to reform of the UN and other such interstate instances (Held, 1991), others proposing new standards such as "The Right to Communicate" (Hamelink, 1995), and yet others focusing on the structure and functioning of global social movements (McCoy & McCully, 1993). There are, finally, increasing efforts to consider the interrelationship between the interstate organizations, the NGOs (nongovernmental organizations) modeled on these, and the global movements that go beyond territorially defined constituencies (Brecher, Childs, & Cutler, 1993; Galtung, 1980; Havens Center, 1994).

Global civil society is no paradise of nonterritorial liberty, equality, solidarity, ecological care, and pluralistic tolerance. It may be the privileged space for the civilizing and surpassing of capitalist, statist, technocratic, and so on, structures, processes, or ideologies. It should be understood as a habitat to be continuously and jointly constructed rather than as an existing structure even imperfectly represented by international social movements or NGOs. Within this space global movements will inevitably express their external and internal tensions, and negotiate their internal and external relations, often revealing or reproducing traits they claim to have surpassed. Increasingly, however, the ambiguity of their own practice is recognized by people in the movements:

> We make compromises, we open new processes. . . We are facing complexities. We make declarations of interdependence. We take money from the powers that we fight, we try to confuse them and are confused. We go along with the carelessness of using and thoughtlessness of production and consumption. We try to live with the system and escape it. We are crushed under the bulldozers of capital and technology; we die from hunger and get used to producing statements in the name of the oppressed and the dying; we live within the grids of the Norths and Souths within and against each other. (Charkiewicz & Nijpels, 1993, pp. 18-19)

Insofar as civil society depends on, struggles against, and is articulated with state and capital, the development of a global civil society depends on and stimulates the democratization, deconcentration, and decentralization, of interstate organizations and of global capitalist companies and institutions. For auto and other transport worker unions, or consumer and ecological movements, for example, this could and should mean proposing a worker, democratic, and ecologically friendly plan for the world auto and transport industries.[6]

Such a global civil society requires a concept of world citizenship appropriate to the era of globalization. This can no longer be simply that of the religious universalist, the liberal cosmopolitan, or the socialist internationalist. Bart van Steenbergen (1992) identified as hypothetical global citizens the "global capitalist," the "global reformer," the "environmental manager" and the "earth citizen," His "earth citizen" would seem the relevant successor to past types of international citizen:

> Ecological citizenship emphasizes the importance of the planet as breeding ground, as habitat and as lifeworld. In that sense we could call this type of citizen an *earth citizen* who is aware of his [sic] organic process of birth and growth out of the earth as a living organism. This is based on the notion of care, as distinct from the notion of control. The development of citizenship from the city, via the nation-state and the region to the globe is here not just a matter of an increase in scale. With the notion of the "earth citizen" a full circle is made. The citizen is back to his roots; the earth as Gaia, as one's habitat. (emphasis in original)

GLOBAL SOLIDARITY: AN INTERNATIONALISM FOR A WORLD BOTH REAL AND UNIVERSAL

The 19th century was the "century of progress," in which the "iron law of capital accumulation" gave rise to an equally deterministic and inflexible opposition. Marxism has it that "freedom is the recognition of necessity"—hardly an encouragement to either dialectical or ethical thought. The gradual transition from industrial to information capitalism, the multiple crises of growth, a spreading ecological awareness, all these encourage or provoke dialectical thinking, the recognition of long chains of

---

[6]When I proposed this at an international autoworkers' consultation, at the Transnationals Information Exchange (TIE), Amsterdam, around 1985, an international officer of the major Dutch trade union confederation, the FNV, confessed total bewilderment. For people like himself, even though supporters of the peace, ecological, and human rights movements, such a notion was totally utopian. It appears to be no longer so. By 1993, TIE, now increasingly supported by FNV affiliates and members, was organizing its first "Car and Society Conference" (Transnationals Information Exchange, 1993).

cause and effect (and the impossibility of separating these), and the increasing necessity of truly fundamental choices concerning ever wider definitions of the social. In 1968, "demand the impossible'—the obverse of Marxist thought—became a political slogan. Ours is a period in which we are increasingly condemned to choose. Such choice is the terrain of ethics, or of an ethically aware, ethically informed politics. This seems to be well understood by Collier (1992):

> The whole planet has become a shared world, even for those who never leave their village. Thus, a tie which is both real and universal has arrived; not yet in the form of a real collectivity embracing humankind, but of real relations of mutual dependence through the sharing of the world; and it is from just such relations . . . that values and obligations arise. (p. 87)

Globalization creates a world that can increasingly be experienced by growing population sectors (although differentially and unevenly) as both real and universal, thus allowing for a universalism that is more than faith or obligation, a global solidarity that is more than a merely imagined community. The new global solidarity projects descend from, selectively rearticulate, allow for, but go beyond, religious, liberal, and socialist universalisms. Proposing neither a return to an unchanging golden past nor a leap into a perfect future—here or hereafter—they allow for and require a dialogue of civilizations and ages, a solidarity with both past and future.

A UNIVERSALISM FOR PLURAL WORLDS

There are two possible pitfalls. The first is that of producing or reproducing a universalism that is either perverse in intention, particularistic in effect, or philosophically illegitimate. The second is that of producing or reproducing a sentimental humanistic universalism, of which the welcoming bark and wagging tail are accompanied by little bite on our infinitely divided, complex, and slippery global reality. I now deal with the first challenge directly, whereas the second is the topic of the rest of the chapter.

The major contemporary philosophical challenge to global solidarity is the widespread current condemnation of foundationalism, universalism, essentialism, rationalism, and any grand narratives that offer universal statements of reality, value, and obligation, based on initial assumptions or arguments about the universe, nature, man, society, and so on. Such grand narratives are those that have descended from Judaism and Christianity, from the European Enlightenment, Liberalism, and Socialism—the sources of most internationalistic doctrine. They are suspect for presenting their story as truth and for imposing this truth on others (and an always excluded Other). There are "right" and "left" versions of such criticism, sometimes directly targeting globalization theories, humanist universalism, or any general international solidarity ethic. I deal only with the left versions.

There has been much left criticism of Marxism—both classical and contemporary—in these terms. Mires (1989) convincingly deconstructs traditional internationalistic discourse, preferring the cautious language of "international cooperation" and "coordination" to that of internationalism. We may also note the related plea of the green economist Alain Lipietz (1990) for a "modest internationalism," a "minimal universalism." There is, on the left, an explicit or implicit fear of once again imposing on those from different (and less powerful) worlds the universalizing claims of Western or Westernized intellectuals or movements. Two arguments may be relevant here: an abstract one relating to universalism and civil society, and a concrete one relating to globalization and universal responsibility.

Following Alexander (1991), we may recognize that cultural universalism has been essential to the development of liberal democracy, its place of residence being civil society. We may further recognize with him how the themes of "civility, civil society, universalism, and citizenship" (p. 167) have been central to the development of the Western nation-state, as well as to the expansion of concepts of citizenship from the legal to the political and social spheres. And we may, finally, recognize with him the manner in which "societal community" can expand beyond the nation-state:

> With the construction of a civil society . . . particularistic definitions of membership are broken through; they are replaced by abstract criteria that emphasize simple humanity and participation . . . . Citizenship, then, can be understood as a form of social organization that is anchored in universalistic bonds of community that define every member as equally worthy of respect. . . . Members of a civil society can refer to these universalistic values to gain distance from their immediate relationships, in order to change or criticize them. (p. 168)

Civil society, in other words, implies not the existence of public consensus or consent, but the very existence of a public, and therefore the possibility of political skepticism, criticism and moral outrage—as well as global civil society. Alexander's (1991) argument provides, in principle, a conceptual basis for notions of global citizenship and civil society. What Alexander does not do is relate his model to actually existing capitalism, nationally or globally.

Collier (1992) offers a case for an ethical universalism that is related to capitalism in general and to internationalization processes in particular. Collier recognizes that Marxists have tended to argue for an ethical universalism either *despite of* or *as* the self-interest of the working class. He is concerned to escape the horns of this dilemma: that is, of appearing either as a "shamefaced altruist or a shameless collective egoist" (p. 76). He does so on the basis of what he calls a relational ontology. Society, he argues, is not a collection of individuals, a group, or organism, but a network:

> Such a network—"society"—is not a count-noun. It does not make sense to ask how many societies there are in the world—nor is there only one society. There is society—not societies or a society. Society is an open-textured network, which can be divided in various ways for the purposes of description and analysis, but these divisions are always more or less artificial. (p. 82)

The ethical implication of this understanding is that it is the lattice of all the relationships within which one is enmeshed that is the source of values and responsibilities. Relating to others is to be understood not so much as something we do as what we are. This position, again, allows us to see that insofar as global society exists, it provides a source of values and responsibilities to be weighed against those coming from membership of a nation-state, class, ethnic group, and so on. It is the worlds we share with others that provide the social basis for morality. Whereas existence in the world of the market may push us in the direction of individualism and egoism, we also exist in other social worlds that allow us to be moved by the needs of significant others.

RECOGNIZING THE NEEDS AND VOICES OF OTHERS

How are we to avoid foisting another Westocentric universalism on the rest of the world? How are we to recognize the needs and voices of such others? Nancy Fraser (1986) is interested in "a discourse ethic of solidarity," which she also characterizes as an ethic of discourse for social movements. She points out that the means of interpretation and communication (the vocabularies for pressing claims, the idioms for communicating needs, the narrative conventions for constructing individual and collective histories, the paradigms of argument considered authoritative for judging competing claims, etc.) cannot be value-neutral. These means of interpretation tend to express the experiences, interests, and self-images of dominant social groups. In the case of the West, the dominant vocabularies constitute people as rational, self-interested individuals, engaged in exchange with others in utility-maximizing relationships. Such a standpoint is characteristically that of White European male bourgeois property owners.

Fraser argues that this vocabulary can hardly express relationships of ongoing dependency, such as that of mother and child, nor account for such experiences and feelings of connection as exist in "more extended networks of community and solidarity," as are to be customarily found in the subcultures of the subordinated. The latter are going to be hindered from participating on equal terms with the dominant groups in communicative interaction:

> Unless they were to contest this situation and organize to win a greater measure of collective control over the means of interpretation and communication, it would appear that members of subordinated groups would have only two options: they could either adopt the dominant point of view and see their own experiences repressed and distorted; or they could develop idiolects capable of voicing their experience and see these marginalized, disqualified and excluded from the central discursive institutions and arenas of society. Or they could do both at once. (1986, p. 426)

To surpass this situation, what is necessary is the replacement of a monological ethic by a discourse or dialogical ethic. The latter implies recognition the unequal relationship to the dominant means of interpretation, making such means themselves a matter of negotiation, and allowing the subordinated to propose alternatives to such. Fraser here provides an effective critique of, and alternative to, the monological universalisms of the past.

Fraser proposes not only a form of discourse, but a content for it—a solidarity ethic. Although she develops her argument in relationship to the women's movement, she herself argues that it is equally appropriate to other social movements of the subordinated or excluded. She also considers it necessary to avoid basing her ethic on either the "individual" or "humanity":

> Here one would abstract *both* from unique individuality and from universal humanity to focalize the intermediate zone of group identity. The most general ethical force of this orientation would be something like this: we owe each other behaviour such that each is confirmed as a being with specific collective identifications and solidarities. The norms governing these interactions would be . . . norms of collective solidarities expressed in shared but non-universal social practices. (p. 428; emphasis in original)

The reference here to group identity and shared practices requires that we address ourselves to—and reflect on—the practices of groups themselves claiming to contribute to global solidarity. I now consider one such group.

WHAT ABOUT THE WORKERS?

Suppose we agree that: (a) globalization processes provide the ground for a realistic contemporary universalism; (b) this is understood as related to specific emancipatory projects of a democratic and pluralistic orientation (i.e., neither self-prioritizing nor other-exclusionary), and (c) this requires both principles of solidarity and procedures for the development of such. At least two moves are still necessary. One is to turn these general philosophical principles into political statements. The other is to specify them in a manner relevant to potential collective actors of a quite specific and problematic nature, for example, semi-skilled White male factory workers in industrialized capitalist democracies. I now describe these moves simultaneously.

We have already seen that globalization is a multifaceted, multileveled, and multidirectional process, affecting all people in all parts of the world, although evidently in different ways and with different effects. One crucial aspect is that of the changing and moving nature of work internationally, creating highly changeable, differentiated, and interdependent working classes. Now, workers in the West are less secure and less homogeneous than they have been for many decades. This can evidently make them more corporatist and racist. But it can also lead them to feel more like workers in other countries, or with other local social identities and concerns. Struggling against the effects of globalization are, as we have seen, women, ethnic minorities, socialists, and people in the South and East as well as the West. Insofar as the worker has other identities, interests, and aspirations (as he or she always has had)—as urban resident, as churchgoer, as gay or lesbian, or as species being—these are also being challenged by globalization. In other words, the real and inevitably particular worlds of workers are increasingly invaded, interconnected, or interdependent.

The need for solidarity in this globalized world does not, furthermore, have to be presented to the Western worker in moralistic terms. I mean this in several senses. In the first place, insofar as we recognize their interpenetration, we need no longer oppose egoism and altruism, the short term and the long, the local and the distant. In the second place, because the worker is no longer conceived of as the privileged revolutionary subject, he or she cannot be conceived of as having a primary moral responsibility for internationalism. Recognition of this could be tension reducing. In the third place, insofar as interdependency is a global condition, any appeal to such a moral responsibility must be addressed to workers and labor movements also in the non-West (although the nature of the appeal would have to be relevant to the local experience and possibilities). This, also, can reduce moralistic demands on and expectations of Western workers and movements. Finally, appeals to workers from above, below, or outside (and these will continue) can be increasingly expressed in terms of worker self-activity, exploration, imagination, and creativity. Global solidarity can thus be seen less as a duty, of ourselves or others, than as an adventure in which all are potentially involved. It can also be increasingly experienced as enjoyable.

CONCLUSION: A WORLD TO SAVE

Developmentalism (reformist), Third Worldism (radical), and Proletarian Internationalism (apocalyptic) are dependent on old internationalization /internationalism theories, with all the superiority, guilt, dependency, and resentment that these imply. A critical and socially committed globalization theory would seem to provide an infinitely richer, more complex, and more open view of the world, and one in which superiority and guilt, dependency, and resentment can be traded in for recognition, responsibility, and reciprocity. The meager or miserable results of 150 years of communism, 50 or so years of developmentalism, and Third Worldism, suggest this may be a more rewarding field to plow.

Ninety hundred eighty-eight will be the 150th anniversary of the *Communist Manifesto* , which ended with a rhetorical slogan of biblical grandeur: 'Workers of the world, unite; you have nothing to lose but your chains; you have a world to win!" The slogan echoed around the world of industrial capitalists, churning the stomachs of crowned and uncrowned heads alike. It inspired massive movements—mostly of a decidedly nonproletarian and noninternationalistic nature or result. Today the slogan is less likely to frighten crowned heads than to frighten off nonworkers—and cause even Third World workers to worry about other things they might lose in addition to their chains (an electric fan? a refrigerator? a VCR?). Yet, like Paris 1968 and the anti-nuclear movement, we too need our slogans, symbols, and rituals. But would a simplifying slogan be appropriate to a world of such complexity, to a project so sensitive to ambiguity, to a period in which maximum optimism of the will must be combined with an equal skepticism of the intellect? How could it address the world's workers, peasants, and petty traders, with their possession of, or desire for, ecologically problematic consumer durables? And, if such a slogan is necessary, what on earth (globe?) could it possibly be?

3

Global Experience as a Consequence of Modernity*

John Tomlinson
Nottingham Trent University

Toward the end of *The Consequences of Modernity*, Anthony Giddens (1990) sketches what he calls "a phenomenology of modernity." He offers the central image of modernity as a juggernaut, "a runaway engine of enormous power which, collectively as human beings, we can drive to some extent but which also threatens to rush out of our control and which could rend itself asunder" (p. 139). The experience of modernity is thus one of "riding the juggernaut"—an ambivalent experience of exhilaration, the realization of potential, and a certain precarious control combined with risk, insecurity, powerlessness, and existential anxiety. He goes on to analyze this essential ambivalence in terms of four categories or "intersections" of experience. Each category describes a dialectical tension between opposed tendencies in modernity as they present themselves to experience: displacement and reembedding, intimacy and impersonality, expertise and reappropriation, privatism and engagement. In each of these categories he tries to demonstrate that the experience

*An earlier version of this chapter appeared in my paper "A Phenomenology of Globalization? Giddens on Global Modernity," *European Journal of Communication, 9*(4), 149-172.

of modernity is one of ambivalence rather than—as has so often been claimed—simply one of alienation or anomie.

Thus, for example, in his discussion of intimacy and impersonality, he argues that it is a mistake to think that we live in a world of strangers. We do not lose the intimacy of personal relations in the modern world; rather, intimacy is transformed by the abstract systems of modernity. People can use money to purchase the expertise of a psychologist to help them to explore their personal relations, and intimacy can be sustained at immense distances via the telephone. There is, indeed, an immense industry of counselors, self-help books, and so forth that attest to the centrality of intimate relations to modern social experience. This does not mean that modernity is unproblematic. Personal relations, he argues, are peculiarly fragile in modern societies, precisely because of the degree to which self-identity is invested in relationships that demand self-scrutiny, self-revelation, and high degrees of interpersonal trust not found in premodern societies. The point is that these problems are the problems not of a loss, but of a complex transformation, of intimacy (see Giddens, 1992) that is dialectically related to the impersonality of the abstract systems of modernity.

The category of experience with which I am particularly concerned here is the first one. In his discussion of displacement and reembedding, Giddens describes the ambivalence arising from the intersection of estrangement and familiarity—the complex of experience produced by the intrusion of distanciated events and forces into everyday, familiar "local" contexts.

What is implied here is, in fact, the experience of globalization, which Giddens (1991) describes as a consequence of modernity's "stretching" of the relations between local and distant events and processes:

> Globalization concerns the intersection of presence and absence, the interlacing of social events and social relationships "at distance" with local contextualities. We should grasp the global spread of modernity in terms of an ongoing relation between distanciation and the chronic mutability of local circumstances and local engagements. (p. 21)

The process of globalization clearly represents an important aspect of the phenomenology of modernity. But what can we say about the specific experience of globalization?

In the first place we should, perhaps, make clear of whose experience we are speaking. Throughout his discussion of modernity, Giddens (1990) writes with reference to the experience of people in the developed world, and he is, of course, conscious of the vast sectors of the world this leaves unconsidered. Globalization is an uneven process which, as McGrew (1992) says, "tends on the whole to reinforce (if not to increase) the inequalities of power and wealth, both between nations and across them" (p. 76). Clearly any full account of the phenomenon of globalization needs to address this unevenness (Hall, 1992; Massey, 1993; McGrew, 1992; Spybey, 1992). However, the issue here is more particular. The "we" that Giddens invokes in his discussions of the experience of modernity and globalization is necessarily the "we" of the developed world—including, of course, the "cosmopolitan" sectors of underdeveloped societies. It is this "world" and this specifically "global modern" experience he is, in the first instance, trying to understand.

As a starting point, we can reflect on a passage from Giddens's *Modernity and Self Identity* (1991), which develops the idea of the intrusion of the distant into the local:

> In conditions of late modernity we live "in the world" in a different sense from previous eras of history. Everyone still continues to live a local life, and the constraints of the body ensure that all individuals, at every moment, are contextually situated in time and space. Yet the transformations of place, and the intrusion of distance into local activities, combined with the centrality of mediated experience, radically change what "the world" actually is. . . . *Although everyone lives a local life, phenomenal worlds for the most part are truly global.* (p. 187; emphasis added)

I focus here on this last sentence. The claim is that there is an experience of the global in the everyday, "situated" lives of people in local circumstances. What is the nature of this experience, and how does it come about? We arrive at an answer from three directions.

THE GLOBALIZATION OF PLACE

The first and most direct approach is through Giddens's reflections on the nature of "place" in modernity. To understand this, we must first look briefly at Giddens's theory of "time-space distanciation," which underlies his view of the globalization process.

The peculiar dynamism of modernity, in contrast with the premodern ("traditional") world, derives, Giddens argues, from a transformation in the social perception and institutionalization of the relationship between time and space. This reordering of these fundamental ontological categories is, in fact, the central discontinuity that Giddens identifies between the modern and the traditional world.

In traditional societies, Giddens argues, the reckoning of time was limited, for the majority, by its reliance on a connection with place. Before the invention and mass diffusion of the mechanical clock, it was impossible to tell the time of day without referring to the particularities of a locality of interaction, especially natural time-space markers. Thus, for example, "dawn," "dusk," and "noon" were not only imprecise markers of time, they were intrinsically tied to the locality in which they were used. The same could be said of a statement such as "when we finish work in the fields and go back to the village." Such a time reference, although almost certainly indirectly governed by the natural span of the working day, is not conceptually tied to the circadian cycle. But it is still dependent for its meaning on the "presence availability" of local communities—that is, the degree to which people can physically come together. The limitations of traditional (nonclocked) time reckoning can thus be seen in the impossibility of statements such as "at three o'clock" or "in half an hour"—not merely impossibilities in terms of precision before mechanical clocking, but, more significantly, in terms of abstraction. The uniform abstract—"empty"— nature of clocked time freed time reckoning and therefore the coordination of social activity from the particularities of place.

This "emptying of time" is, for Giddens, a crucial feature of modernity's break with tradition[1] and has direct implications for the globalizing tendencies of modernity, for example, in the standardization of time across geographical regions (the institutionalizing of global time zones). However, the thrust of his argument, for our purposes, is in the implications that "the emptying of time" has for "the emptying of space." "Empty space" refers to "the separation of space from place," which abstract time reckoning makes possible. Giddens argues that in premodern societies, space and place (grasped as locale—"the physical setting of social activity as situated geographically"; 1990, p. 18; see also, 1984, pp. ff.) largely coincide. This is because here relations of presence (local face-to-face interactions) dominate social life for most people; and clearly this derives from—among other technological limitations—the limitations imposed on social coordination across distance by premodern time reckoning.

Modernity thus simultaneously liberates time and space from the particularities of place, allowing distanciated interaction between absent others and, crucially, the institutionalization of this distanciated interaction via the modern social organization. Giddens (1991) considers organizations to be distinctive features of modern societies, not so much in the classic Weberian sense of their "bureaucratic" form, but in terms of "the concentrated reflexive monitoring they both permit and entail" (p.

---

[1]See also Anderson, 1983. On the general significance of time in social theory, see Adam, 1990; Brunn & Leinbach, 1991; Elias, 1992; Hassard, 1990; Lash & Urry, 1994.

16). This capacity for reflexive monitoring of action is what distinguishes modern organizations from any premodern interactional form: "the regularized control of social relations across indefinite time-space distances" that they entail (p. 16). Modern organizations are, indeed, the prime instance of the potential for the reintegration of time and space, which, Giddens (1990) argues, is characteristic of modernity: Once time and space are separated from the constraints of presence availability, their recombination in organizations (up to and including nation-states) produces the dynamic mode of life we recognize as the modern world: "Modern organizations are able to connect the local and the global in ways which would have been unthinkable in more traditional societies and in doing so routinely affect the lives of millions of people" (p. 20).

The emptying of time and space, therefore, allows social relations to be established at distance from local contexts of presence. Giddens (1990) expresses this in another new concept: disembedding— "the 'lifting out' of social relations from local contexts of interaction and their restructuring across indefinite spans of time-space" (p. 21). Giddens's use of the term *local* is, admittedly, rather vague here as elsewhere in his discussion of modernity. He uses it at different times to refer to anything from the subjective sphere of the self (1991, p. 184), through personal living spaces (actual living rooms; 1991, p. 189), to more public localities such as shopping malls (1990, p. 140) and broader notions such as neighborhoods or communities (1990, pp. 141-142). The common feature seems to be the sense of the local as the "habitual settings though which an individual physically moves" (1991, p. 188). We can thus understand Giddens, in this context at least, to use *local* in a phenomenological sense rather than a strictly geographical one. What is important is the experience of the places we habitually move through.

Time-space distanciation and the disembedding of social relations thus imply a distinctive experience of place in modern societies no longer dominated by relations of presence. The places we inhabit are still, of course, peopled by "real" others with whom we interact in relations of presence, but, increasingly, relations with absent others shape our experience. Giddens (1990) expresses this in a striking image by describing modern places as increasingly phantasmagoric:

> That is to say, locales are thoroughly penetrated by and shaped in terms of social influences quite distant from them. What structures the locale is not simply that which is present on the scene; the "visible form" of the locale conceals the distanciated relations which determine its nature. (p. 19)

Why *phantasmagoric*? The term has its most general sense as a deriva-
tion from *phantasm*, meaning an illusion or a deceptive appearance. But
it has an interesting subsidiary usage as "a supposed vision of an absent
(living or dead) person" (*Oxford Encyclopedic English Dictionary*, 1991,
p. 1087). Giddens's use of the term seems to trade more on this subsidiary sense, to suggest a situation in which locales are not so much
illusory as peopled by the "absent" as much as the "present." The influences of distant social forces and processes are the phantasms—the
"ghostly presences"—in locales.

He offers an illustration of this idea in his discussion of the phenomenology of modernity referred to previously—the "intersection of
estrangement and familiarity." Here he argues against the familiar claim
that modernity means the simple loss of the existential comforts and
assurances of local communal experience in the face of increasingly
abstract social forces that structure our lives. Rather, he argues that we
retain a sense of familiarity in our day-to-day experience of local contexts, but that this familiarity no longer derives from the particularities of
localized place. People are somehow aware that their experience of
localities are of phantasmagoric places in which familiar features are
often not unique to that locale and part of its organic development but,
rather, have been placed into the locale by distanciated forces:

> The local shopping mall is a milieu in which a sense of ease and
> security is cultivated by the layout of the buildings and the careful
> planning of public places. Yet everyone who shops there is aware
> that most of the shops are chain stores, which one might find in any
> city, and indeed that innumerable shopping malls of similar design
> exist elsewhere. (Giddens, 1990, p. 141)

This is to argue that the experience of place in modernity is not
one of alienation, but of ambivalence. People "own" their local places
phenomenologically in a sort of provisional sense, always recognizing
the absent forces that structure this ownership. It might be argued that
this ambivalence is produced in large measure by the realization that
there is increasingly less local ownership of public spaces in a direct
material sense. The corner shops run by local families that were once
ubiquitous in the U.K. have been largely displaced in the last 30 years by
supermarket and "High Street" chains. Such shops in the mall—an
ambivalent public/private space unknown before the 1960s—appear and
disappear at the behest of (global) market forces, not, normally, as the
expression of local decisions.

Giddens's discussion of the transformation of place thus suggests an experience of distanciated relations in modern everyday life.
But does this experience answer to the claim that phenomenal worlds

are for the most part truly global? It will be recalled that Giddens (1991) defines *globalization* in terms of distanciation—"the intersection of presence and absence, the interlacing of social relations 'at distance' with local contextualities" (p. 21). Clearly not all the distanciated forces that we might be aware of in modern locales are "global" in the sense of, say, being part of giant transnational enterprises that span the globe. The chain stores in a mall may belong only to national or regional chains. Nonetheless, it does make sense to think of distanciation as a process of virtual globalization. "The world" is in a sense the virtual context of all local transformations. This is so, for instance, in the sense that Giddens suggests of the influence of global capitalist markets on the economic fates of local neighborhoods. Our day-to-day experience of locales is certainly structured by forces that are, ultimately, global. But does this imply that our phenomenal worlds are global? Well, not necessarily.

We can agree that distanciated relations enter into our phenomenal worlds, but this is rather different from saying that people have an ongoing experience of the global in their local affairs. Indeed, if "the global" refers here to the virtual context of "the world," which is the domain of, for example, currency and commodity markets, it seems unlikely that this will have any more than a dim presence in anyone's consciousness. As Fredric Jameson (1991) has plausibly argued, the world system of multinational capitalism represents a totality—"a network of power and control [too] difficult for our minds and imaginations to grasp" except in the representations of "high-tech paranoia of cyberpunk fiction" (p. 38). The world as a complex political-economic system that may be the ultimate determinant of our local experience is surely not a central figure in most people's everyday awareness.

Arguments about the transformation of place do not by themselves justify the claim about global phenomenal worlds. However, Giddens's work is highly integrated, and the arguments about "displacement" shade into arguments about our interactions with global media that we now consider.

THE MEDIATION OF EXPERIENCE

There is a sense, as Giddens recognizes, in which almost all human experience is mediated, if by this we mean that experience is given to human beings through the symbolic order of language. No doubt one could argue for some "immediate" sensory experience (e.g., of body states), but in terms of the social and cultural orders of human existence, language is the medium through which we grasp and relate to the world. Giddens (1991) puts a distinctive spin on this, by expressing the mediation of language as the "prime and original means of time-space distanciation, elevating human activity beyond the immediacy of the experience of animals" (p. 23). This gesture toward a philosophical anthropology is not developed, but it does have interesting implications for the way Giddens presents the concept of mediation. There is some slippage between the idea that language takes us out of the "immediate" (in the sense of unsymbolized, unrepresented) experience of animals and the idea that it enables us to handle time and space in ways that are unique to human existence. It is not that these two ideas are not closely connected, but one aspect of the notion of mediation thereby becomes dominant. Thus, Giddens defines *mediated experience* as "the involvement of temporally/spatially distant influences with human sensory experience" (p. 243).

Now this makes a lot of sense, of course, for the arguments he presses about global experience. However, it does tend to de-emphasize a central part of the concept of mediation, that is the idea of experience passing through an "intermediary" and thereby having a qualitatively different nature from immediate experience. If we think of mediation only in terms of time-space distanciation, we are in danger of obliterating questions of the different phenomenological orders of the immediate and the mediate. Clearly there is considerable philosophical depth to this issue in relation to language, and this is not the place to pursue this. However, there are issues to do with the nature of "mass mediated experience" as contrasted with other "everyday experiences," which, as will be discussed, pose problems for Giddens's claims about global phenomenal worlds.

As one might expect, Giddens goes on to argue that the mediation of experience is vastly accentuated in conditions of modernity as a consequence of the development of media technologies and their related forms. The distinction between oral and literate cultures is, of course, often made in relation to the tradition/modernity distinction (Giddens, 1984; Levi-Strauss, 1968; McLuhan, 1964; Ong, 1977). However, Giddens (1991) suggests that printed texts differ from handwritten ones in significant ways that mark a more central distinction between the modern and the pre-modern:

> When books were produced by hand, readership was sequential: the book had to pass from one person to another. The books and texts of pre-modern civilizations remained substantially geared to the transmission of tradition, and were almost always essentially "classical" in character. Printed materials cross space as easily as time because they can be distributed to many readers more or less simultaneously. (p. 24)

Thus he argues that it is with the coming of print technology that the distinctive mediations of modern experience are born, and with the integration of print and electronic media typical of "high modernity" that these mediations achieve global dimensions (p. 26).

The most significant feature of the impact of these media technologies on everyday experience, for our purposes, is what Giddens (1991) refers to as "the intrusion of distant events into everyday consciousness":

> Distant events may become as familiar or more so, than proximate influences, and integrated into the frameworks of personal experience. Situations "at hand" may in fact be more opaque than large-scale happenings affecting many millions of people. (p. 189)

This is best illustrated in terms of some examples he provides:

> A person may be on the telephone to someone twelve thousand miles away and for the duration of the conversation be more closely bound up with the responses of that distant individual than with others sitting in the same room. The appearance, personality and policies of a world political leader may be better known to a given individual than those of his next-door neighbour. A person may be more familiar with the debate over global warming than with why the tap in the kitchen leaks. (p. 189)

Each of these examples seems to express the central claim about the intrusion of the distant into the everyday locally situated lifeworld of people. And we have to agree that "the world out there" is neither any longer phenomenologically separate from the local lifeworld, nor is it intrinsically alien to everyday experience. In this general sense, the phenomenon is, perhaps, best expressed in Giddens's phrase, the "'openness of the world' to the individual" (p. 189). This idea is highly suggestive for a phenomenology of globalization.

The Mode of Media Awareness: A World Opening to Us

It is also worth noting the distinctions that could be made between these examples. In the first example, it might be argued that we are dealing with a fairly low order of mediation as contrasted with the other two. The telephone conversation, although clearly different from face-to-face conversation in terms of its semiotic structuring, is sufficiently close to it for the significant issue to be simply the one of the eradication of distance. The very "intimacy" provided by telecommunications technology reproduces a familiar context of local experience—the conversation—across distance. True, there are other aspects to the texture of experience of telephone conversations that distinguish them from the immediacy of face-to-face interaction (Aronson, 1986), but these are, I think, less significant than the distinctions that may be drawn between telephone conversations and, say, television viewing.

Thus, the second example, the experience of familiarity with a world political leader, seems to me to be a much more complexly mediated experience. Most people's experience of the personality of, say, President Clinton will have been gained through television, in particular through the carefully orchestrated presentation of his media persona by his public relations team. So much is obvious. But there is a more general question that may be asked about the "familiarity" we experience with "media figures." This is the question of the context within which we recuperate media representations. Without being drawn into the fine grain of debates about media reception, we can at least say with confidence that the extension of individual lifeworlds offered by the television screen is categorically different from the extension provided by direct social interaction. Televisual experience is obviously highly mediated in terms of the technical determinants of the form (pictures on a screen) and of the complex set of semiotic codes, conventions, formats, and production values it employs. Perhaps more significantly, it is experienced as mediated; that is, people, for the most part, claim to be able to routinely distinguish between televisual experience and "real life." Indeed, all the studies that stress the "active audience" (Leibes & Katz, 1993; Lodziak, 1986; Morley, 1980, 1992; Richardson & Corner, 1986) logically depend on this basic discrimination. For how could viewers bring their "lived experiences" to a negotiation of the meaning of a text if they did not maintain at least this fundamental phenomenological distinction?

Now, of course, this does require quite careful conceptualization. I am not suggesting that televisual experience is somehow superficial or does not significantly enough engage the viewers' attention or emotions for it to be taken seriously. Indeed, it may be that people often fail to maintain a strong "reflexive," self-monitoring awareness that they are "watching television" as opposed to engaging in less mediated forms of cultural experience. As Giddens (1991) argues, in extreme cases, feelings of "reality inversion" may arise from the familiarity of televisual experience: "The real object and event when encountered seem to have a less concrete existence than their media representation" (p. 27). An example of this might be the psychological difficulties people in modern societies often experience in contact with the dead and dying: routinely represented on television, but socially sequestered in real life.

However, none of this undermines the case for maintaining the basic phenomenological distinction between the mass-mediated and the real-life. Reality inversion, on the contrary, logically preserves the distinction. Nor do the occasionally reported cases of people confusing soap opera reality for real life—sending flowers to fictional funerals, and so on—necessarily challenges the distinction. A more plausible and less patronizing gloss might be that people here are deliberately and consciously integrating these experiences for their own creative satisfaction.

We have to take seriously the claims the vast majority of people would surely make about their ability to distinguish these types of experience. Consider how offensive would be the imputation that you were not able to distinguish your feelings of emotional involvement in a soap opera from your involvement with "real" close relations. The fact that people take offense to such imputations surely says something about the existential importance of the priority of "real" social relations in the constitution of the lifeworld. It also appears that the availability of the category of mass-mediated experience would be threatened if we assumed along with some postmodern theorists (Baudrillard, 1985; Kroker & Cook, 1988) that the media had so blurred people's experiential fields as to create an undifferentiated "hyperreality." Just as media theorists would be conceptually impoverished without this discrimination—which of course grounds all descriptions of the nature of the televisual—so we must assume audiences routinely use the distinction in monitoring and evaluating their experience.

There is clearly more depth to this argument than can be addressed here (see Tomlinson, 1991). The point I press is that the distinction between mass-mediated and non-mass-mediated experience needs to be preserved, even in the face of some general theoretical suspicion of the status of immediate lived experience. Those suspicious of the normative privileging of face-to-face communities in the critique of modernity often stress the point that all experience is mediated (e.g., Young, 1990). We can agree with this but still maintain that some experiences are more mediated than others. This is necessary not only to avoid the fall toward the hyperbolic rhetoric of postmodernism,[2] but to appreciate the subtleties and complexities of different modes of experience available to human beings in conditions of modernity.

Therefore, the experience of "the world opening to us" via the mass media needs to be seen as a distinct mode of experience within the lifeworld. President Clinton may be present in our homes and familiar in a way unthinkable before the dissemination of the electronic media. We may, indeed, be more familiar with his appearance, ideas, tastes, and so on, than with those of our neighbors. This clearly has enormous

---

[2]As, for example, in Kroker and Cook's (1988) extravagant claim that, "TV is, in a very literal sense, the real world of . . . postmodern culture, society and economy" (p. 268).

social significance, not the least in its implications for the political process (Meyrowitz, 1985). But I argue that the televisual Clinton could never be familiar to us in precisely the same way the next door neighbor or the distant telephone partner could be. One reason for this is that he never appears to us as a dialogue partner. The Clinton we "know" is constituted in the monological mode of televisual communication. This is a point I return to later.

The point of maintaining this distinction between modes of experience is that it qualifies the claim about distanciated events being integrated into the frameworks of personal experience. Although the mass media provide the most obvious access to the world for the majority of people, this experience is always, in a sense, contained within the lifeworld as mass-mediated experience. To compare this with Giddens's claim about the provisional sense in which we experience localities, we might think of mass-mediated experience as a very provisional sense of the global: instantly and ubiquitously accessible, but insulated from the local quotidian order by virtue of its very form. If this is so, it has implications for the idea that the world becomes open to us via the mass media. Zygmunt Bauman (1990) is skeptical of the idea that television overcomes cultural distance by giving us insight into the lives of distant "institutionally separated" others:

> Contrary to widespread opinion, the advent of television, this huge and easily accessible peephole through which the unfamiliar ways may be routinely glimpsed, has neither eliminated the institutional separation nor diminished its effectivity. McLuhan's "global village" has failed to materialize. The frame of a cinema or TV screen staves off the danger of spillage more effectively than tourist hotels and fenced off camping sites; the one-sidedness of communication further entrenches the unfamiliars on the screen as essentially incommunicado. (p. 149)

What Bauman is implicitly questioning is the degree to which the mode of mass-mediated experience engages with the lifeworld so as to produce a real hermeneutic engagement with the distant other. This, as he implies, raises problems for notions of the global community made available via the media, problems to which we return in a later section.

Global Awareness and Local Lifestyle

None of this denies the enormous influence that sheer access to information about the world via the mass media may have on the way we live our local lives. Giddens (1991) insists that global awareness is not limited to a vague background knowledge of events, but may directly shape individual lifestyles:

A concern with global warming, for example, might form part of a distinctive lifestyle adopted by a person. . . . She might keep in close contact with scientific debates and adjust various aspects of her lifestyle in relation to the practical measures they suggest. (p. 190)

This is, I think, an important aspect of the claim about the openness of the world to the individual. There is something of a dialectic discernible in the relation between local lifestyles and global contexts. However, there are some complexities in this dialectic that are revealed, particularly in the example of global environmental awareness that Giddens cites.

In the first place, it appears that such lifestyle choices are made within an experiential context that remains, in important ways, stubbornly local. There are, for example, the simple pragmatic constraints on action that derive from our local material situation. To adapt a phrase from Marx, we could describe these constraints as the "dull compulsion of the quotidian": the priority imposed by routines that are more "immediate" in their demands—commuting, working, shopping, caring for a family—than lifestyle orientations built on an awareness of global issues. It is just these constraints that are at stake in the Green maxim "Think globally, act locally." This indicates the possibility of intervention in global ecological processes via, for example, consumption and other lifestyle choices expressed at the local level—for example, the purchase of "green" products such as CFC-free aerosols or the rationalizing of car use. But the practical difficulties of following this maxim arise from the very "local" nature of the pressures and demands of everyday routines. For example, the most environmentally aware people may find it "necessary" routinely to use a car for commuting, shopping, transporting the family, and so on, simply because of the structural integration of the automobile into social life and the consequent problems of "managing" a modern lifestyle without one. Claus Offe (1984) expressed this situation in his concept of the structurally imposed needs of capitalist modernity.

To pursue a principled local "green" lifestyle is thus practically difficult and poses problems of motivation. The rewards of adopting these inconvenient, laborious, and perhaps even socially limiting lifestyle choices are not immediate. Very few direct indications of the effectiveness of this sort of local action on global problems are available, and yet the logic of local-global integration seems to place the responsibility of environmental protection on individuals. As Ulrich Beck (1992) puts the problem, in conditions of global modernity, "how one lives becomes the biographical solution of systemic contradictions" (p. 137). Thus the awareness of global issues made possible through the mass media imposes a peculiar moral responsibility on the individual:

> The biography is increasingly removed from its direct spheres of contact and opened up across the boundaries of countries and experts for a long-distance morality which puts the individual in the position of potentially having to take a continual stand. At the same moment as he or she sinks into insignificance, he or she is elevated to the apparent throne of a world-shaper. (p. 137)

Beck goes on to suggest that the burden of such responsibility "can only be tolerated through the opposite reaction of not listening, simplifying, and apathy" (p. 137). If this is so, then, as discussed later, it does not auger well for concerted local intervention in global problems.

To return to the central issue, these reflections lend some weight to the idea that local exigencies maintain a certain priority even in a lifeworld opened up to the global. This derives in part from the sheer material demands of local routines tied to the satisfaction of basic needs. But it also derives from the distinctions people routinely make between an immediate local world and the mass-mediated experience of the global that is, for most people, the most common way in which the world is opened to them. Clearly the mass media represent a highly significant linkage between local and global experience, and there is a lot of work to be done investigating the phenomenology of this linkage: the precise sense in which, for example, television can be said to bring the world into our living rooms (Meyrowitz, 1985, 1989; Morley, 1992; Wilson, 1993). What I have tried to suggest is that this problematizing of mass-mediated experience is a necessary qualification for Giddens's claims about the intrusion of distant events into everyday consciousness.

So far our understanding of a global phenomenal world has been in the sense either of an awareness of global presences in or determinations of local contexts, or of the elimination of distance and the openness of the world (primarily via the mass media) to the individual. Neither of these senses is unproblematic, but we have also glimpsed another sense: that of a consciousness of the world, in Roland Robertson's (1992) words, "as a single place" (p. 132). Or, as both Giddens and Ulrich Beck have expressed it, a sense of a world in which there are no "others."

GLOBALIZED COMMUNITIES

> The "emptying" of time and space set in motion processes that establish a single world where none existed previously. . . . Taken overall, the many diverse modes of culture and consciousness characteristic of pre-modern "world systems" formed a genuinely fragmented array of human social communities. By contrast, late modernity produces a situation in which humankind in some respects becomes a "we," facing problems and opportunities where there are no "others." (Giddens, 1991, p. 27)

Our final approach to the idea of a global phenomenal world engages with this sense of globalization as (in very significant scare quotes) "unifying." Giddens's comment about the unifying nature of modernity is made to offset contrary claims about social fragmentation; claims typical of, although by no means restricted to, theorists of postmodernity.[3] Consistent with his overall approach, he suggests a dialectical interplay between the unifying and the disaggregating forces of modernity. For present purposes I focus on the unifying moment of this dialectic.

One reason why the notion of unifying has to be so heavily qualified is the utopian resonances it has in the context of talk about globalization: its naive sense of a "global village." Another is the dystopian vision of cultural homogenization it could imply (Hannerz, 1991; Tomlinson, 1991, 1995). Giddens's (1991) most direct approach avoids both these problems, for he focuses on the unity implied in a common set of global risks.

A Global Community of Risk?

Principal among these are the risks we all face of ecological catastrophes. As Giddens says, referring to Beck's work, the realization that "Chernobyl is everywhere" suggests a sense in which there are no "others" in relation to environmental risks. Not only do the dangers of disasters like Chernobyl spread beyond the political boundaries of nation-states, they to some extent transcend other social and economic differentials such as class positions.[4] This applies not only to high consequence risks, but to chronic problems of environmental pollution as the result of industrialization. As Beck (1992) pithily puts it, "Poverty is hierarchic, smog is democratic" (p. 36). Global environmental risks, then, suggest a curious sort of unity in adversity, in which, "no specific individuals or groups are responsible for them or can be constrained to 'set things right'" (Giddens, 1990, p. 131).

Giddens (1991) thinks that people are generally aware of global risk and its relation to local practices. It may be that he exaggerates the degree of this public awareness, extrapolating from the base of the articulate environmentally aware. But his point is that this sort of knowledge—at least in the developed societies of the West—is not "confined to the specialist awareness of professionals" (p. 211), and in this he is

---

[3]See also, Giddens (1990) for a summary of his distinctions between the presuppositions of postmodernity and late modernity. Although it would take too much space to argue the case here, in general I share Giddens's view that the present period is more usefully and accurately described as "late modernity" than as postmodernity.

[4]But see Beck's (1992) qualification to this.

surely correct. Thus, in a section called "Personal Lives, Planetary Needs" in *Modernity and Self Identity* (1991), he comments on the rise of ecological issues on the political agenda:

> A clear part of increased ecological concern is the recognition that reversing the degradation of the environment depends upon adopting new lifestyle patterns. Ecological problems highlight the new and accelerating interdependence of global systems and bring home to everyone the depth of the connections between personal activity and planetary problems. (p. 221)

This awareness, in the sense of simple information, however, does not exhaust the phenomenology of risk, which seems likely to be complex. Both Giddens and Beck point out that the very enormity of the risk of global environmental or nuclear catastrophe is liable to produce coping reactions that involve forms of distancing of such threats. For Beck, as we saw in the previous section, this may involve not listening, simplifying, or apathy. For Giddens (1990), it may involve the resurrection of premodern dispositions to trust in fortuna: "a vague and generalized sense of trust in distant events over which one has no control" (p. 133). Thus the apprehension of global risks may be inseparable from a sort of fatalism: "the feeling that things will take their own course anyway" (p. 133). However such coping strategies are conceived,[5] it seems clear that the phenomenology of global risk awareness is unlikely in itself to involve a moment-to-moment sense of positive global unity—of being, in Sartre's sense, "embarqué." Paradoxically, the most pressing sense of a global "we"—unity of purpose in the face of potential annihilation—seems likely to be routinely backgrounded in consciousness.

Ulrich Beck (1992) makes a connected point when he discusses the problems of political organization on the basis of perceived common risk. There is a sense, he says, in which global risk makes "the utopia of a world society a little more real or at least a little more urgent" (p. 47). However, when we come to think about the unifying principle involved, the notion of a community of mutual risk looks much more uncertain:

> The driving force in the class society can be summarized in the phrase: I am hungry! The movement set in motion by the risk society, on the other hand, is expressed in the statement: I am afraid! The commonality of anxiety takes the place of the commonality of need. The type of the risk society marks in this sense a social epoch in which solidarity from anxiety arises and becomes a political force. But it is completely unclear how the binding force of anxiety operates, even whether it works. (p. 49)

---

[5]See here Giddens's (1991) discussion of Goffman's concept of the *Umwelt*.

Uncertainty about the binding force of anxiety Beck expresses can be put in terms of the phenomenology of global risk awareness: Can anxiety shared with others produce the experience of a global "we"? To assume that it can might be, as Beck (1992) has it, "jumping much too casually from the global nature of dangers to the commonality of political will and action" (p. 49).

Where does this leave us in assessing the experience of global risk as an example of Giddens's claim about global phenomenal worlds? It leaves us with what we might call a "weak sense" of global commonality. The simple perception of common risks might give some sense of global unity, but this is liable to be fragile and easily displaced from the foreground of consciousness. What is required if the local lifestyle changes necessary to confront global ecological risk are to emerge is a much stronger sense of global commonality. This stronger sense can be expressed, if with some hesitation, as a sense of a positive global community, that is a sense of global belonging that does not solely derive from mutual threat. This is the possibility examined now.

Mass-mediated Communities?

There are several reasons, as Giddens recognizes, for caution in invoking the concept of *community* in discussions of modernity. Principal among these is the need to avoid the romantic connotations that the term has collected: the sense of cozy, cooperative *gemeinschaft* supposed to characterize premodern social relations and polarized with modernity's impersonality, anonymity, abstractness, and so forth. The popular sense of the loss of community in modern societies thus often carries a burden of problematic historical surmise (Giddens, 1990; Plant, 1974). However, Giddens (1990) employs a less controversial use of the term, as "an embedded affinity to place" (p. 117) and, in this particular sense, he agrees that modernity has largely meant the end of community.[6] Indeed, this is implicit in his analysis of the disembedding of social relations and the transformation of place.

---

[6]Of course, not all senses of the communal depend on a relation to the local, even in premodern societies. Anderson (1983), for example, discusses the "great transcontinental sodalities of Christendom, the Ummah Islam and the rest" (p. 40). However, as he argues, the loss of the binding character of these spatially stretched communities is precisely related to the "disenchantment" of modernity— for example, the loss of the unquestioned authority of sacred scripts and so the decline in significance of sacred script languages. It was these reference texts that provided the element of commonality uniting ethnically distinct peoples. The problem of constructing a global sense of community in modernity seems to be intrinsically related to this post-Enlightenment loss of any convincing existential narrative that could unite people across distance (see Tomlinson, 1991, Chap. 5).

The question then arises as to whether any experience of community can be retained in global modernity. In an interesting comment in *The Consequences of Modernity* (1990), Giddens seems to suggest that the mass media may give us access to a sort of communal experience:

> A feature of displacement is our insertion into globalized cultural and information settings, which means that familiarity and place are much less consistently connected than hitherto. This is less a phenomenon of estrangement from the local than one of integration within globalized "communities" of shared experience. (p. 141)[7]

Clearly the scare quotes are all-important. This experience will not be identical with the experience of community linked to locality. The question is: What sort of communal experience can we derive from the mass media?

In the first place, we have to separate this transformed concept of community from what might be called the ideology of global community: the images projected in corporate advertising—"a World of Coke," the "United Colors of Benetton." Although these images might register some popular attraction to the idea of belonging to a global community, they probably do little in terms of constituting this sense of belonging. Furthermore, tied as they are to promoting a consumerist lifestyle, they are obviously unlikely to promote the lifestyle changes required to confront global environmental hazards.

There have, however, been some suggestions from critical cultural and media theorists that "participation" in global media events might be thought of as constituting a more genuine community of shared experience. Some of these ideas were prompted by consideration of the significance of events like the Live Aid concert in the 1980s, which seemed to combine entertainment with some sense of common moral or political purpose. So, for example, Hebdige (1989) argues:

> The simultaneously most spectacular yet most participatory examples to date of the kind of bonding made possible across transnational communications systems have been the televised events organized by Band Aid, Sport Aid, Live Aid and the Free Mandela movement. . . . such phenomena suggest the possibility of a new kind of politics existing primarily in and through the airwaves and organized around issues of universal moral concern. (p. 91)

---

[7]Giddens follows Meyrowitz (1985) in this as in much of his discussion of the mass media. But see, for example, Kirby's (1989) critique of Meyrowitz and Meyrowitz's (1989) reply.

It is, of course, easy to be skeptical about the political significance of such events, which Hebdige admits are "superficial and transitory alliances" (p. 91). However, it cannot be denied that some kind of experience is happening here, and the question is not that of the direct sense of political solidarity or mobilization involved but, rather, what sort of communal experience it represents. Perhaps the way to appreciate this is to understand the differences between these events and the experience of local communities. There seem to be at least three obvious ones.

The first is simply in terms of scale. The satellite audience for the Live Aid concert has been estimated at 1.5 billion people across 160 countries (Meyrowitz, 1989, p. 329). It might be thought that the experience afforded by such a horizon is liable to be, as Meyrowitz says, "a broader but also a much shallower sense of sharing" than that of the local community (p. 329). The very idea of a global community might then seem to involve a certain abstractness or "shallowness." But this does not necessarily follow from the sheer scale of things. Benedict Anderson's (1983) well known description of the nation as an "imagined community" implies the possibility of a sense of community with millions of fellow nationals who will never meet each other. The scale of a national community does not seem to inhibit the (generally strong) imagined sense of national belonging, so why should scale vitiate a sense of global community? The answer, I think, is that it does not. The difference between the experience of national community and global community is not one of scale but of the cultural, symbolic, or ideological work that has been invested in the constitution of the former. It is because of these factors that Anderson can plausibly describe the sense of national belonging as a "deep horizontal comradeship" (p. 16). If the sense of global community is by comparison shallow, this seems to indicate a comparatively undeveloped global political culture, not an inherent problem of scale. I return to this point presently.

The second obvious difference between mass-mediated experiences of global community and the experience of local community lies in the dispersed nature of the former. People experiencing global media events like Live Aid are obviously doing so, in the main, in small groups in their living rooms. This is true, of course, for the television audience in general, and there has been some interest among media theorists in how audiences can be considered to constitute "communities" rather than being simply absorbed in the private consumption of media products. Dayan and Katz (1987), for example, compare watching televised public occasions (in this case, a British royal wedding) to the diasporic ceremony of the Jewish Passover seder:

> Characteristically the seder has served through the ages as a powerful means of unifying a scattered people, offering a ceremonial

structure despite geographic dispersion by translating a monumental occasion into a multiplicity of simultaneous, similarly programmed, home-bound micro events. By . . . transferring public celebration to the home, the model of the seder seems to have solved a problem very similar to that now experienced by the dispersed mass of television viewers. (p. 195)

This is a tempting, if not exact, analogy for the sort of national public occasions that Dayan and Katz discuss. The "ceremony" of television viewing might not have quite the same sort of significance as the seder, given the difference of context between historic diasporas like the Jews and the "dispersed" but not actually diasporic audience for national media. However, we can allow this degree of slippage. David Morley (1992) believes the model can be extended to include:

the regular viewing of the nightly television news or of a long-running soap opera . . . as a discourse which constitutes collectivities through a sense of "participation" and through the production of both a simultaneity of experience and a sense of a "past in common." (p. 287)

These suggestions—which recall Benedict Anderson's analysis of the role of national newspapers in the constitution of national identity—seem quite plausible when applied to institutionalized collectivities like the nation-state. However, the problem with applying this model to the global television audience is precisely that it lacks that "past in common" which defines both a national and a diasporic community. The whole point about the constitution of a global community via global media is that it must be achieved, if not exactly ex nihilo, at most out of ideas of global belonging that have few strong political-ideological, institutional, or linguistic supports.

This returns us to the point made earlier about the comparatively underdeveloped political culture of the global in relation to the national. Identification with the nation is a process stimulated and encouraged by a complex set of cultural practices meshed into the political institutions of the nation-state. But such practices simply do not exist in any institutionalized form at the global level. It is important here to distinguish the global from the international (categories Giddens (1990) in places seems to conflate). Many international institutions do of course exist: the United Nations and its subsidiary bodies like UNESCO are obvious examples. However, the defining characteristic of such bodies—that they are organizations of member (nation) states—makes it rather unlikely that they could easily transform into truly global organizations. This is because such international bodies only exist at the behest of their national membership and to protect their members' individual interests as nation states. This is obvious if we consider the limitations placed on the actions of UN peacekeeping forces by the political structure of the UN. The distance between UN forces and a "world police force" is precisely the distance between international organizations and a transcendent global polity. The global interest—world peace, environmental protection, global development, and so on—is only served in bodies like the UN insofar as this does not threaten the status quo—and of course the established power differentials—of the nation-state system. The ultimate sanction in the event of such a threat is simply withdrawal from the international community, as the United States and Great Britain did from UNESCO in 1985 and 1986. So, although international communities exist, these are far from being global.

Furthermore, it could be argued that the very strength of institutionally promoted national identity depends on the continuance of a weak sense of the global, for a sense of national identity draws not only on a national language or the representation of a common cultural heritage, but on the existence of a system of "others" against whom identity can be forged. As Featherstone (1993) puts it:

> The process of formation of [national] culture cannot be understood merely as a response to forces within the nation state, but must be seen in relation to forces outside of it: the potential for the development of national identity and cultural coherence as relationally determined by the structure of the shifting disequilibriums of power and interdependencies of the figuration of nation states within which a particular country was embedded. (p. 173)

It is not that identification with the nation and the world are mutually exclusive. But, insofar as a strengthening identification with the world as a whole implies a weakening sense of what divides us as national cultures, it could be argued that simultaneous "nation building" and "world building" is, in a certain sense, a zero-sum situation. It should not, therefore, be surprising that no real global—as opposed to international—institutions exist in a world that, as Giddens (1990) recognizes, is ordered by the mapping of the reflexive political system of nation states onto the extents of global space.[8] My point here is that the lack of such

---

[8]Giddens sees the nation-state system as one of the key dimensions of globalization. However, there is also a growing body of thought that suggests globalization—in particular the global economic system of advanced capitalism—is undermining the integrity of the nation-state system (e.g., Rosenau, 1990), although this is disputed by others (Gilpin, 1987; Gordon, 1988). There is no space here to develop this debate, but it appears that Giddens is correct to assume the continuing power of the nation-state system is significant, even if in transformed, ways. This is also the conclusion of McGrew's (1992) excellent discussion of this debate.

global institutions makes the cultural imagining of the global community a far more problematic task. Certainly, as Featherstone (1993) says, it can in no way be conceived "as the culture of the nation state writ large." It is precisely this particular, exclusive cultural imagining that needs to be overcome to achieve a widespread sense of "a world without others." Yet what the sources of such a universalizing cultural imagination might be remain obscure. A key problem facing aspiring "global social movements"—for example, a global women's movement (Morgan, 1984)—is that they are trapped both within the structural/institutional context of the nation-state system, which inhibits their actual political development, and within an equally powerful system of cultural difference (different experiences of patriarchy), which undermines the claim to universal "global sisterhood" (Mohanty, 1992).

The final distinction I raise lies in the nature of mass-mediated communication. I have already commented on what I believe to be the distinctive mode of experience provided by the media, but we can add to this another obvious consideration relevant to the idea of communal experience. This is the fact that media communication is, for the most part, monological rather than dialogical in nature. This is a fact so obvious that it is not often seen as worthy of comment. Mark Poster (1990), however, intent on establishing the distinctive "mode of information" of television, spells the point out:

> One communication pole transmits virtually all of the messages; the other simply receives. For three, four or five hours a day, individuals tune in, voluntarily becoming spectator-participants, mutely receiving messages, choosing to observe, but observing selectively. The spectator recipient is structured to constitute his or her own programming schedule from the available offerings. But that is the extent of active involvement. (p. 45)

Poster, in fact, paints this picture of the passive media consumer only to deny it. He goes on to argue that the monological mode of television talk generates an active response in viewers by inviting them "to play with the process of self-constitution, continuously to remake the self in 'conversation' with differing modes of discourse" (p. 46). The viewer thus engages in a conversation with media texts at the subjective level of the self. He is right, I think, to point out that the monological mode of television does not imply viewer passivity. But what is more interesting is his distinction between this mode and other modes of communication:

> The language/practice of TV absorbs the functions of culture to a greater extent than face-to-face conversations or print and its discur-

sive effect is to constitute subjects differently from speech or print. *Speech constitutes subjects as members of a community by solidifying the ties between individuals.* Print constitutes subjects as rational, autonomous egos. . . . *Media language replaces the community of speakers* and undermines the referentiality of discourse necessary for the rational ego. (p. 46; emphasis added)

Being addressed in the monological mode of television, Poster implies, creates a sense of the self that is distinct from that created by direct speech and that specifically replaces the sense of communal identity speech provides. Without following him too far down the poststructuralist path of his reflections, we can take something from this suggestion. It is not that the experience of television viewing is particularly individualistic or isolating. It is simply that dialogue is not its intrinsic communicational mode.[9] Television viewing might provoke dialogue between fellow viewers, and it may involve the sort of internal self-formative conversation Poster suggests. In both these senses monology does not imply audience passivity. But this is clearly not to say that the experience of television viewing involves dialogue as usually understood. It also seems clear that a sense of communal identity must depend on opportunity at some point to engage in a dialogue—to have a sense of others as dialogue partners.

Perhaps the simplest way to express this is to say that the media audience remains an audience rather than a community. Whatever sense of unity events like Live Aid provide may derive from a sense of simultaneous involvement in the televisual event. This, although experienced in dispersed form, may be very similar to the experience of being part of a "live" audience (given sufficient emphasis on the event's "quasi-live" status by the presentation). Audiences may also be communities—like religious congregations—or they may not—like cinema audiences or spectators at an accident. But what seems clear is that the supporting factors that allow an audience to be a community—particularly the opportunity for dialogue—are not provided routinely via television.

CONCLUSION

Of the various interpretations of the idea of a phenomenology of globalization considered here, that of the sense of a global community—a

---

[9]I discount the obvious, but also obviously feeble, examples of "dialogue" presented in television phone-ins, telephone polls, or even "representative" studio audience discussions. Whatever the impact they may have in the political process, these seem to be in many ways paradigm cases of the shortfall from Habermas's (1984) ideal speech situation.

world without others—seems to be both the most important and the most elusive. Theorists like Roland Robertson (1992) claim that "the trends towards the unicity of the world . . . are inexorable" (p. 26); if we assume unicity to mean the "world as a single place," then this is in certain senses entirely true. However, as Robertson recognizes, unicity—even when it is conceived as a matter of global consciousness (that is, awareness of the world as a single place)—does not imply "unity" in the morally and politically binding sense of community

Giddens is right to argue for the importance of the mass media in "opening the world" to the individual, but the arguments of the previous section suggest skepticism toward the capacity of mass-mediated experience to furnish us with a robust sense of global belonging. However, this should not be taken as a criticism of mass-mediated experience itself. After all, why should we expect television to provide solutions to the problems of global modernity? The point is, rather, that when we come to look for sources of global identity, we struggle to find any more plausible ones than the easily accessible electronic images of television. Ultimately our lack of a positive sense of global community is not to be blamed on the limitations of these images, but on the lack of any coordinated project of "world building" at an institutional level.

All of us, as Giddens says, continue to lead local lives within a globalized socioeconomic context. But lacking anything approaching a global "public sphere," it is not surprising that our sense of the global context remains largely that of a set of determining structures, not of a potential political and cultural community. Throughout his work on modernity Giddens insists on a dialectical push and pull between opposing tendencies: the local and the global, disembedding and reembedding, and so on. Although I agree with this general position, my sense is that the push and pull between the disembedding of socioeconomic relations characteristic of globalizing modernity and reembedding in the sense of global cultural and political belonging remains heavily unbalanced at the present time. Lash and Urry (1994) make a related point at the level of political economy when they argue: "Broadly speaking . . . local powers tend to be reactive, to resist decisions from centers, and to devise institutional and policy responses through identifying niches in existing forms of social organization" (p. 284).

Translating this into political-cultural terms, it might be argued that reembedding is simply a form of local resistance to globalizing forces. Indeed, the sort of examples Giddens (1990) gives of reembedding—"the recreation of places of relative smallness and informality" within "the impersonal cluster of city center buildings" in the landscape of modernity (p. 142)—suggests just this sort of reactive process.

What is needed to construct a global community is a much more proactive political-cultural mobilization. I have argued that mass-mediated global experience alone cannot be relied on to establish this properly antithetical—rather than reactive—moment in the dialectic of global modernity. However, what is surely clear is that the sort of political institutions needed to address global problems cannot be separated from the need for a new global discursive arena—a public sphere—disengaged from the interests of the nation-state system. Were this ever to emerge (and it is difficult to imagine this without the use of global media technology), then the new political agenda that might follow could make Giddens's local-global dialectic look much more plausible.

4

"Re-membering" and "Dis-membering" Europe: A Cultural Strategy for Studying the Role of Communication in the Transformation of Collective Identities*

Dov Shinar
The New School of Media Studies, Tel Aviv

SOCIAL CHANGE AND COLLECTIVE IDENTITY

The 1990s will be recorded in history as a decade of geopolitical, socioeconomic and technological transformation, and of psychological and institutional restructuring—of cultures, religions and ideologies; of nations and states; of social control; and of communication. The magnitude of these changes can be compared with the invention of print, the Industrial Revolution, the introduction of leading ideologies and the processes of decolonization.

In the West and in "other worlds"—known until recently as second, third, and less developed—collective identities and aspirations are being reshaped and reframed. Traditions that had maintained social networks have become obsolete; and better models for understanding major change are being sought along global and local dimensions, in an

*I am grateful to Professor Mihai Coman, Dean, Faculty of Journalism, University of Bucharest, for his valuable contribution to this chapter.

interdisciplinary effort that includes, at least, sociology (Giddens, 1990, 1991), political science (Barber, 1995), and communications (Katz, 1986; Sreberny-Mohammadi, 1991).

Europe is well seasoned in dealing with such challenges. In recent years, the idea and practice of a supranational community have created expectations that new types of economic and political structures and a budding European identity can confront new realities. But this internationalist spirit has not yet found effective ways of confronting the power of ethnic, religious and regional factions in a fragmented Eastern Empire and of rejuvenated secessionary trends in a unifying Western Europe.

Communications and Change: Means and Meanings

Uncertainty and confusion are typical of the transitions between order and disorder in a changing Europe. They affect global unification and factional separatism alike. The demand for communication is intensified in such circumstances of enhanced public awareness and mobilization and of increasing needs for information, integration, and emotional support (Singh, 1979; Tehranian, 1979; Turner, 1977).

Communications are recognized as a crucial element in the creation of new orders and in the transition from older to newer conceptual frameworks. However, as

> the role and shape of communications . . . [are] by no means very fixed or very clear, and neither are our theoretical models for explaining/exploring communications in an international scale, [this] seems to require a newer set of terms and vantage points than are offered by older perspectives. (Sreberny-Mohammadi, 1991, p. 119)

The disparities between the belief in media power and the modest achievements of modern communications in processes of social change have traditionally been considered to be a result of inadequate media models (Katz & Wedell, 1977). Although some progress has been made, the effective formula for using communications for evolutionary and revolutionary change has not yet been found. The failure to arrive at the correct formula might result from the fact that scholars and practitioners alike have accepted the meaning of change as a given, while putting exaggerated emphasis on the means of attaining effective change. Indeed, communications as a discipline has focused much more on media models than on paradigms of change and development.

Based on the premise that a critical appraisal of models of change is necessary for assessing the roles of communication therein, this chapter offers a critique of older and alternative perspectives and a conceptual framework for looking at communications in social change, with particular reference to the global and local dimensions of the European context.

The Dominant Paradigm: Shortcomings of Modernity and Development

The theoretical criticism of the dominant paradigm of modernity and development has focused on its artificial dichotomy of the traditional/modern and on ethnocentric, determinist, and historical biases. Marxist critical theories have not provided viable alternatives, given their own determinist bias, deductive and single-factor logic, and explanations anchored in deus ex-machina ideologies (Portes, 1976; Rogers, 1976; Sreberny-Mohammadi, 1991). In practical terms, the collapse of communism has further disqualified USSR-inspired Marxism from being accepted as an overall interpretive or planning tool. But the apparent victory of Western liberal ideology and capitalist praxis has not concealed their own shortcomings. In this sense, a sociocentric attitude is outstanding: the term *Third World* (or its current synonym, *Eastern Europe*) usually refers to societies that failed to absorb Western values and became disintegrated, bankrupt, and polarized.

This has stood in contrast with the now outdated rhetoric of a prosperous and stable liberal-capitalist West. In glorifying this image, practitioners and researchers have ignored the increasing rates of unemployment, homelessness, poverty, illiteracy, disease, and pollution in the "developed" world. They have failed to recognize that social and cultural gaps, economic crises, rehabilitation efforts, and "quality of life problems" are all now typical of East and West, North and South; that processes of change have global and local dimensions; that change-related problems in the West and in the "other worlds" differ in degree and volume rather than in substance; that blueprints of social change cannot be copied or imposed in their entirety; and that particular cultural identities have to be considered. The "rediscovery" of culture by the social sciences has helped to suggest some alternative models based on premises, contexts, rhetoric, and imagery that can accommodate these theoretical and practical demands and clarify the limitations of some approaches that challenge the dominant paradigm (Geertz, 1973; Shinar, 1987; Worsley, 1984).

ALTERNATIVE APPROACHES

Rejection of the Five M's

Some scholars have adopted the path of rejection (Latouche, 1986; Mowlana & Wilson, 1990). Learning the lessons of major events in this century, they refuse to accept modernity and development as just and effective concepts for understanding and planning viable change. On the one hand, such an approach emphasizes the destructive effects of modernity, which include the "homeless mind" psychological syndrome (Berger, Berger, & Kellner, 1974); processes of ethnocide, defined by Clastres (1988) as cultural genocide; and processes of economicide—the replacement of traditional economic structures and mechanisms by modern market rules (Temple, 1988). Scholars have also identified processes of mediacide (Shinar, Olsthoorn, & Yalden, 1990)—the elimination of traditional media systems—that had been vital components in the transmission of information and for social regulation, such as the Iranian story teller (Motamed-Nejad, 1979) or the West African village gong man (Ugboajah, 1974). On the other hand, evidence has been produced of attempts made by traditional cultures to resist the pressures of modernizing Westernization (Wang & Dissanayake, 1984).

This approach has had some appeal, particularly in its criticism of the five M's that had supported the dominant paradigm: missionaries, the military, merchants, Marxism, and the media (Latouche, 1986; Shinar et al., 1990). However, some weaknesses are apparent, such as the claim for abolishing the nation-state. A flourishing European ethnonationalism suggests that the current course of events is not likely to be reversed, and that a return to a primordial state is highly improbable. Also, the meaning of primordiality is problematic in itself. First, the claim, inspired by the Iranian revolution, that the globalism of religion is an alternative to local nationalism, ignores the variety of religions and the variety of their roles in secular affairs. Second, the focus on the destructive effects of modernity displays a victimizing attitude and underestimates the self-determination potential of non-Western societies.

Geertz: Interplay of Essentialism and Epochalism

In contrast with the determinism of the dominant paradigm and the limitations of rejectionist approaches, Geertz (1973) views social change as an interplay of "institutional change and cultural reconstruction" (p. 244), based on the coexistence and interaction of tradition and modernity. Emphasizing a convergence of essentialism (the inherited course of tradition and indigenous symbols) and epochalism (the work of ideological, technological, economic, and other foreign influences), this approach focuses on an open-ended interaction of social forces rather than on a predetermined orbit. In contrast with the linear, progressive assumptions of the dominant paradigm, in this approach sociocultural change is recognized as multidimensional and uncertain. Time and space are considered through the acceptance of precolonial history and of geographic dimensions, and qualitative empirical methods are employed.

Geertz's freedom from determinism and his consideration of certain global and local aspects in the convergence of essentialism and epochalism are an improved basis for interpreting change. Yet some problems cannot be ignored. First, Geertz's (1983) reductionist preference for "local frames of awareness" (p. 61) leads him to "brilliant readings of individual situations, rituals and institutions," without, however, specifying how they "relate to each other or to general processes of economic and social change" (Walters, 1980, pp. 550-551). Thus the global perspective is incomplete. Second, the implication that essentialism refers to non-Western underdevelopment, and epochalism to Western modernity (Geertz, 1973), displays at least some sociocentrism. Third, Geertz is aware of "the vices of interpretation," such as losing touch with "the hard surfaces of life—with the political, economic, stratificatory realities within which men are everywhere contained" (p. 30). But an undifferentiated treatment of detail, and a lack of specifiable evidence and evaluation criteria (Biersack, 1989; Crapanzano, 1986; Shankman, 1984), lead his analysis away from these realities. In order to accommodate the idiosyncrasies of different cultures and to render them effective analytical tools, essentialism and epochalism need to be considered in a differentiated conceptual and operational framework, made of specific variables. One such framework is presented in the following sections of this chapter.

THE WORK OF VICTOR TURNER

Order, Disorder, Re-membering and Dis-membering

Victor Turner's (1977) work provides a significant contribution to improving the interpretation of change through an approach that helps avoid a determinist attitude, that accommodates global and local dimensions in a universally applicable model, that reduces sociocentrism, and that considers the multidimensional nature of change. His concept of fluid and indeterminate social change stands in agreement with Geertz's open-ended approach: All social groups, or "natural units of socio-cultural process" (p. 78), have a temporal structure with successive phases. They feature processes of regularization and situational adjustment, but also contain elements of inconsistency, ambiguity, discontinuity, contra-diction, paradox, and conflict.

Turner does not address the causes, origins, purposes, or effects of social change, nor the forces or ideologies that generate it. His attention is centered on collective reactions to change and on cultural strategies used to cope with change. He focuses on symbolic and insti-tutional tools utilized by all human groups to make sense of the interplay of order and disorder present in the processuality of life, in transforma-tions of nature, and in the appearance of the unexpected, sometimes in the form of crisis and disaster. In Turner's approach, transitions from order to disorder, and vice versa, take place in a complex institutional and symbolic interplay, typified by *liminality* and *communitas*. Liminality is "a legitimized situation of freedom from cultural constraints and social classifications" (Turner, 1968, p. 581), whereas communitas is "an unstructured or rudimentary structured and relatively undifferentiated community" (Turner, 1969, p. 96). Both function as an ambiguous link between the past and the future of any given unit of sociocultural process. Liminality and communitas are typical of ritual, a cultural mech-anism of temporal change, structured by a well-defined linkage of sym-bolic units. Such structuring is functional in creating a mental model that gives cyclical meaning to social and cultural ruptures and consecrates transformation, thus enabling a group to feel that it controls reality.

Turner (1977) makes a clear distinction between ceremony, which is linked with integration, stability, "social stages and statutes" (p. 77), and ritual, which is associated by definition with social transition. Ceremony is a regulatory process. It introduces liminality "through the interstices of structure" (Turner, 1969, p, 128), in the form of perfor-mance, public spectacle, or media events: elections, party gatherings, and debates; religious processions and pilgrimage; and artistic festivals and major sports events, such as the Olympic games. In such circum-stances,"the social drama is an eruption from the surface level of ongo-ing social life, with its interactions, transactions, reciprocities, its customs for making regular, orderly sequences of behavior" (Turner, 1986, p. 90).

Ritual, in contrast, emphasizes crisis, disorder, and disintegra-tive processes that emerge in periods of sudden or radical change. Being "a major source of change rather than an embodiment of a logical antithesis" (that typifies the ceremony; Turner, 1977, p. 76), ritual liminal-ity is "future-oriented" and provides unusual, illogical, or potential options that can be both regenerative and destructive. A constant source of anxi-ety, they cannot lean on constraints imposed by familiar (but weakened) cultural models. Thus every historical moment of crisis and transition can be understood as a liminal construct.

Units of sociocultural process (big or small, in Europe or else-where) may be "neither here nor there, betwixt and between the positions assigned by law, custom, convention or ceremonial" (Turner, 1964, p. 8). As in *rites de passage* (van Gennep, 1960), liminality is the "separation" from a preliminal state that leads to a postliminal stage. Depending on the cultural resilience of societies, postliminal phases range from regenerative renewal to oblivion and from "reaggregation" or re-membering to total dismemberment.

Three variables help to contextualize the model and to specify Geertz's essentialism-epochalism convergence, offering a variety of "re-membering" and "dis-membering" options. First, *re-membering* involves a "formulative effort," a concerted search for a new consciousness (Myerhoff, 1980). Second, this effort is oriented by *root paradigms*: consciously recognized cultural models of an allusive, metaphorical kind, cognitively delimited, emotionally loaded, and ethically impelled that give form to action in publicly critical circumstances (Turner, 1977, p. 74). Third, formulative efforts are conducted through *transformative agents*, such as collective memory or an increased awareness of a unique collective self (Myerhoff, 1980).

Thus, re-membering processes involve the action of transformative agents in formulating, applying, and regularizing a new or renewed collective consciousness, based on a root paradigm. A good example is Ataturk's revolution in Turkey, in which transformative agents were mobilized by power-based governmental formulative efforts to promote re-membering, inspired and legitimized by root paradigms of modernity, secularism, and Europeanism.

Dis-membering processes involve the action of transformative agents in the dilution and destruction of identities and root paradigms, and/or their replacement by alien root paradigms, and/or their fragmentation caused by conflicting pressures. Examples include the dissolution of the USSR and Yugoslavia. The plight of the Lebanese Shi'ite minority is another illustration of such processes (Ajami, 1986).

Examples of historical and contemporary root paradigms include the past and tradition; modernity, development, and change; kinship, race, language, and culture; religion and ideology; ethnicity and class; nationalism, regionalism, and internationalism; justice and law; and other values, symbols, and principles of social order. They can be used universally and can appear with culture-bound contents, in "pure" or composite form. Root paradigms can be invented, revived, and imported by both sovereign and stateless nations, such as European states (Hobsbawm & Ranger, 1983); the Shah and the Islamic movement in Iran (Tehranian, 1979); Israelis and Palestinians (Shinar, 1987); and separatist movements in Quebec, Spain, or Yugoslavia (Barber, 1995). Research on the origins of traditions reveals the complex nature of root paradigms. Hobsbawm argues that it is quite easy to trace the sources of traditions that are deliberately invented and constructed by a single initiator, such as the invention of the Boy Scouts by Baden-Powell, and of traditions based on officially instituted (and thus well documented) symbolism, such as in Nazi Germany. However:

> It is probably most difficult to trace where [they] are partly invented, partly evolved in private groups . . . or informally over a period of time, as, say, in parliament and the legal profession. . . . We should expect it to occur more frequently when a rapid transformation of society weakens or destroys the social patterns for which "old" traditions had been designed, producing new ones . . . or when such old traditions and their instrumental carriers and promulgators no longer prove sufficiently adaptable and flexible. (Hobsbawm & Ranger, 1983, pp. 4-5)

In order to become more than abstract ideas, root paradigms need some form of practical organization and power that can be provided by governmental machineries, political parties and movements, religious establishments, trade unions and professional organizations, or bureaucratic structures. These are formulative efforts that enable root paradigms to evolve into action-oriented structures. Formulative efforts get legitimacy and contents from root paradigms.

Transformative agents enable combinations of formulative efforts and root paradigms to reach the masses and to mobilize support for change by disseminating ideas and symbols through formal and informal, established and improvised channels. They can include (a) specialized media of various types, ranging from traditional to modern, interpersonal to mediated, and local to global; and (b) performance of communications roles by social institutions such as religion, family, the arts, educational and political systems; and (c) other vehicles of seduction, bribery, coercion, and terrorism.

The Interactive Dimension: Relations between Components

Historical research provides abundant evidence on the total dis-membering of empires, nations, and cultures. Re-membering processes have also been documented in Europe and elsewhere. Nationalism, for example, served as the major root paradigm for the formulative efforts made in the creation of federal Switzerland in the 19th century. The transformative agents utilized in this process included customary traditional practices—folksong, physical contests, marksmanship—modified, ritualized, and institutionalized for the new purposes.

The statutes of the Swiss Federal Song Festival clearly demonstrate the re-membering purpose of these transformative agents: "to develop and improve . . . the awakening of more elevated sentiments, for [the root paradigms of] God, Freedom and Country, union and fraternization of the friends of Art and the Fatherland" (Hobsbawm & Ranger, 1983, p. 6). This example of local re-membering brings to mind a modern globalizing counterpart: the Eurovision Song Contest, organized since the 1950s by the European Broadcasting Union (EBU) from its Geneva headquarters to foster European solidarity.

However, it is probably impossible to identify total re-membering. Turner's dialectical approach postulates that any postliminal stage, including instances of re-membering, can become preliminal and then liminal. Thus, the stability and prevalence of any re-membering set (of root paradigm—formulative efforts—transformative agents) is always threatened by other re-membering or dis-membering sets. In every society many such sets are active at any given time.

This is where the dimension of power becomes relevant. Root paradigms expressed in terms of effective organization and action are bound to become consensual or dominant. If such a dominant set declines in popularity or credibility, or is weakened in organization and action, it enters a liminal stage, typified by competition with other sets, in which the previously dominant set either recuperates or collapses and is replaced by another re-membering or dis-membering combination.

The re-membering and dis-membering of Yugoslavia provides an example of collapsing sets: in the late 1940s, after 600 years of dis-memberment, Tito's successful formulative efforts, called by Galtung (1993) "statecraft," led to re-membering around three root paradigms. The first was "brotherhood and unity," the slogan used by the state machinery, that "stuck because they had had enough for the time being" (p. 6). The second was Tito's anti-Stalinist socialism. The third was the Non-Aligned Movement, which gave Yugoslavia an identity in the world. All three collapsed in the 1990s, because tribal affinity proved stronger than "brotherhood and unity"; because the socialist root paradigm collapsed altogether; and because "you cannot be non-aligned between something and nothing. . . . There was no rationale any longer to keep the construct going" (p. 6).

In considering the interaction of values, images, and symbols (root paradigms); power and organization (formulative efforts); and action (transformative agents), the model departs from linearity. The absence of specific ideological, organizational, or action-oriented judgments and points of departure allows for analyzing multidimensional relations, such as between the re-membering of one group and the dis-membering of another. Although possible (as in Yugoslavia), a dysfunctional relationship between such processes is not automatic. The re-membering of Europe does not necessarily imply a corresponding dis-membering of its components. The voluntary dis-membering of Czechoslovakia has not proved detrimental so far; on the contrary, it seems to have been functional for the re-membering of its components.

Moreover, the re-membering/dis-membering model allows for dealing with many possible scenarios of change. There are a number of possible combinations.

The "Avis-Syndrome" ("We know what we want and we try harder"). This is the case in which promoters of existing root paradigms search for organizational and power structures (formulative efforts) and action agencies (transformative agents) in order to reach re-membering dominance or consensus. Examples include European or Quebecois separatism; the establishment of Israel as the sociopolitical expression of Zionism, and the concept of the Greater Israel promoted by Israeli irridentists; the struggle for Palestinian statehood as an expression of self-determination rights; and Islamic political fundamentalism that has achieved substantial degrees of "re-membering."

The "Pirandello Syndrome" ("Six Characters in Search of an Author"). This is when members of organizational/power structures (formulative efforts), sometimes accompanied by action agencies, seek the legitimacy supplied by root paradigms in order to reach re-membering dominance or consensus. Examples include radical groups, such as the Nicaraguan Sandinistas or the Algerian F.L.N., after their revolutions; and Eastern Europe, in which power structures remained operative after the collapse of the communist root paradigm.

The "Che Guevara Syndrome" ("Exporting Transformative Agents"). In this case, action agencies (transformative agents) search for the legitimacy supplied by root paradigms and the strength provided by organization/power structures, in order to achieve re-membering dominance or consensus. Examples include media-based political personalities and movements, "perpetual revolutionaries," terrorist groups, and subversive organizations around the world.

THE THREE SCENARIOS AT WORK:
POSTREVOLUTIONARY ROMANIA

The following summary of Coman's (1993) analysis of postrevolutionary Romania between 1990 and 1992 shows the occurrence of the three scenarios in separate and simultaneous instances.

A prolonged liminal period started with the December 1989 revolution and the end of Ceausescu's dictatorship. This was expressed in a fierce struggle between sets of root paradigms, formulative efforts, and transformative agents, whose proponents have been seeking dominance through violent conflict, political and economic struggle, and ideological strife. The occurrence of all three syndromes illustrates a complex situation, as shown by the following brief account of the political scene. Chronologically, the Pirandello syndrome came first, with the advent of the Front of National Health, before the revolution. A people's coalition of all anti-Ceausescu forces mobilized from many ideological backgrounds, the Front appeared as the only power able to conduct the revolution. This ideologically incoherent alliance of political dissidents, which included the military, students, intellectuals, and others, was pledged to be a transitional structure, and was expected to be dismantled after the 1990 election. The leadership decided, however, to participate in the election as a political party. The Front's transformation from a loose revolutionary coalition— around a narrow anti-dictatorship root paradigm, intended to dis-member Ceausescu's regime—into a re-membering formulative effort demanded the adoption or invention of another ideology. The pragmatic nature of the Front, and its vague ideological identity, led to the construction of a tailor-made root paradigm. A populist stand was adopted, featuring the Front as a product of the antitotalitarian revolution and as the true representative of the people's democratic aspirations. The Front's victory in the election can be explained by its systematic refusal to take specific ideological positions, and by the justification of all strategic decisions in universal terms of democracy, prosperity, national health, and consensus.

However, search for an appropriate root paradigm did not end with the electoral victory. Facing economic and social problems, changes in the political scene, and its own eclectic nature, the Front experienced a deep crisis, which eventually led to its reorganization into two movements. One was the new "Democratic Front of National Health," under President Ion Iliescu, that pledged to maintain the original goals, under a "social protection" platform geared to the middle class. The second was the old "Front of National Health," under former Prime Minister Petre Roman that, under a neo-liberal platform, opposed neo-communism and "conservatism" and promised to implement a "shock-therapy" strategy, designed to achieve economic and political reform that catered to the new technocratic generation.

Between 1990 and 1992, the Front used a wide range of transformative agents. Following a revolutionary media strategy, it has made extensive use of television, particularly the first channel, which provided nationwide coverage. A Front newspaper was established (*Today*), and rallies, public conferences, and cultural events were organized on a regular basis. A strong emphasis was given to building a network of local branches around the country and to activating the church. Legitimacy and mobilization have been sought through public services in the memory of revolutionary heroes (thus emphasizing the role of the Front in the revolution) and visible participation of Front leaders in religious celebrations.

The Avis syndrome developed after the immediate postrevolutionary trauma, out of a massive adoption of an anticommunist ethos and out of interpretations of democracy that gave different emphases to human and minority rights, freedom of expression, the market economy, and civil society. These values were an alternative to the former root paradigm, based on Ceausescu's personal and ideological regime. They served as an overall umbrella of legitimacy for the adoption and invention of alternative root paradigms under the sponsorship of cultural and spiritual personalities—not necessarily political leaders—who acted as cultural catalysts.

Attempts to translate these root paradigms into organizational power produced a variety of formulative efforts: in the 1992 presidential election, new political movements—the "Civil Alliance" and the "Civil Alliance Party"— mobilized popular support around a version of the democratic root paradigm that included hatred of the Ceausescu regime, opposition to the left, and vague democratic principles.

Others, who made more specific democratic demands, failed in the election. They included the Democratic Future Party, the Anti-Totalitarian Party, the Down with the Nomenklatura movement, and the Alliance for Anti-Totalitarian Dignity. Another trend combined democracy with traditional and particularist values, ranging from the revival of pre-1945 movements (the Farmers National Party—Christian and Democratic; the National Liberal Party; and the Social Democratic Party) to the establishment of ethnic-nationalist associations, such as the Democratic Union of Romanian Hungarians and the Romanian National Unity Party. Left-wing democracy, inspired by Gorbachov's perestroika, was promoted by organizations such as the Socialist Labour Party.

In order to translate ideas and organization into mobilizing action, transformative agents were activated in the process, based on rallies, student meetings, and mass communications, including the extensive use of revolutionary rhetoric, popular songs, and an exceptionally prolific printed press.

The Che Guevara syndrome developed as a product of the chaotic disintegration of value systems, power structures, and action agencies in Romania. Following the collapse of former system-structuring norms, Romanian society became open to ad hoc action that depended on immediate circumstances, rather than on institutional frameworks. A communitas-like context developed, in which orderly communication systems and action principles were replaced with informal exchanges typical of liminal "performance" such as in ritual, carnival, and pilgrimage (Turner, 1969). This was expressed in spontaneous meetings and rallies, street demonstrations, violent confrontations between factions, and the proliferation of the printed press to some 1,000 daily newspapers in 1990.

Two types of transformative agents are particularly worthy of note. The first—the "communication explosions" in the Bucharest University Square and in the printed press—represents a search for legitimacy and power that did not go beyond the liminal stage. The second type of transformative agent—the "Great Romania" party—featured the development of this search into a relatively stable structure. Total communication, unstructured action, and mass identification with collective ideals took place until mid-1990 in University Square, temporarily renamed the Communist-Free Zone. Day and night, from morning to evening, workdays and holidays, the square featured nonstop group singing, public prayers, unison shouting of revolutionary slogans, and free speech. From university balconies and street corners, ad hoc orators addressed the public in typical revolutionary discourse, complete with confessions, slogans, and calls for action. A special place was reserved for the protesters who went on a hunger strike to force the Front of National Health to resign from government. The setting, the rhetoric, and the imagery all created a new gallery of popular heroes, martyrs, and charismatic leaders. These colorful events did not develop, however, beyond the liminal ritual stage. They did not win full recognition and legitimacy, nor did they coalesce into direct re-membering organized action.

The "press explosion" followed the same disorderly path. A flourishing postrevolutionary Romanian press offered a printed dis-membering version of University Square. Most newspapers constructed ambiguous realities, in which everything was possible. An aggressive style and an apocalyptic dramatization of events served to launch constant attacks against any form of authority and to offer spectacular and rumor-based news that was usually denied the day after publication.

The establishment of the aggressive nationalist Great Romania party and its participation in the 1992 election were exceptions to this trend. The party emerged and borrowed its name from a newsmagazine whose editor had political ambitions. A colorful and violent style, viewed by some as demagogic, and the adoption of a legitimizing nationalist root paradigm, enabled the magazine to build a significant readership that served as a basis for the formulative efforts to establish an effective political structure.

CONCLUSION: COMMUNICATION SYSTEMS AS TRANSFORMATIVE AGENTS

These scenarios of change describe transitions from a liminal to a postliminal stage. Each of the factors—root paradigms, formulative efforts, and transformative agents—can function as "triggers" or "releasers" of processes aimed at the structuring of communitas. In order to succeed, such a trigger has to attract the two other factors so as to establish a stable system, to disseminate information, and to justify and/or impose the new order. In such a transition, from an unstable state, rich in potential alternatives, to a relatively stable and "closed" structure, a decisive role is performed by communication systems—whether language, literature, or the arts, or through the "public sphere," the church, mass, or traditional media. They are the only phenomena that can assure the penetration and survival of a given model of social organization in complex societies.

Consequently, transformative agents play ambiguous roles. As agents of transformation, they equally assure its effectiveness, but being mere agents (even though they can act as triggers or "process releasers"), they never reach the autonomy of root paradigms or formulative efforts. Their effectiveness depends on a successful fusion with root paradigms and formulative efforts. If a transformative agent is not effectively fused in a compatible set of values and organization (represented by a root paradigm and formulative efforts), if communications dominate the postliminal configuration, then the postliminal phase will most probably result in dis-membering.

Thus, within the Avis syndrome, persons or groups acting on behalf of root paradigms (that enjoy some legitimacy) search for organizational power (formulative efforts) and utilize transformative agents to form and maintain a strongly structured configuration. Likewise, in the Pirandello syndrome, persons and groups with organizational power look for value systems in order to gain legitimacy and use transformative agents in order to impose their formula of order. It is quite evident that if these processes function effectively, the outcome of liminality will be directed toward re-membering in both cases. On the other hand, the Che Guevara syndrome features transformative agents seeking both legitimacy and power, in order to focus transition around free communication. This focus undermines order, hierarchy, and classification, leading to communitas. The type of change typical of free communication cannot accept order (i.e., restrictions on the freedom to communicate), except when submitted to the power and logic of the other factors. This explains why the Che Guevara syndrome leads to dis-membering as a cyclical reproduction of the liminal state.

Why should one use the re-membering/dis-membering approach in analyzing social change? One answer is provided in the discussion of the ways in which the model helps to avoid the pitfalls of previous theories. Moreover, the model adds a dynamic dimension to the present body of knowledge on value systems, organizations, and action agents, through a detailed treatment of their internal relationships and interactions. This helps to pose relevant questions about historical and contemporary processes of change.

First, internal transitions within ideological constructs, power structures, and media of communication can be analyzed in depth through the study of questions such as: How are root paradigms adopted, invented, and transformed? How is the root paradigm of local nation-state sovereignty being replaced by global perceptions, and vice versa? What types of formulative efforts and transformative agents are utilized by nation-states in processes of globalization, by secessionary groups in integrated entities, by budding sovereign states in disintegrating empires, and by stateless groups?

The model also allows for studying the joint operation of its parts and the construction of one component under the influence of others through questions such as: How do supporters of a root paradigm make use of formulative efforts and transformative agents? What is the behavior and contribution of different model components and scenarios in re-membering and dis-membering processes? How do re-membering or dis-membering sets of root paradigm—formulative efforts—transformative agents compete in different circumstances?

Third, the model helps to study questions of social change in particular geocultural areas. The following types of questions are relevant to the European case: What are the components of European identity/identities? Which mechanisms are shaping them? Is it feasible and desirable to foster one single identity? What are the roles of communications in such processes? Analyzing the dynamics of remembering and dis-membering offer fruitful avenues to answers.

5

Freedom and Its Mystification: The Political Thought of Public Space

Shalini Venturelli
The American University

Recent European struggles in the East, but also in the West, over the basic terms of human dignity, a better life, the good society, and the deepening of the democratic revolution demand examination, not merely of the scientific "facts" of political and social change, but of the foundations of the very meaning of common existence. The success of liberal democracy over alternative schemes of social organization is not in itself historical evidence that further investigations and discussions of late modernity from this point on can be reached through a process of "emancipation from moral judgments" (Strauss, 1973, p. 18). This chapter addresses one category of moral judgment that remains to be adequately problematized in terms of contemporary democratic reality: the relationship between the theoretical grounds of public space assumed within communication policies in transnational arrangements and the question of political freedom.

Among the most significant aspects of the European problem of common existence is the reconstruction of democracy around policies favoring the notion of transnational public space, or transnational communication (Commission of the European Communities, 1987, 1989,

1990a, 1990b). The significance, of course, is implicit in the central value placed on free speech, free press, and equal and open access to communications within the historical legitimation of liberal democracy according to a standard of freedom, justice, and civil society (Habermas, 1989; Kant, 1793-5/1991; Mill,1859/1974; Rawls, 1993). But the centrality of communication to democracy is also evident in the link between the mode of public space and the potential for political liberty, and between the ideals of modern emancipation and its realities in the arrangements of political space.

The assumptions underlying the form of communication policy can be regarded as the constitutive theory of associational life and democratic relations that defines a given social order. In the reorganization of European systems of public communications over the last 10 years (Negrine & Papathanassopoulos, 1991; Sepstrup, 1991; Servaes, 1992), questions have been raised (Curran, 1991b; Garnham, 1990; Porter, 1993a) regarding the political reality of the values of free speech, thought, opinion, and knowledge at the heart of democratic belief. Indeed, recent transformations of the communication environment—both audiovisual and telecommunication—render problematic the philosophical grounds of the whole concept of transnational communication in global relations. Those who promote the concept generally assume an enlargement, via new communication technologies, of the liberatory capacity for opinion, action, and thought among individuals worldwide (McLuhan, 1964; Pool, 1990). It invokes, therefore, the notion of a transnational public sphere, or global public space (Jameson, 1991; Sakamoto, 1991; Tomlinson, 1991), and of mutual constitution developing as a natural consequence of convergence in systems of information production and distribution among diverse societies, as well as convergence in communication technology access and delivery.

In an attempt to reassess the political foundations of major modes of thinking about public space, this chapter examines the conceptual and normative grounds of validity in theories of public space underlying contemporary transnational communication policy assumptions and claims. The notion of the "transnational" denotes a universal reality distinctive from that of the "international" in processes that (a) transcend the political and economic orbits of the world's state actors (Mowlana, 1994), (b) produce a structure of multinational arrangements grounded in a world economy managed by a set of commercial-state proprietary powers with more influence on the lives of individuals and societies worldwide than the national governments they have elected or been forced to endure (Tomlinson, 1991), (c) construct a globally enframing architecture of communication-cultural formats that render the boundaries of indigenous and exogenous cultural production obscure (McQuail, 1992), and (d) provoke the need for response to the dominance of such transnationalized forms of remote oligarchy by means of a radical restructuring of reigning national-communal political cultures toward the progressive extension of participatory rights of knowledge and public freedom to all.

Transnational communication policies in these historical circumstances are those fundamentally implicated in multinational arrangements to enlarge the sphere of liberal economic culture of negative freedom and its social basis of participation by consumption; to eliminate all barriers to capital flow and transferability in modes of production and labor, thereby fueling growing inequalities and concentration of power; and to reduce, regulate, and manage all political systems by the terms and conditions of private proprietary interests in a laissez-faire world economy. Such policies may arise from multilateral agreements, as in the new World Trade Organization (WTO); from intergovernmental institutional networks such as the institutions of the European Union (EU); or from nations such as the United States, the policies and social power of which exert a formative influence on world institutions and the world economy.

The modes of transnational communication policy draw on national and regional precedents and traditions. They can be said to represent contemporary framework options facing any construction of a transnational public sphere, particularly with respect to the claim within intergovernmental policy deliberations — such as the European Union, the General Agreement on Tariffs and Trade (GATT), and the North American Free Trade Agreement (NAFTA)—that a calculative expansion of global processes implies a progression in the qualities of freedom, justice, and political liberties for mankind. Theories of the press and of media responsibility in modern democracies have been extensively treated, most recently by Curran (1991b) who sheds important light on the divergent interests of these approaches and their social consequences for media systems. The discussion here devolves a stage beneath press theory to question fundamental conceptions of the good society and the free life within the political thought of modern communication policy. The aim is to suggest the principal forms in which a transnational public sphere would be imagined, structured, and institutionalized within intergovernmental arrangements. Examining the intellectual grounds of theories of public space, in effect, amounts to asking the meaning and possibility of common identity in a given political order.

In a wider sense, communication laws and policies ought to be regarded as theories of public space and, therefore, as political theories of associative relations. For instance, press laws protecting freedom of expression as an intrinsic value can be seen as being founded on a certain concept of the good society; that is, a society in which justice, freedom, and human dignity would be impossible if public language were expunged of honest debate and the critique of existing social conditions, or in which knowledge of political, cultural, and social life was unavailable to citizens. Increasingly, however, legislators, policymakers, and corporate institutions in advanced industrial democracies take pains to differentiate factual questions about innovations in communication technology and global competition from normative questions about the correctness of regulatory arrangements. That is, the momentum of privatization is moving in the direction of separating the "is" from the "ought." Even so, the possibility of the emergence of a more enlightened rationality in policy matters becomes questionable because the resulting laws and policies could not possibly gain social legitimacy, or even coherence, if they did not resuppose a concept of the "good." One may conclude, then, that arguments in defense of the neutrality of contemporary democratic policies for communication can only be regarded as rationalizations seeking to evade a decision about the form of their political, and therefore ethical, theory.

Such evasions are no doubt routine in the legal and policy histories of liberal democracies. But in no other sphere are the consequences of unacknowledged motivation and the confusions to which it gives rise greater than in the communication policies and practices that define the public realm of democratic civil states. This is because the actualization of political freedom is fundamentally tied to the potential, conditions, structures, and organizations of public space where common interests are proposed, enacted, deliberated, struggled over, and determined. One of the purposes of this chapter, therefore, is to set aside any notion of the validity of the idea of a context-free technological imperative in legislation, policy, and jurisprudence governing transnational public communications. The perspective presented here recognizes that a substantive change in moral outlook in the advanced industrialized democracies since the 1970s regarding the meaning of a free society and the status of its citizens has been required in order to accept that no "ought" in communication regulation can be derived from the "is." Instead, the principal forms of contemporary communication policies must be explicitly connected to certain moral positions these policies presuppose but generally do not acknowledge. The purpose of disengaging communication laws and policies from political theory is abundantly clear. Weber (1946) points to the systematization and rationalization of conceptual and administrative structures of liberal law, suggesting, especially today in the case of communication regulation, the imposition of policies and laws in the name of technology, efficiency, and market exigencies. Weber's basic insight into the encompassing, pervasive reaches of reason reduced to technological rationalization within all spheres of jurisdictional, political, and market processes is central to grasping the reality of contemporary laws and policies of the public realm. These policies (e.g., Commission of the European Communities, 1994; U.S. Congress, 1994) seem to increasingly project the independently established, rational, and undeniable premises of "legal reasoning" Weber identified by which communication policy options are rationalized as natural consequences of the laws of technological innovation rather than the outcome of the will of the members of a policy or the participatory requirements of a democratic social order.

With respect to the materialist perspective (Murdock, 1993; Tomlinson, 1991) on the social reality of transnational communication, although one might posit a correlation between capitalism and liberal democracy, the argument here is that the conditions of emancipation, such as freedom, rights, equality, and justice, are in fact the measure of democracy and must be regarded as the products rather than the conditions of the political process. Opposing Locke, Kant, and Marx on this issue, I suggest that in the exposition of modes of public space economic freedoms—whether the right of private ownership, or the right to creative labor free of domination—do not have any pre-political historical reality. Political community, the terms of associational life, precedes economics and therefore creates the central values of economy and society (Arendt, 1975; Aristotle, 335-323 B.C./1962, 335-323 B.C./1981; Barber, 1984; Hegel, 1821/1974) as it creates the values of private rights and freedoms. Theories of freedom that envision prepolitical, a priori natural states for human freedom (Hobbes, 1651/1991; Kant, 1784-5/1990; Locke, 1690/1960) constitute harmful, even destructive, fantasies (Taylor, 1993) whose social consequences have been the systematic dismantling of the moral foundations of common existence and possibilities for effective political self-determination in late modernity.

To address these problems in the conceptualization of transnational communication policies, I elaborate four ways of thinking about theories of public space prevailing in democratic policy frameworks and in the global political struggle over the meaning of a transnational public sphere. All derive from distinct, although related, modes of apprehending individualism and privatism, even though the fourth may project itself as a unitary or fraternal approach to conceiving the public world. I focus the discussion on questions that arise from private versus public conceptualizations of the public sphere, or private as opposed to public reasoning in defining the terms of associational life. The relevance of assessing the political foundations for the regulation of modern communication policies may seem obvious, but it has rarely been explored in the context of the meaning of political freedom in public policy and global relations. The problem is not merely that of constructing transnational democratic communications by some specific terms of political theory, but of defining particular historical forms in which democracy's promise of political emancipation through access to the public realm for all citizens and social groups is embodied in contemporary policies that define that realm.

Finally, this chapter suggests the need for further reflection on modernity's accelerating departure from the ideals of political liberty that has been the core of the modernist political enterprise; not simply as an alternative to other principles of associated life (Dewey, 1939/1963), but as the idea of the just and free political community itself. Criticism of the distance between the ideal and political realities of modernity has been most notably developed by Rousseau, Marx, and Weber. For the most part, however, the critique of modern life has tended to ignore or marginalize the relation between the theory and structure of public space and human emancipation. Although some may argue this has been forcefully developed by Habermas (1989), I attempt to show the political inadequacies of his theoretical project that derive from its grounding in Kantian liberalism, whereas other historical and conceptual problems in his argument about the nature of the public sphere have already been extensively taken up elsewhere (e.g., Curran, 1991a, 1991b).

Other critiques of modernity under the loose rubric of "postmodernism" parallel the discrediting of Marxism-Leninism as a theory of society and attempt to force a shift from the very postulate of a normative account of human life in favor of a self-defined free play of human interpretation as world force. This collapse into subjectivism, as Nussbaum (1992) defines it, is taken up more fully under the two modes of public space that illustrate the political and conceptual outcomes of the legitimation of the subject as cultural practice. It is held here that postmodernist rejection of the political project of modernity, as exemplified in Rorty's (1983, 1989, 1994) and Lyotard's (1984) arguments for the eclipse of universalism, ought to be regarded philosophically as the continuation of intellectual Romanticism that began in the mid-18th century and has provided an eclectic, although persistent, criticism of the expansion of social science and modern progressivism. Consistent with its historical roots, this Nietzschian revival, as some have called postmodernist thought (see Lowenthal's extended reflection in Jay, 1987), is not autonomous of modernity, but exists only within and in relation to the structures of modern social experience, the instrumental rationality of which it attacks from an expressive, radically subjectivist orientation. And like its conceptual predecessors, the political consequences of postmodernist perspectives reify the status quo through retreat to celebrations of the private, thus reinforcing conservative threats to progressive democratic politics. Evoking the meaning of the modern political project is therefore consciously employed in this chapter to distinguish the emancipatory struggle for the democratic revolution that began in the 18th century and is still far from complete, from Romanticist postmodernism (see Keane, 1988, 1991; Laclau, 1988; Mouffe, 1988) and its quest for the authentic, passionate, radically indeterminate, empty signifier imagined as "the subject."

   This chapter instead argues the historical need for a reconstruction of the philosophical grounds of political freedom by returning to account for the central condition that makes freedom politically contingent: the organization of public space (Arendt, 1975; Aristotle, 335-323 B.C./1981; Barber, 1984; Montesquieu, 1748/1989; Tocqueville, 1834-40/1945). This problem of actualization that freedom presents for the globalization of democracy is addressed in the context of theoretical assumptions about the transnational public sphere.

PUBLIC SPACE AS INSTRUMENT OF PRIVATE CHOICE

The notion we allude to as democracy is far from coherent. Although applied most often as a law-like explanatory thesis, it comprises, in fact, disparate conceptual systems defining the meaning of freedom. Macpherson (1973) notes that political modernity has at least two traditions, liberal and democratic, that are not necessarily related. But in order to sort out the complex motivations, terms, and implications of communication policy, it is necessary to distinguish democracy even further by more specific sets of assumptions regarding public space and political liberty.

   Committing the resources of society to developing maximization of choice in products and services is commonly recognized today as the meaning of freedom and the primary goal of public policy. This idea of the good society has become so powerful a model in the postsocialist age that sometimes, as Barber (1984) observes, "the very future of democracy seems to depend entirely on its fortunes" (p. 3). There is historical need, therefore, to seriously address the premises about the political aspects of human nature and associational conditions that may be genuinely progressive, in the sense of their effects as transformational forces, but not intrinsically democratic. I limit the discussion of the provisionality of contemporary public policy based on market-centered democratic values to a particular foundation within the works of Locke and Hobbes.

   In the critique here of the utilitarian foundations of public space, the term *civil society* is not employed in the sense of society versus the state, but rather signifies the entire complex of the democratic social order whose system, in the Hegelian meaning of civil society (see Hegel, 1821/1974; taken up by Gramsci, 1971; and more recently by Cohen & Arato, 1992) both incorporates and differentiates the spheres of state, economy, and nonmarket or noncommercial social networks. Although the complexity of this order may be irrelevant to the assumptions of utilitarian thought, the notion of civil society as political society points to the totality of social life, thereby invoking the democratic social contract. It is the grounds of political reasoning with respect to this contract that concern the discussion here, for what is at stake in the debate over theories of the public realm that underlie communication policies is not simply the defense of society against the state or the economy, but, rather, the issue of which version of civil society is to prevail. Failing in an understanding of the premises and assumptions of the democratic social contract for civil society, it is not possible to grasp the mode and place of public freedom, the public realm, or the value of citizenship as opposed to other constructions of the individual within liberal political theory.

In this system of thought, the principal moral legitimation for the argument that the preferred setting for the good life is the market, in which individual men and women—consumers, rather than producers—choose among a maximum number of options, and in which the autonomous individual confronts his or her possibilities of ultimate being, is definitively supplied by John Locke. In *The Second Treatise of Government* (1690/1960), he argues forcefully that "the great and chief end therefore of men uniting into commonwealths and putting themselves under government is the preservation of their property" (p. 395). The identity of freedom with property, with "possessions and a right to them" (p. 335), renders it unsurprising that liberal democrats regard political community as an instrumental rather than an intrinsic good, and that they should hold the idea of public life and participation in disdain.

Locke's particular understanding of natural law as individual self-preservation and property acquisition forms the basis of his argument that the contractual motive for civil society derives from the individual's need for encoding and enforcement of these laws of nature in order to ensure his or her preeminence over all other codes of association. He imbues property with a prepolitical validity that is the defining characteristic of humanness: "Though the earth, and all inferior creatures be common to all men, yet every man has a property in his own person" (p. 328). The aim of common existence is not to share in power or to be a part of a community, but to contain power and community and to judge them by how they affect the freedom of property ownership.

Thus, to live well in this democratic vision is not to make political decisions, as the ancients suggested, nor to make beautiful objects by one's own labor, as Marx suggested, but to make personal choices about possessions. The market within which ownership and consumption choices are made, like the socialist economy, largely dispenses with politics. It requires at most a minimal state—not the regulation of common interests and political freedoms— along with a military to guard against external threats and a police to guard the rights of property. The laws of nature, therefore, suggest only a minimal state for human happiness.

This naturalization of the character of democracy—as with naturalization of other aspects of human existence—renders the form of political society to be immutable and beyond questioning; eliminating the con- ceptual terms signifying its essentially constructed reality functions to shield democracy's existing formation from broad social challenge. The impact of rationalizations by appeals to inherent naturalism in the political thought of utilitarian liberalism is deepened, albeit less cheerfully, by sig- nificant contemporary implications of Hobbes's construction of human nature and his rationale for the civil state. In the *Leviathan*, Hobbes (1651/1991) claims that human life comprises the perpetual pursuit of desires, and that man's natural condition is one of incessant competition oriented toward a "war of all against all" (p. 88). The consequences of this competition in the state of nature is "a general inclination of all mankind, a perpetual and restless desire of power after power that ceased only in Death," and its primary cause is "because [we] cannot assure the power and means to live well . . . without the acquisition of more" (p. 70). The realities of human history, no less in the present than in the past, continue to vindicate Hobbes's uncomfortable hypothesis that brutality, injustice, tyranny, and persecution arise wherever democratic civil society has been absent or inattentive. Yet, it is less a matter of engaging Hobbes on the correspondence of his theory of man's natural condition with human history than of questioning the grounds of his solution to the inevitability of such a fate. His political state for deliverance from a fate of mutual self- destructiveness is a government empowered to do all that is necessary to bring into being and keep a civil peace—but nothing more.

The core of civil society, therefore, is a state that exists to enforce a minimal set of laws demarcating property rights and civil disci- pline (Gray, 1993; Oakeshoot, 1975). Hobbes's (1651/1991) notion of the importance of adjudicating property rights does not emerge from some belief in the identity of freedom and property, as Locke proposes, but in order to keep common peace and security:

> The distribution of the materials . . . that is to say, in one word prop- erty, belongeth in all kinds of commonwealth to the sovereign power. For where there is no commonwealth, there is a perpetual war of every man against his neighbor. . . . Seeing therefore the introduc- tion of property is an effect of commonwealth . . . which we call law and define justice by distributing to every man his own. (p. 171)

The source of freedom in the Hobbesian minimal, but authorita- tive, civil state is the condition in which individuals can pursue their pri- vate appetites:

> Felicity [happiness] is continual progress of the desire, from one object to another; the attaining of the former, being still but the way

to the latter. . . . That the object of man's desire, is not to enjoy once only, and for one instant of time; but to assure for ever, the way of his future desire. (p. 70)

Thus, the good life, which creates the most opportunities for the freedom of pleasure, can only be accommodated by the potential of the commercial market. In modern liberal reasoning, if there is no final or higher good than progressive, that is, ever-advancing desire, there can be no political context other than the minimal civil state, the essence of which is the marketplace relevant or instrumental to that end. With the historical acceleration of entrepreneurial capitalism into monopoly capitalism, this conceptual foundation has become structurally fused to the globalization of commercial and democratic practice, thereby assuming considerable formative influence on the policy, trade, and political arrangements of worldwide liberalization.

The value of the citizen, the individual member of such a state, is as consumer or entrepreneur, the latter being the hero of autonomy who competes to supply whatever all the other consumers desire or might be persuaded to desire. Entrepreneurial activities track consumer preferences or desires, and their aim is to increase their market power, to maximize both the options of entrepreneurs and the options of consumers, and, most of all, to enlarge entrepreneurial assets. Competing with one another, entrepreneurs maximize everyone else's options as well, filling the market with objects of desire. The market, in other words, fixes the meaning of public space and of the common welfare and is preferred over the idea of a political community and the cooperative economy because of its promise of plenitude and increased ownership.

The issue of justice is highly problematic for market-centered democracy. This theory overlooks the fact that individuals come to the marketplace with radically unequal resources—some with virtually nothing at all. Not everyone can compete successfully in commercial production. The market is not, therefore, a good setting for mutual assistance. As Walzer (1992) observes, "I cannot help someone else without reducing my own options and compromising my drive to desire" (p. 95). Individuals have no reason, in the philosophical system of Locke and Hobbes, to accept any reductions of any sort for someone else's sake. Democratic freedoms of the marketplace provide no support for any concept of social solidarity. Indeed, defenders of this theory of freedom—which contains no concept of political space (Hayek, 1982; Nozick, 1974)—argue that social justice is a "myth" and the notion of "society" illusory.

All the same, this view of public life has to confront the reality that the successes of commercial production, the good life of property ownership and consumer choice, is not widely available. Large numbers of people drop out of the market economy or live precariously on its mar-

gins. Philosophically, however, the reality of gross inequalities in property is consistent with this doctrine of a natural right to property and a natural necessity of desire, even though it is irreconcilable with Locke's
view of the right of the majority to rule. As MacIntyre (1966) observes, a
Whig theory of democracy is unable to explain the contradiction that to
give the rule to the majority will be to give the rule to the many whose
interests lie in the abolition of the right of the few to the property the
minority has acquired. The private choice theory can only hold if it
assumes that the majority of citizens in a democratic social order will
accept, and benefit from, an oligarchic government controlled by property owners, privileging by law and property—in the name of each citizen—the interests of owners of large-scale property.

Participants in this social order are not conceived as active in
the state order other than to articulate claims for enforcing, regulating,
and guaranteeing the market economy. Thus, in its ideal form, democracy understood primarily as an environment that facilitates the processes
of private choice, does not make for citizenship. Defense of this theory
(see Johansson, 1991, for a survey of the literature; see also Buchanan,
1975; Buchanan & Tullock, 1962; Gray, 1989; Hayek, 1949; Jasay,
1990) as the only valid meaning of democracy interprets citizenship
purely in economic terms. Such a view increasingly supports public policies in a number of spheres, from communication to childrearing, favoring the transformation of citizens into consumers or property owners who
must then seek out the party or program that most persuasively promis-
es to strengthen their market position. Members of democratic civil society need the state, but have no moral relation to it. Instead, they seek its
capture for gaining advantage with the buying or not buying of what they
make. Because the market has no political boundaries, commercial ownership, production, and consumption also tends to transcend state control. The state is required for determining rules of fair play, but there is
no loyalty to the state, which brings the political order into continual conflict and struggle with the basic principles of guaranteeing freedom.

As Barber (1984) observes, the reality of the preeminent value
placed on private choice in the marketplace has been a major historical
obstacle to achievement of democratic experience: "the giantism of the
modern, monopolistic multinational corporation [is] the liberty-corroding
heir to the independent, small-scale firm" (p. 253), suggesting that multinational corporate institutions today stand outside, and to some extent
against, every political community. In other words, the practice of political liberty in public life, the value of public space, deliberation, and public
debate on matters of common concern and political solidarity, are by and
large irrelevant to the more pressing concerns of consumer preferences,
the dismantling of trade barriers, and the flow of global investment. If the
conditions of the marketplace can now be guaranteed and regulated in

the international arena, the national democratic civil state becomes an anachronism. The intractable paradox, therefore, of the utilitarian private choice theory of public space is that, by its own logic of the meaning of freedom as property and desire, this version of the democratic state threatens to enact its own effacement in the face of historical realities favoring the transnationalization of the market.

To the extent that those who have formed transnational policies have appeared to unquestioningly adopt—whether consciously or not—Locke's and Hobbes's articulation of selfhood, because it is a framework of freedom most favorable to commercial culture, conceptions of political liberty deriving from justice and common interest are rendered historically impossible. This is because alternative conceptions of these basic requirements of human experience are at variance with the central features of the modern order and, more especially, the characteristics of an emphasis on individualism, acquisitiveness, and elevation of the values of the market to the status of public space, that arena of human association that facilitates the conditions and practices of political liberty (Arendt, 1973). The fundamental idea of political community is at odds with transnational conceptualizations of communication because the latter have generated policies that do not ensure the public conditions for the narration, deliberation, or imagination of ethical relations among the inhabitants of such a community. As a set of institutional arrangements of communication, in which the idea of society is constructed as an aggregation of emotive beings who lack any genuine moral consensus, the commercial content of the public spheres of transnational media cannot but render the nature of political and public obligation to the meaning of democracy systematically unclear. MacIntyre (1984) calls this condition "a rejection of the modern political order" (p. 255), referring to the erosion of the political enterprise for progressive emancipation of social groups from all spheres of domination, a process of thought and political action that began in the 17th century.

For the transnational public sphere, the wholesale adoption of a position like that of Locke's notion of civil society and citizenship in transnational communication policies—such as in the European Commission's policies on transfrontier communication, or in GATT demands for elimination of public interest regulation for global information flows—will result in the formation of global cultural space with characteristics fundamentally opposed to the requirements of a democratic public sphere. As can be observed in the United States and some other industrialized nations, the public realm of modern communications is a narrative and deliberative world in which a particular kind of moral vocabulary consecrating the self has created an historical disjuncture with the idea of political community. What European or worldwide users of global information networks can therefore expect to possess are no more than the fragments of a conceptual scheme of the possibility of society (MacIntyre, 1984). If this is the case, as Tocqueville (1834-40/1945) anticipated in his study of the pathologies of Anglo-American individualism, then democracy will be a mere fiction in the cultural or transnational communication. The basis of this claim is that the particular character of a market-driven, monopoly-oriented electronic public sphere generates a set of social conditions under which audiences and users are powerless to detect the disorders of political thought and practice in the face of forms of commercial cultural content and their catastrophic deification of the universal consumption-driven being (Ferguson, 1992).

The significance of this monological state of rights and self-interest, of individualism and utilitarianism, is not merely at the level of private belief. This late modern condition has succeeded in establishing a moral culture through fundamental transformation of institutions and social arrangements. The actions and policies of government and all other social institutions, such as schools and economic organizations, answer only to this standard of value: the primacy of private interest (Taylor, 1989a, 1989b). Thus, adopting a private choice approach to the regulation of communications offers regulatory and structural legitimacy to organize society by the standards of private, not associational or common, ends, with the expected consequences for public life, justice, and the practice of political freedom.

Media policies under this system of thought are largely concerned with protecting the rights of media ownership and are thus rapidly subsumed under ownership laws (Porter, 1993b), the most important and defining category of laws for this type of civil society (Oakeshoot, 1975). Moreover, recent political changes in the countries of East Asia, Latin America, and the postsocialist states of Eastern Europe indicate the emergence of a model of civil society that leans more heavily in the direction of a Hobbesian state. That is forms of civil society offered as alternatives to totalitarian orders are seeing the enactment of laws and policies guaranteeing private property and contractual liberties, but not necessarily the political and human rights of participation, free press, free speech, a fair trial, and so on (Gray, 1993). This is an historical development that further fixes the central values of economy and society in favor of ownership laws over democratic political freedom. The trend is now global in scale, compelling nations through powerful multilateral pressures to abandon alternative assumptions of the organization of a free society in favor of policies of deregulation, privatization, and entirely market-based criteria of public reasoning and policymaking.

In Great Britain, for instance, a commitment to some version of a public space philosophy for communications policies during most of this century, especially since the end of the World War II, is being steadily dissolved at all levels of public communications, both audiovisual and telecommunications (Curran, 1991a, 1991b; Garnham, 1990; Scannell, 1992; Smith, 1989). Elsewhere in Europe, and especially in the European Union, this view is being written into policies and laws regulating communications, despite existing policy frameworks emphasizing social, political, and cultural goals with which the former are in fundamental conflict (Servaes, 1992; Venturelli, 1993). The Lockean-Hobbesian vision of human nature and a free life, although lately called by other names, is also being held forth as the ideal policy standard of political and social liberation for the countries of the former Soviet Union.

Despite its contemporary historical power over global relations, it should be recognized that a maximization of private choice approach to public space is a singular form of rationality. It is unable to conceptualize inequalities of access to social goods and information, and it is unable to articulate a set of principles for democratic political association. It ignores one of the central questions of late modernity: Given that there is no alternative to the market, what degree and what kinds of public intervention in markets does "justice" require?

PUBLIC SPACE AS PRACTICES OF THE SELF

Conceptually intermingled, but nevertheless distinct from a Lockean-Hobbesian approach to public space, is another instrumental approach that regards the civil state as a vast store of assets to service contending projects for the political protection of subjective identities. The state is an instrument of predation, the arena within which a legal war of all against all is fought by rules and laws specifying not only property rights and contractual liberties, but every type of private right and personal freedom. Individuals and collusive interest groups engage in lobbying and colonizing regulatory authorities, legislative bodies, and the judicial system to mold these rules to suit their own interests on the assumption that if they do not alter the legal and regulatory framework to their advantage, their competitors will do so against their interests. Individuals and enterprises are constrained to organize collusively so as to capture the democratic state, if only because they know that if they do not others will. What they seek from government is not equal freedom under law, but particularistic political recognition and legal privilege. They seek political endorsement not of common values emerging from public deliberation, in which citizens are allowed opportunities for participation on issues of common concern, but of their private values and interests. Although this view could also be articulated from the perspective of Locke's oligarchic individualism, here I attempt to address the philosophical basis of another form of individualism from which the inflation of the rhetoric of private rights can be said to emerge; namely, from a consideration of Kant as the ultimate defender of the moral value of subjectivism (Rawls, 1993).

The paradigm of a rights-based theory of public space sets out from the assumption that a chronic, low-intensity civil war on personal rights is the natural condition of a free society (Gray, 1993). The moral validation for private rights as the highest, unconditional end of a good society emerges from Kant's construction of the rational, hence free, being who utters the commands of morality to him or herself, and obeys no one but him or herself. The absolute sovereignty of the subject emerges from Kant's (1784-5/1990) "categorical imperative" in the *Foundations of the Metaphysics of Morals*, in which he constructs the individual as a morally sovereign member of the social order, able to abstract universal principles or maxims of social relations from private reason, and obligated to no authority external to him- or herself. The categorical imperative states: "Act only according to that maxim by which you can at the same time will that it should become a universal law" (p. 38).

This power of the individual will to endow itself with moral sovereignty releases it from obligation to the political order because we are each empowered a priori by reason to give ourselves our own laws without taking into account associational concerns or public debate on common ends. Individual members of civil society, therefore, stand outside the social order and have no duty other than to personal, prepolitical rights against the state. If you modify Locke and Hobbes by Kant, you arrive at the conclusion that the purposes to which the public world is instrumentalized are found within us. These purposes are self-preservation as embodied in the pursuit of happiness or property or of both as they are given by nature, but actualized under the control of far-sighted, calculating, and generalizing reason.

As Taylor (1993) observes of this philosophical system, reason in a rights-based theory of freedom is no longer defined substantively, that is, in terms of a public notion of the good that action brings about, but, rather, formally, in terms of procedures that the private subject should follow in rationalizing private rights and actions to social ends. Thus, freedom takes on a new meaning, entailing breaking loose from any external authorities in order to be governed solely by one's own reasoning procedures, the "absolute worth of the [private] will alone, in which no account is taken of any use [existing conditions]" (Kant, 1784-5 /1990, p. 10), social, political, cultural, or otherwise.

In Kant's "search for and establishment of the supreme principle of morality" (p. 8), he puts forward a rights-based deontological theory based on universal rights that are not public but private, and which if you follow will be moral regardless of the ends:

> The good [private] will is not good because of what it effects or
> accomplishes or because of its competence to achieve some intend-
> ed end. . . . Usefulness or fruitfulness [either in a personal sense or
> in terms of the common interest of political society] can neither
> diminish nor augment this worth." (p. 10)

Self-interest is morally valid, but not by the wrong rules. The state is there
not to facilitate the practice of political self-determination, but to prevent individuals from infringing on each other's rights and to defend and enhance the
sphere of private rights. Kant's regard for the laws of democratic society,
therefore, comes from the perspective of hindrance. The rules are "statutes
and formulas, those mechanical tools of the rational employment or rather
misemployment . . . [which] are fetters of an everlasting tutelage" (p. 84).

The condition of liberty for Kant arises far less from the form of
political community than from the immanence of private reason. "If only
[private] freedom is granted," he writes, "enlightenment is almost sure to
follow" (p. 84). It is the role of government, therefore, to "divest the
human race of its tutelage and [to] leave each man free to make use of
his reason in matters of conscience" (p. 88). In short, conscience, the
inner, private world of the self, replaces citizenship, whereas the voca-
tion of private reason and thought displaces public life and political participation. We may conclude that this theory of freedom has no concept
of public space—other than from the utterances of private reason—and
therefore so long as communication policy frameworks are centered on
the question of private rights, there is no conceptual foundation on which
to articulate public space in laws, policies, and political practices.

The moral foundation of subjectivism in Kantian thought assures
that the notion of human dignity derived from private reason gains a new
importance, because human existence is now removed from the context of
obligation by its own status as a sovereign reasoning being demanding
the use of rational control. The imagination of this sovereignty has pervad-
ed social thought and cultural practice in late modernity, despite the realities of rampant irrationalism in practices of the self, because the idea of
human dignity is invoked from Kantian moral categories. Thus, the good
life socially translates into our freedom to be disengaged from political
society and from the common welfare and to indulge our private desires,
or "emotivism" as MacIntyre (1984) calls it, without moral compunction.

The question for a rights-based theory of democratic relations is
whether a theory of atomism, however morally worthy notwithstanding its
reprehensible social and political uses, demonstrates any fundamental
capacity to articulate the need for justice or the practice of broad participatory inclusion in deliberations over policies of state or economy, or the
value of public space. The requirements of justice, citizenship, and widespread access to public space is, after all, what is supposed to distin-

guish democratic society from other forms of polity such as oligarchy, authoritarianism, and totalitarianism. The question arises as to what political fate are we inexorably drawn in this trend toward privatization of all reasoning by which moral principles are removed from the political sphere and placed in the private sphere? Insofar as democracy requires the active commitment of citizenry in the preservation of political freedoms for all, the argument here is that, as with the private choice view of public space, the logical terminus of rights-based freedom is the evacuation of political, that is, common reasoning from most, if not all, domains of human experience. The consequences are a return to prepolitical human existence, to the end of democracy, and to its epitaph: the private.

The most influential embodiment of this theory for communication is the First Amendment to the U.S. Constitution:

> Congress shall make no law respecting an establishment of religion, or prohibiting the free exercise thereof; or abridging the freedom of speech, or of the press; or the right of the people peaceably to assemble, and to petition the government for a redress of grievance.

This collection of rights with respect to conscience, speech, and political self-determination has served as the historical standard for the ideal of freedom. Yet, under a rights-based theory, this ideal is subject to certain social and political uses the consequences of which are not always to further the interests of a democratic political community that must enable the practice of citizenship in order to survive (Gray, 1993). Insofar as any social entity can assimilate to itself the moral sovereignty of private rights (Porter, 1993b), the rights-based theory gives rise to media laws, public policy, and jurisprudence increasingly tilted against retention of the most minimum standards of public interest, the encouragement of citizenship practices, or the furtherance of information, knowledge, public reason, and constitutional community (see critical legal analysis of free speech jurisprudence in Streeter, 1990; Unger, 1983).

For this reason, policies in the global arena that are rationalizations for advancing democratic freedoms focus on forms of media ownership, not only under the necessity to protect ownership rights, but also as a result of a process granting a growing moral equivalence between the individual rational being and the individual corporate or institutional being (Porter, 1993b). Kant's idea of human beings as ends in themselves and therefore deserving of dignity and respect in their public speech has been extended to special interest groups, corporate, institutional, and bureaucratic beings as ends in themselves also deserving of dignity and respect in their public speech; and this public speech itself is becoming increasingly commercial rather than political, as Habermas

(1989) points out in his critique of the modern democratic public sphere. The current historical trend, therefore, is for artificial entities to somehow absorb more and more of the status of the individual human citizen and therefore more and more of the private rights originally intended by the Enlightenment founders of modern democratic thought for the emancipation of humans from oppression, tyranny, ignorance, and injustice.

This tension is apparent in media policies within the European Union, in which speech is acknowledged as a moral necessity for individuals who seek to actualize their true freedom, but is also placed within communications regulations that are tilting increasingly in favor of artificial individuals and their rights of media ownership, cross-ownership, monopoly ownership, multimedia ownership, and transborder ownership (Porter, 1993a, 1993b; Tomlinson, 1991). Communication policies in the transnational public sphere seem to be shifting away from the rights of individual citizens to receive substantive knowledge and information of their surrounding world in order for them to practice their freedom in the first place (Curran, 1991b). This is also why media laws of the new post-socialist states contain so many ambiguities regarding free speech. They pay ample homage to its necessity, but when applying Western models of public space, become confused and politically fragmented over the issue of how to translate laws favoring freedom to own, buy, and sell media enterprises into the realities of freedom of participation, information, and knowledge for their citizens. Hence, we find long lists of exceptions, mostly in the form of cultural and social exceptions, as well as exceptions to ensure the continuity of governments in power (Jakubowicz, 1992; Johnson, 1993).

Thus, contemporary communication policies defining the public space of democratic societies are caught between an ownership discourse and a rights discourse, with the increasing tendency of the two to converge in the permanent fixing of government policy to favor media ownership rights and corporate media rights of free speech. Those who make communication laws, therefore, cannot conceive of how to apply the criterion of public interest, even when that seems to be the intention, as with U.S. Vice President Gore's vision of an information superhighway ("Gore outlines data highways," 1994; "Uncle Sam's superhighway," 1994), which pleads for the common good without providing the principles by which it ought to apply to communications; or the vision of Jacques Delors, former President of the European Commission, of an advanced telecommunications infrastructure for the entire European continent ("Delors' grab-bag," 1993; "Heavy weather ahead," 1993), which regards the enterprise more as a public works undertaking than a project to facilitate political self-determination and common interest among a plurality of social groups, the latter being the normative purpose of democratic public space (Arendt, 1975; Aristotle, 335-323 B.C./1981; Habermas, 1989).

PUBLIC SPACE AS AN INSTRUMENT OF RADICAL INDIVIDUALISM

The third individualist theory of public space in a free society is less influential in terms of social reality, but significant in terms of the modern intellectual struggle to present an alternative conception to existing forms of organization. Critical legal studies and critical theory are theoretical manifestations of a broader debate over the meaning and reality of civil society in advanced industrialized democracies. As self-conscious reflections on the place of the individual in the late modern age, the general movement distinguishes itself from preceding approaches in the following ways: Far from rejecting individualism or being indifferent to legal protections for basic human rights, as in a Hobbesian civil state, critical approaches seek to solidify these values more deeply in the structure of society. Instead of choosing either to fully reject or embrace the privatism of the market or the self, a privatism that wields a formative power in contemporary democratic policies, these approaches see subjectivism reconciled to the founding ideals of individualist thought.

Civil society is thus rearticulated as the legal, institutional, and economic realization of individualism's philosophy and prophecy implicit in contemporary legal and political doctrines, but absent in their corresponding practices. Employing different forms of intellectual justification, a critical individualist view of public space attempts to unmask the halo of naturalness and necessity that enshrouds the canonical forms in which democratic society is ordered and shielded from scrutiny. It advocates a civil society more closely representative of the ideal of radical subjectivism, which implies a rearrangement of the fixed order of society to liberate the self from social, political, legal, and economic constraint. As Unger (1983) observes of this reconstructivist program,

> It pushes the liberal premises about state and society, about freedom from dependence and governance of social relations by the will, to the point at which they merge into a large ambition: the building of a social world less alien to a self that can always violate the generative rules of its own mental or social constructs and put other rules and other constructs in their place. (p. 41).

To achieve reconciliation between political practices generated by an approach based on individualism and the political ideals of individualism, Habermas (1979, 1984, 1987, 1989) advances an enormous theoretical project for civil society in which he retools Kant's idea of freedom grounded in reason to reinvigorate the moral grounds of democratic relations. The central propositions of this project are first, purification of the public sphere of civil society by restoring reason and open disclosure, and, second, defining the procedures of discourse ethics that establish rules of reasoning for arriving at common consent among sovereign individual beings. In this attempt to reconstruct the Kantian philosophy of freedom, Habermas makes no serious departure from Kant's theoretical focus on the sphere of individual social action in the definition of the political order. What may be considered substantive, perhaps, is Habermas's attempt to shift discussion from the entrapments of a monological perspective of the subject, that dominates Kant's theory of individual reason and rights as well as Locke's theory of self-interest, to the notion of "intersubjective relations."

A theory of society based on the atomized individual is thus partially transformed into a theory of society based on the dialogical individual oriented to mutual understandings of the other. Furthermore, theories of political freedom derived from Kant's categorical imperative and from Locke's natural necessity of property ownership is transformed into a theory of freedom derived from the rules of uncoerced argumentation in an undistorted public sphere. Thus, civil society is still largely conceptualized by the categories of individual life, private relations, and ethical procedure, regardless of social outcomes. Habermas insists on the value of private reason and distinctive modes of rationalization legitimate to intersubjective relations (the "lifeworld"), on the one hand, and institutional relations (the "systems world"), on the other. The differentiation of forms and contexts of rationality is a recognition he regards as essential to the very possibility of civil society in late modernity. In this sense, Habermas reclaims the validity of modern reason from the legacy of despair in Weber's (1930, 1946) account of the devastating consequences of instrumental reason, or rationalization, for the authentic conditions of a free life.

This portion of the Weberian legacy is best understood when contrasted with Marx's (1839/1978c, 1867/1978d) theory of modernity, which attempts to demonstrate how the universalization of capital exchange relationships leads to conditions of exploitation, scarcity, and the intensification of economic crisis. Despite the grim prognosis, and following the dialectics of Hegel (1821/1974), the theory also holds that processes of capital accumulation carry the seeds of their own negation, which conceptually permits the emancipation of humankind to be prefigured in the dynamics, the crises, and the logic of capitalistic social development. Clearly, the notion of liberation implicit in Marx's critique of modernity owes most, if not all, of its inspirational power to Hegel's (1837/1953) philosophy of history, which emphasizes the creation of unity through reconciliation of opposites and the ultimate synthesis of the dialectical progression at the end of history: the state of universal freedom. Because a Hegelian theory of reconciliation between the individual and the community is absent from Weber's critique, he concedes little, if any, emancipatory hope in his explanation of modernity, both in terms of its processes and in terms of its ultimate consequences. Modernity as the process of advancing rationalization signifies for Weber (1946) an increase in formal rationality in all spheres of social experience, but without bearing the seed of its own negation as capitalism does for Marx. Thus, the absence of an immanent utopian orientation in Weber's assessment of reason has left a difficult theoretical legacy to critical philosophers like Habermas who wish to reclaim its virtues in the interest of preserving modernist emancipatory development.

The critical approach to public space is also advanced by Keane, who describes it as inherently indeterminate and therefore open to perpetual self-invention by the subject. Keane (1988) dismisses the idea of consensus over public goods, because this would threaten the requirement of systematic uncertainty essential to the subject's self-construction. In fact, he regards the civil state's role in guaranteeing certain public goods as "ideology": "To defend democracy in this sense is to reject every ideology which seeks to stifle this indeterminacy" (p. 47). Elsewhere, however, Keane (1991) argues that communications media are defensible as a public service in order to "serve as the primary means of communication for citizens living, working, loving, quarreling, and tolerating others within a genuinely pluralist society" (p. 150). He favors the "decommodification" of communications in order to liberate the subject as "empty signifier" to its indeterminate or contingent practices of the self. Keane's approach, therefore, is an extension of rights-based theories, which construct civil society as an aggregation of private sovereignties, with the important distinction that his defense of radical subjectivity converges with a developed critique of free-market liberalism.

Unger, Habermas, and Keane represent three main currents of thought in the critical democracy movement and, although distinctive in many ways, share certain key features regarding the normative foundations of public space and membership in political community. One common feature is an intensification of the moral category of the subject and its autonomy from any constraint on discretionary rights. Another is an attention to the problem of theorizing interpersonal discourse, the sphere of experience, in which the immunity of the subject from social obligation must be tempered by the need for relations outside itself. For those occasions, Habermas has developed the procedures of dialogics that are ethical insofar as their validity is deontological—that is the rules of intersubjective relations impose a certain duty or a condition on discrete subjects. In order for a norm to claim validity, the subject's absolute autonomy from history and culture in the zone of self-actualization must be scaled down within the intersubjective experience in order to meet with the consent of all affected in their role as participants (Habermas, 1990).

Because of this theoretical advancement in the recognition of those who speak from the perspective of individualism of personal associations within the larger context of private autonomy, as compared with Lockean-Kantian concepts of insular private freedom, those who present critical theories are able to articulate a concern for public space in their attention to it as a feudal sphere (Habermas, 1989) of oligarchic structures, irrational relations of social power, and political domination. Consequently, Keane proposes the "decommodification" of communications media, Habermas the intersubjective use of private reason, and Unger (1983) the "destabilization rights" of the subject to disrupt established institutions and social practices. Thus, a critical individualist concept of public space is the only one of the four individualist modes of defining freedom explored in this chapter that can articulate a challenge to the moral legitimacy of the market in the determination of public space.

However, in terms of a political understanding of the civil state and public policy, critical individualism perpetuates its root tradition of defining the state negatively, that is, defending the absolute claim of the subject to security against the state. Civil society has a single purpose: to provide an environment conducive to the practice of passionate individualism, the liberation of the individual into newer forms of subjective excitement. Practices of the self within political and social surroundings free of domination either by state or market is the overriding moral virtue, whereas self-invention is the only duty. In other words, those who take the position of critical individualism, as its more liberal counterparts, still cannot articulate the notion of political community—although they can recognize communal claims (e.g., see, Unger, 1983). Habermas's procedures for achieving mutual consent notwithstanding, ideas of justice or common welfare are implausible if they arise from any category beyond individual interest. Although those who make public policy, in this way of thinking, may drop market metaphors and choose not to invoke moral assumptions regarding the free market, their articulations must remain confined, as with Lockean and Kantian bases of democratic reasoning, to questions concerning subjective rights and entitlements. Keane's argument for a public service approach in communication cannot, therefore, be reconciled—despite his critique of the market economy—with his theory of democracy as radical subjectivity.

The political foundations of this general approach bear some debt not merely to liberal sources of individualism, but to Marx's theory of individualism as well. Although I take up Marx's view of public space and political community at more length elsewhere, I merely point out here key aspects of his theory of history relevant to the issues addressed. Marx (1832/1978a) seems to share in common with Locke several categories by which the question of freedom is problematized, including a disdain for the state and a high regard for prepolitical human life, which they both hold up as more "authentic." They also share an emphasis on the sanctity of the individual's labor, and thus both articulate labor and ownership theories of freedom. In *The German Ideology* (1832/1978a), Marx defines the preferred setting of the free life as the cooperative economy in which we can all be producers—artists, inventors, and craftsmen. The picture Marx paints is of creative men and women making useful and beautiful objects, not for the sake of this or that object, but for the sake of creativity itself, the highest expression of our ontological condition as man-the-maker:

> The mode of production must not be considered simply as being the reproduction of the physical existence of individuals. Rather, it is a definite form of activity of these individuals, a definite form of expressing their life, a definite *mode of life* on their part. As individuals express their life, so they are. (p. 150; emphasis in original)

Thus, Marx and Locke regard the economy as the substance, boundary, and constitution of civil society itself; the key difference between them being that whereas Locke regards private property as the essential, perhaps sole, condition of human freedom in the state of nature, Marx regards private property as the source of the division of labor and thus of the eventual alienation of individuals from authentic conditions of production in his account of the state of nature.

Given this construction of what is meant by freedom, Marx and Locke both view the civil state in instrumental terms. The state, as Marx (1832/1978a) sees it, ought to be managed in such a way as to set production free, following which politics simply ceases to be necessary. The disappearance of the state, apparently, requires its replacement by some administrative agency for economic coordination of production in some form of regulatory structure that is nonpolitical; the implication is that the individual producer, as the consumer-entrepreneur in the private choice or private rights theories of public space, is freed from the burdens of citizenship. Thus, Marx's conception is seriously anti-politics because the free life requires a worker-controlled factory in which men and women make decisions and make things without any concept of how a system of justice, political self-determination, or participatory common interest will apply. The vision of a cooperative economy is set against an unbelievable background: a nonpolitical state and regulation without participation, deliberation, or conflict. This literal effacement of the conception and structures of a public world, and therefore disregard for the value or utility of political freedom, is woven into the very structure of critical theories derived from a convergence of Kantian and Marxian critical individualism, tied to the notion of prepolitical, radical subjectivism. It is one among several reasons that a critical individualist theory of public space cannot transcend the subjective and private categories of reason by which those who take this approach articulate apolitical associational life.

For communication policy, critical theories of public space imply that all sectors of civil society, including its system of public communications, are regarded from the standpoint of their potential instrumental use in the liberation of the individual to a more authentic condition of selfhood, nonsubjugation to visible and invisible constraints, expanding social entitlements, and communal experience—although not necessarily in the sense of a political community. The theory of public space is thus nothing but the theory of the political conditions of the existence of a "subject," as Touraine (1992) has defined it. Principles of communication policy emerging from this politics of the subject include media representation of the social diversity in modes of subjective being, disengagement of communication systems from both state and commercial control, enhancement of a plurality of public communication sources to reflect the plurality of subjective realities, and the general weakening of the power of reified notions of ownership in legal thought to determine communication structure and content.

PUBLIC SPACE AS CULTURAL COMMUNITY

One of the most powerful ways of apprehending freedom in the period of postsocialism and late modernity is via the idea of nation or community grounded on the essential and preexistent "nature" of a people. The building of community posited on archaic identities of "blood" and "cultural tradition" was recognized by the Romans as distinct from constitutional, and therefore political, community. *Natio*, in Latin, refers to peoples and tribes not yet organized in political associations, a term the Romans employed to distinguish communities of people of the same descent, integrated geographically and culturally, but not yet politically (Lepsius, 1992). Since the 17th century, the term *natio* has been used interchangeably with the nation of the citizen, a meaning that does not include a concern for common ethnic properties, but with the relations of citizens who believe and enact some concept of civil society. In seeking an explanation for modern occurrences of the supposedly premodern tendencies to xenophobia, ethnic conflict, and the imagination of a common cultural history, recent analyses of cultural and national identity (e.g., Gellner, 1983; Hobsbawn, 1990; Smith, 1992) do not seem to make the Roman distinction.

However, as Hayden (1991) and Bowman (1992) have determined in their study of ethnic persecution in the states of the former Yugoslavia, there has not been sufficient recognition in intellectual thought that nationalisms we see today are neither manifestations of a will to overcome traditional modes of organization, as Hobsbawn (1990) suggests in his theory of nationalism as the process of dissolution of tribal identities, nor is it an attempt to reestablish the historical condition of preexisting cultural formations, as Geertz (1973) suggests. Both explanations locate modern nationalism within a progressive context of the quest for communal liberation and freedom. Instead, as Bowman points out, mobilization of imagined identities provides not a return to the world that existed before modernity effaced it, but to yet another modern "alternative," albeit antidemocratic community—this time constituted by narratives of sameness and common descent, and often by perceptions of persecution by an external antagonist.

Contemporary investigations and rationales in international relations for the most part have failed to stress, therefore, that the notion of national identity as citizenship completely parts company with the idea of identity in an imagined prepolitical community integrated by descent—although both may be modern in conception and practice. Although the community of citizenship in civil society and that of membership in nationalism have sometimes fused as catalysts, the democratic nation-state has not always forged an historical and constitutional link between *ethnos* and *demos* (Francis, 1965). Citizenship has rarely been conceptually tied to ethnic national identity, because the term *freedom* has completely different meanings for each. For *ethnos*, that espousal of distinct states for supposedly distinct "peoples," *freedom* is collective self-assertion not generalizable to other social groups. For *demos*, *freedom* is political liberties of participation, self-determination, and deliberation in the public realm of constitutional civil society, liberties that are universally conferred on all social groups and that exclude in principle any connection between ethnic or religious ascription and one's political status as citizen.

Thus, cultural notions of public space implicitly incorporate the legitimation of defensive violence against threats to narratives of cultural self-construction, sustained by the reification of progressively essentializing notions of culture derived from the dynamic construction of cultural origins. This modern tendency has continuously confounded the modern philosophy of freedom because there has been little serious attempt to distinguish nationalist movements for statehood or public policy from democratic movements for statehood or public policy. Patterson (1991) argues that *private* freedoms, whether for individuals or distinct groups, have been historically founded not on the dignity of human self-determination, but on the social deaths of others. In the late 20th century, nightmare scenarios of social death, slaughter, and population transfer are being acted out; nebulous markers of cultural identity are being filled out by the imagined common history in one discourse of public space, endangered by the imagined common history in others.

The problem with the notion of communication policy as cultural policy or cultural self-defense is that the sovereignty of the ethnic nation-state to preserve its imagined cultural legacy against hostile forces has very little to do with arguments for a politically self-determining community arising from universal civil liberties and the conditions of open communication and open access in the deliberations of public life. There is no conceptual connection between nationalism and citizenship because the idea of citizenship is not based on sharing the same ethnic or cultural origins. Rather, the political culture of citizenship depends on the creation of a constitutional community of guaranteed political liberties and open public communications. In a participatory theory of public space, one's ethnic, religious, or racial identity becomes irrelevant to one's identity as a citizen. The problem, of course, is that not only the contemporary resurgence of xenophobia with its romantic appeals to the Volk, but also democratic theories of public space based on maximization of choice, private rights, or critical subjectivism as the highest social goods are all equally unable to translate into political reality the moral ideals of participatory democracy oriented toward public, not private, ends.

Thus, France's recent victory in the GATT negotiations ("With time waning," 1993) to temporarily gain a "cultural exception" for transnational trade in audiovisual program production and transmission, although applauded by many for inserting recognition of noneconomic issues into global negotiations about communication, and although significant as a counter discourse to the supposedly "natural" imperatives of the global market, nevertheless fails as an alternative articulation for a public sphere that serves democratic ends. France's success, although notable in its attempt to provoke an international debate on the organization of public space in late modernity, remains bound to the untenable arguments of cultural self-defense. Consequently, the French argument remains unpersuasive from the normative standpoint of what is required in communication policies to facilitate common interest among a plurality of social and ethnic groups: deliberative citizenship practices; equal and open access to public space; and the citizen's need for substantive knowledge of social, cultural, and political matters. The competing views of the United States and France on the problem of communication policy neither fully nor accurately represent the range of significant policy options for the transnational public sphere. The differences in negotiating positions in the GATT comprise, in a sense, a false opposition with respect to the role of intergovernmental policy in supplying the necessary preconditions of public space in order to facilitate the practice of political freedom.

Similarly, reforms of the press and broadcasting in Eastern Europe may indeed be undertaken to provide legal guarantees for free political speech in the public space of postsocialist civil states, but these laws have also been crafted by those who choose to engage in policies espousing the preservation of shared ethnicity and nationalist solidarity. Poland's version of *l'exception culturelle* is codified in a broadcasting law passed in 1993 stipulating that both public and private programs must adhere to a "Christian value system" and "should not promote activities that violate the law or the interests or the state nor opinions that conflict with morality and the public good" (quoted in Johnson, 1993, p. 13). In Hungary, nationalists have been mobilizing to push for policy requirements to increase religious broadcasting as well as programs to preserve Hungarian culture (Pataki, 1992). Furthermore, in Russia, Slovenia, and other states, the equation forged between nationalist discourse for inscription of the "pure nation" into the laws and policies of representative democracies, on the one hand, and the ostensible spread of movements for democratic reform, on the other, has made it difficult to disentangle antidemocratic theories of "public space as cultural solidarity" from the modern promise of common citizenship, human rights, and political self-determination for all.

Approaches to the problems of nationalism for communication policy must therefore recognize that the question regarding interethnic peace is inseparable from the question of the fate of political culture in a globally restructured social environment. Analysis of the transnational public sphere must be built on the recognition that the potential for the enhancement of peace in the postsocialist era will emerge, not so much from the dismantling of trade barriers, creation of common currencies, privatization, and deregulation of economies, or, for that matter, from the hope for an enlightened regard among ethnic groups for each others' fundamental right to exist. But rather, the stability of democratic states is conditional on the creation of a genuine form of common citizenship—not merely codified in law, but also actualized by access to and participation in the political and technological arrangements of shared public space. This can only come about by guaranteeing the conditions of deliberative public participation in the electronic public sphere, not merely for artificial citizens—that is, institutions that own the systems of public communication and thus have a monopoly over their forms, content, and accessibility—but especially for human citizens and an expanding diversity of social groups. The democratic political process can only be accountable if the public sphere is both representative of differences in point of view regarding the conditions of life as well as structured, regulated, and organized to facilitate the emergence of common interests.

Ultimately, therefore, the struggle to determine the form of public space in the name of cultural identities, private choices, private rights, or critical subjectivism leaves the citizens of free societies with only a single mode of public space to choose from, in reality: a model of public space that facilitates private reason, personal and exclusive privilege, and the recognition of subjective claims.

BEYOND PRIVATE MODES OF PUBLIC SPACE:
CONSIDERATIONS TOWARD AN ALTERNATIVE VIEW

There is a pressing need to conceptualize alternative political foundations for communication policy in the transnational arena. In this chapter I have attempted to challenge prevailing conceptualizations and to demonstrate by exposition of their philosophical premises that the development of human potential and the deepening of democratic freedoms can have no historical reality outside of the constraints of the form of public space, by virtue of which common citizenship, human rights, private freedoms, and the idea of justice are possible. The structure of this space, which political freedom necessarily requires, and its capacity to facilitate a deliberative environment and make possible real knowledge of the social, cultural, and political life of democratic society, are both the conceptual and empirical challenge of communication policy research. There is a need to reorient communication theory and political theory to the problem of human freedom and public space in the hope of demonstrating by argument and evidence that the practice of democracy is contingent on the practice of citizenship, which depends in turn on the reactivation of political agency in the "public sphere."

The concept of a public sphere for late modernity is not, I suggest, completely identical with the meaning of a public sphere advanced by Habermas (1984, 1987, 1989). The historical validity of his argument has already been contested (Benhabib, 1992; Curran, 1991b; Fraser, 1992), yet the normative and theoretical validity remains to be addressed. As I have argued, the theoretical problem of Habermas's public sphere for associational life is that he grounds his conception in a procedural theory of "intersubjective" rather than public reason, principally because he is constrained by the monological and procedural liberalism of Kant's moral philosophy. Habermas (1990) has tried to address this problem, of course, by expanding Kant's universality of the monological conscience to a dialogical concept of communicative relations. This is not enough, because this concept of human emancipation continues in the prepolitical, procedural, and ultimately subjectivist domain. This is not the place for extensive critical examination of Habermas's theory for communication policy; I simply suggest that the notion of public space that needs proposing in a theory of communication policy ought to be closer to the idea of "political space," a substantive, not just procedural or interpersonal, space between individuals, in which citizens can act collectively and engage in common deliberation about all matters affecting the political community. It is anachronistic to limit one's understanding of this space to the analogies of the village square, the proverbial townhall, or dialogical experience. Certainly, this space could possess many forms, but today its predominant mode is technological, mass mediated, and global.

Regardless of the form or structure of political space, the principles of emancipation and political liberty that derive from this space should remain unaltered. Ultimately, it should be argued, human freedom cannot be actualized under the realities of a dysfunctional, distorted, and inaccessible public or political space, whose structures and realities exclude the development of knowledge, deliberation, the enlargement of public opinion to include all major social groups, and the constitution of public identity in the practice of citizenship that necessitate transcending subjective, even interpersonal, interest and private reason.

Here, I suggest three key categories of consideration that ought to be accounted for in any theoretical policy model for a genuinely democratic public sphere.

Justice

The distinctive feature of the identity of citizen, as opposed to that of consumer, producer, owner, or communal member, is its constitution within a web of egalitarian-participatory relations based on justice, not merely equality. The difference between a citizenship of justice and a citizenship of equality is fundamental to the distinction between communication policies, the aim of which is to advance a participatory public sphere and policies that seek to facilitate the interests of the private sector in ownership, competition, and commercial investment.

As we know from the history of liberal democracy, equality can be addressed by legal procedure or "recognition," yet having achieved this under the law, conditions of inequality may persist. This is not to say that any critique of the codification of the rights of man amounts to an unqualified endorsement of Marx's (1843/1978b) view of human rights, which he treated as nothing but the right of self-interest and symptomatic of bourgeois individualism. Articles 10 and 11 of the 1789 French Declaration of the Rights of Man, for instance—that declare the right of free communication of thoughts and opinion as one of the most constitutive rights of political freedom—do not easily bear Marx's interpretation of them as institutional egoism or a mode of private property. As Lefort (1981) argues, Article 11 at least, makes it clear that

The right of man, one of his most precious rights, is to go beyond himself and relate to others, by speech, writing and thought. In other words, it makes clear that man could not be legitimately confined to the limits of his private wants, when he has the right to public speech and thought. (pp. 58-59)

Lukes (1985) notes that these rights in the text of the French Declaration are passed over in silence by Marx because they do not lend themselves to his interpretation.

Nevertheless, Marx's views of the justice of capitalism provoke serious reflection, for although the positive, world historical significance of human rights equality is unquestionably necessary for any possibility of freedom, it is certainly not sufficient. As pointed out earlier, the logic of Lockean and Kantian paradigms of freedom that form the philosophical foundation of democratic laws and policies tend to result in practices of privatism in which rights are typically the basis for claims by private interests to be treated in special ways. The consequences for communication policy is the monopoly of the meaning of human rights by private institutional interests over the rights of citizens for adequate knowledge, information, and public speech. There is thus a considerable distance between the citizen's right of equality of access to public space in speech, thought, and expression and the right's actualization.

Thus, contrary to Locke's and Kant's assumptions, equality cannot be prepolitical; in itself, it is meaninglessly external to political association, with the fundamental moral basis of such association, as Aristotle points out, being justice. Aristotle's (335-323 B.C./1981) definition of politics as not only the essence of human experience but as fundamentally contingent on justice or ethical reasoning is centrally dependent on concepts of public space, public life, and communication:

Obviously man is a political animal. . . . But nature . . . has endowed man alone among the animals with power of speech . . . [which] serves to indicate what is useful and what is harmful and so also what is just and what is unjust. . . . It is a sharing of a common view in *these* matters that makes a . . . state. (para. 1253a7-17; emphasis added)

For an emancipatory theory of public space and communication policy, the implications here are that human political nature is made possible by the power of deliberation and public reasoning, which in turn are nothing less than the negation of the unjust and the affirmation of the just. What the ethical nature of public communication enables, then, is the "sharing of a common view," without which society itself would not be possible. Thus, justice is the central feature of political community. It is "the arrangement of a political association" (para. 1253a38), of the emergence of common interests; Aristotle understands the terms of the good society not merely by shared history, cultural meanings, symbols, and rituals, but by the terms of the virtues of justice. The second important argument Aristotle (335-323 B.C./1962) makes on the relationship between political association and justice is that he links the problem of justice to the problem of equality. Political justice "is found among men who share their life with a view to self-sufficiency, men who are free and either proportionately or arithmetically *equal*, so that between those who do not fulfill this condition there is no political justice" (para. 1134a30; emphasis added).

Not only does political justice enable associative life, but the qualities of that life, according to Aristotle, are related to the citizen's access to political community, communicative competence, and the conditions of public life—all of which are matters of justice. Access to the public sphere and the competence to practice political liberty in that space are in fact the citizen's claim on lawgivers—namely, an issue of political justice. Thus, justice is the condition by which equality is realized, for it seeks to aim higher than procedural enactment. The original problem of justice, therefore, is not entirely the way Rawls (1971) defines it. Seeking to deny the category of political justice because it derives from association as opposed to the separate lives of individuals, Rawls endorses the moral values of Kantian atomism, stresses equality as the baseline for the good society, and ends up by supplying a rationalization for our existing thought about justice as a term identical with the meaning of codified rights in law and policy. The contrast between Rawls's procedural justice and the idea of political justice is the difference between a theory that holds that there is no such thing as social justice and a theory that starts from the premise that citizens have a fundamental claim on lawgivers for social action to address the requirements of human need and functioning.

In a democratic society, political justice in associational terms requires formulating legal codes that emphasize principles and procedural rules, within a framework of public policy that facilitates the resolution of actually existing human needs in education, communicative competence, health, work, and other fundamental terms of membership in democratic community (Dahrendorf, 1994; Marshall, 1950). These needs must be addressed not merely by codification, or even at the minimum threshold of human survival, but at a level that ensures the conditions under which all social groups have access to public space and possess communicative competence in the practice of deliberative political participation.

The notion of political justice, rather than just equality or rights, provides the only conceptual hope for a universal ground of value by which important conditions and needs in democratic human life can be identified and the only philosophically defensible position from which to ask what the world systems of social and political institutions, organizations, and agencies are doing about them. Are these transnational systems of power giving citizens of democratic societies what they need to practice their freedom and be capable of addressing their conditions of information and competence for enhancing the qualities of political liberty? Are they doing this in a minimal way, as privatist theories of public space would, for the most part, prefer, or are they making it possible for citizens to make authentic, that is, real, nondistorted choices for their well-being in public life? These questions simply cannot be addressed by a vision of the public sphere stemming from a restricted view of human rights that privileges, at the expense of all competing conceptions of democracy and freedom, the procedural recognition of equality.

Civil Society

The second important consideration in any alternative theory of public space is the question: In what sense of civil society do we mean a participatory public sphere? Although the success of capitalism has delegitimized all alternatives to itself and left it with no effective enemies, the forms of civil society that supply its social foundation have degenerated, in terms of democracy, to the point in which the increasing privatization of public life and political dissent, as well as the corresponding depoliticization of the modern technological, mediatized public sphere, represent serious threats to the quality of human freedom. These qualities are not merely at the minimal threshold beneath which life is so impoverished that it would not be human at all, but at a somewhat higher threshold, envisioned by both premodern and modern democratic ideals. Below this higher threshold, conditions favoring opportunities for imagination, creativity, reasoning, conceptions of the good, enriched individual and associational experience, and competencies for critical reflection cannot be sustained.

From a normative standpoint, conceptions of civil society ought to be examined in any theory of communication policy for their telos to deliver the possibilities for the second threshold, the one that ought to concern us most when we argue for a participatory and influential public sphere with respect to freedom and its claim on public policy. We do not want democratic societies to make their citizens capable, as Nussbaum (1992) warns, only of the bare minimum. The move from a minimal human life, as presented in the Lockean civil state, to a "good," or free, human life, is supplied in a participatory public space framework by the capacities of civil society to construct, defend, and enhance a multiplicity of public spheres (both weak and strong, political and cultural) with a diversity of choices for self-definition and nondistorted social discourses representing systemic and authentic sociopolitical alternatives—above the second threshold.

To answer the question of in what sense of civil society we mean such a concept of the public sphere, there is a need to examine the historical and theoretical traditions of civil society available to modern communication policy. I suggest for the present that the cause of democracy can be advanced only from a more powerful understanding of civil society as communicative relations. If the essential possibility of civil society resides in the idea of vigorous public spheres capable of penetrating, fragmenting, decentralizing, and influencing political-economic power in the cause of human freedom, then a stronger sense of civil society demands two things: one, the most widespread and developed conditions of critical communicative competence to resist and defend the system of public spheres from normative depreciation and systematic distortion; and, two, a stronger societal claim on public policy to regulate the conditions under which public communication structures —in which civil society and freedom are constituted—are maintained free of powerful, unequal, and oligopolistic domination.

Such a theory of civil society must be firmly rooted in the recognition: (a) that private, individual, subjective rights of any kind are meaningless without the institutionalization of a democratic political order the citizens of which may participate in and deliberate through an accessible public realm guaranteed in the public interest (Aristotle, 335-323 B.C./1962, 335-323 B.C./1981; Hegel, 1821/1974; Montesquieu, 1748/1989); (b) that securing private rights is not the only goal of political community—justice and the common welfare are of equal, if not greater, value, because they are prerequisites for securing rights in the first place and, in fact, delimit them so that all citizens may enjoy these rights equally under the law (Hamilton, Jay, & Madison, 1787/1961; Preamble to the U.S. Constitution; de Tocqueville, 1834-40/1945); and (c) that the freedom of citizens requires not merely the legal codification of such rights, but the actual conditions for practicing their political liberties in the public deliberations of civil society, the only grounds on which a transnational public sphere could have legitimacy (Arendt, 1975; Aristotle, 335-323 B.C./1962, 335-323 B.C./1981; de Montesquieu, 1748/1989; Tocqueville, 1834-40/1945).

The Public Good

The conditions of the public realm necessary to the functioning of a democracy are conditions held in common among all members. In democratic theories, whether utilitarian or ethical liberalism, republican or communitarian thought, these conditions are said to be in the "public good" or "public interest," constituting, thereby, the essential mandate of the nation-state. Thus, the final consideration I offer regarding how to

think about an alternative theory of public space is the problem of articulating the fundamental terms of common existence in institutional
arrangements and in the role of the state in guaranteeing the public
interest. Any call for a transnational social order must face this test of the
normative basis of civil society conceptualized as a political order constituted by the will and the active participation of its citizens, with its governing institutions expressing this will in laws and policies that guarantee
the availability of certain elements of the public good under three criteria.

First, elements of the public good are goods in those categories
deemed necessary to the functioning of democracy; certainly the quality
of the information environment, which makes citizenship possible in the
first place, would easily qualify for the status of an element of the public
good. Second, elements of the public good that must be provided to all or
to none are the responsibility of the policies of the state, such as universal
education, infrastructure development, and public library services in whatever form, manuscript or electronic. Once again, it would be difficult to justify the exclusion of public communication under this criterion of democratic goods, for that would mean justifying vast inequalities in access to and
the quality of, the public information environment, in the same way that
inequalities in clothing and consumer products may be justified by free
market determinants. Third, goods passing the test of necessity and universality would still not qualify as "public"—that is, the responsibility of law
and policy—unless they could not be supplied in a universal, accessible,
and qualitatively adequate form by the private sector.

Democratic states cannot deny the first two criteria to public
communications because that would imply a rejection of the ideals of
democracy. However, the third criterion involves intense debate in contemporary policy. In global relations, the ascending value of the market,
on the one hand, and of private rights and liberties, on the other, has
allowed communication to be excluded from a public goods status under
the third criterion (Braman, 1990). This is because standards of qualitative adequacy for information in a free society can be reduced to communication technology innovation and commercial content choices made
available by private communication entities. Recognizing both Eastern
and Western Europe's volatile, nationalist histories of fragmentation and
regression, the general market tendency to obstruct the classification of
public communications as a political good guaranteed in the public interest, and to appropriate the structures of information as privately determined commodities, is an exceedingly dangerous policy for the continent's stability in the long term, as it is dangerous to the survival of
democracy itself.

CONCLUSIONS: FREEDOM AND ITS MYSTIFICATION

I have argued that the problems of communication policy for the transnational public sphere are very much problems of theory. In the exposition and critique of prevailing theories of public space, the failure to realize the aspirations of human emancipation within contemporary modes of democratic public space is deeply connected to flawed conceptualizations of citizenship, common welfare, justice, and the meaning of the democratic civil state embedded in the philosophical grounds of their individualistic theory and practice. Modern history has shown that the right to vote, the rule of law, contractual liberties, and private interests can all exist without, in fact, the existence of democracy. Membership in political community does not necessarily bring with it the actual experience of political freedom. Partly, this is related to the ungovernability that afflicts democratic states caught up in the integrative vortex of contemporary transnational relations. We have created a technological world the imperatives of which we can no longer control, and the emancipation of which from all human will and purpose has rendered it extremely difficult for us to govern ourselves, to remain our own political masters.

However, for the most part, the crisis of freedom and its mystification under various ideologies of the public sphere relates to the progressive abdication of public life by democratic citizens, to the ever-advancing relegation of matters of common concern to the private sector, and to the redefinition of politics as the public airing of private interests, which in turn allows public goods to be redefined as private assets. Our public interests as citizens, as Arendt (1975) argues, are quite distinct from our private interests as individuals, and therefore the public interest cannot be automatically derived from private interest. Indeed, it is not the sum of private interests, nor their highest common denominator, nor even the totality of enlightened self-interests. The interests of the world, Arendt's argument implies, are not the interests of individuals: They are the interests of the public realm, the realm of state action and policy, and of citizenship action. As citizens we share that public realm and participate in the pursuit of its interests, *but the interests belong to the public realm.* This is a substantive distinction from atomist, individualist, procedural, and minimal theories of the public realm. Recognizing the destructive consequences of these modes of elaborating the basis of political community, I suggest it is necessary to seek an alternative.

Those who formulate transnational communication policy must be able to conceptualize questions of the security of democracies in terms of free, accessible, and sufficient information environments that facilitate deliberative political practice and participatory citizenship. A proposal for the public responsibility of social thought must argue that the most significant challenge for communication theory and political theory at the end of the 20th century is to contribute to modern understanding that the organization of political culture by information and citizenship, not merely by trade, strategic, or ethnic relations, or for that matter by the false projection of freedom derived from technological and consumption choices within the culture of modern public communications, is the only real and lasting foundation to assure world peace through authentic terms of democratic legitimacy. In short, the struggle for the advancement of the participatory conditions of citizenship in a transnational public sphere has become historically necessary as a political counterpart to proprietary governance of the information networks of the world's economy.

6

Media Charisma and Global Culture: The Experience of East-Central Europe

Gabriel Bar-Haim
The New School of Media Studies, Tel Aviv

The arguments that mass media are either active agents in bringing about instrumental change towards a global culture or that mass media accurately reflect and diffuse underlying ideas that indicate a global trend need to be challenged. The question that should be asked is to what extent mass media inherently create an artificial universal culture, especially under the present conditions of Western societies. In other words, the question is whether, in the present quasi-anomic condition of postmodern society, it is the nature of contemporary mass media and the type of its textuality that provide an apparent emergence of a global culture.

Specifically, the first part of this chapter discusses the "charisma" of media and its implications for an apparent global culture, as well as the fictional nature of the media text and its implications for our question. The second part of the chapter consists of a few brief remarks on the social structure and conditions that underlie the possible formation of a dominant non-nationalistic public opinion in East-Central Europe. I ask what the public expects from local East-European media under the present circumstances and describe briefly how the media fulfill those expectations.

There is no doubt that we are witnessing an intensification in all dimensions of international exposure and exchanges. This exposure filters down not only to the professional middle classes, but also to the working class and rural populations. It is true that the "official" language of this international exposure is, most of the time, English or other Western languages. However, a great deal of exposure and exchange is carried through the profuse world of goods from all over the world that surround even those who live in the most remote places. Beyond any functionality, these goods are a medium of communication about different cultures as well as about the world as a totality. Yet, when people exclaim in awe and wonderment that we live in a "global village," what they have mostly in mind is the world of mass communication.

The charisma of the mass media is derived from two major sources. The first is the popular perception that the media are "connected" with the "center" of society, wherever that may be, and therefore "know" what takes place at that "center." This is the sense that the media know what is most important and what is trivial, thus validating a certain version of reality that in most cases preserves the familiar status quo; hence, the belief that the media are touched by some kind of secular sacredness. The sacredness spills over into expectations for both ethical behavior, such as guarding the underdog and disclosing the corruption of the powerful, as well as into expectations for forecasting, however ambiguous or even farfetched that may be. In short, the media are expected to be "moral oracles," and, in the absence of competitors, traditionally produced in the past by popular beliefs, it is not a small role to fill.

The second factor contributing to the charismatic aura of the media has to do with the assumption that the media attend to what is actual and immediate, a reality from which none can escape. In a world in which the rate of change of events and information is so high, the latest information has an advantage with which nothing can compete. The actual information represents an objective reality, as it were, awarded by the force of the present as opposed to a reality mediated either by interpretation, as that of the past, or touched by uncertainty, as in the case of the future.

The rapidity with which international media networks are capable nowadays of conveying the most current information from all over the world adds a new dimension to its charisma, that is, a sense that the media are connected not only with the center of society, but also with the center of the globe. Whether there is a global order with a definite center or not, the media give an impression of the existence of such an order. Affirmation of such an order is carried through daily international news; documentary programs on various parts of the globe such as ecology in India or business in Japan; international cultural occasions such as the Cannes' film festival or the Ms. Universe Beauty Pageants; and through special media events such as rock concerts in support of the victims of famine in Ethiopia, the opening of the Olympic Games, the Earth Summit in Brazil, or the launching of a new spaceship.

The international news and stories originating in the West are presented from a Western viewpoint, having in mind the sensibilities of the Western audience, Western achievements, Western philanthropies, and Western taste (Howes, 1990). These are in essence glorifying celebrations in which the non-Western are kindly invited to join. Furthermore, annual international media events paradoxically emphasize the divisions by country more than anything else. Organizers make a special effort to positively advertise the individual culture of each of the participants, as in the Eurovision Song Contest or Ms. Universe Beauty Pageant.

International events are contests and competitions, inspiring drama with heroes and heroines. Dayan and Katz (1988) regard these media events as rituals articulating national consensus. Elsewhere, Katz (1986) poignantly observes that television broadcasting in most nations serves as a medium of national integration more in the sense of offering a shared experience and of introducing different population segments to each other than as a medium of culturally authentic self-expression.

Indeed, it seems that many of the international events initiated and carried mainly, but not only, by the electronic media serve the needs of the educated Western middle class, especially Americans, for a broader and yet unthreatening international experience; an experience that sustains the supremacy of the middle-class American way of life, yet aspires to supersede its narrowness. The need for a cross-cultural experience forces the Western middle class to seek out appropriate media programs by setting up international media networks. The American impulse for proselytizing, however, must be mentioned. Missionary work can appear even in the guise of secular cultural events; perhaps CNN should be understood as a natural extension of televangelism.

Western media seem to suggest a kind of global culture that is not an entity with an existence of its own, but is a conglomerate of multiple international cultural events that reflect a multitude of societies whose cultural differences are minimized, although distinctive enough to be perceived as exotic. Hence, it is no wonder that after the sterilization by the Western media all of these cultures appear extraordinarily comprehensible to the Western viewer. There is even an effort on the part of Western cultural elites to prove that intensive Western media entrepreneurship of international events eventually leads to a coherent and controlled global order.

The reality is far from this. Such efforts cannot have an impact on the formation of a world culture, and not only because the efforts are Western-derived. Neither the diffusion of international programs, nor the contrivance of international media events, can even marginally contribute to the creation of a supra-culture. If the assumption is that the exposure of millions of viewers to the same programs, whether Western or not, makes a substantial contribution to a world culture, then the assumption is fallacious. Because active exposure, even if prolonged, cannot change fundamental sociopolitical conditions that stand in stark contradiction to the artificial coherence and putative cultural convergence promoted by these media. The argument resembles the false sense of community created by American and English television in their popular sitcom shows, whereas the disintegration of communities, especially in North America, is a well-known fact.

Media are conservative, preserving conventions and the social status quo as loyal custodians. Reconsidering arguments put forward in the late 1950s about the culture industry, of which the media are central components, Adorno (1944/1990) came to the same conclusions in the 1960s as he did a decade earlier: "The concepts of order which it [the culture industry] hammers into human beings are always those of the status quo." Further on, Adorno continues the argument, observing that the culture industry proclaims:

> You shall conform, without instruction as to what; conform to that which exists anyway, and to that which everyone thinks anyway as a reflex of its power and omnipresence. The power of the culture industry's ideology is such that conformity has replaced consciousness. (p. 280)

The ideas that the major mission of contemporary media is to expose people to other cultures, and that the more such exposure takes place the more likely the generation of a supra-culture, are unfounded. Only through interactions over common problems that require building supra-institutions is there going to emerge a new attitude toward "others," a different perception of reality, a new type of consciousness, a synthetic new language, and a radical mythology that will converge to form a supranational culture. The media facilitate neither unbiased encounters between cultures nor critical debate about such encounters, but rather provide mediated and biased exposure that contributes to the generation of stereotypes and vulgar simplifications.

In contrast to fiction, in which the text is not expected to represent an objective reality but signifies an imagined one, the texts of news stories and media events are perceived by the popular mind to accurately represent and rigorously communicate an external reality. The falsity of such a perception is obvious, yet stubbornly persists among the masses of media consumers. The statements that "it has been written in the paper" or that "we know because the TV broadcast it" are still powerful. At the root of the problem is the popular assumption that there is an objective reality, and that the media can capture that reality in terms that everybody understands. Paradoxically, that reality does not include the media itself, and therefore the texts of the media are all denotative.

The transformation of the social by the media, especially in news reporting, documentaries, and all the so-called factual programs, into cultural significations takes place out of sight and undeclared, in a process opposite to that of fiction. Thus, the fictionalizing of the social carried out by the media is unnoticed by the ordinary viewer and consequently is not perceived as occurring. In the case of literary fiction, the imaginative use of social materials is taken for granted as part of the creative process, whereas in the case of media texts, the use is obfuscated.

In other words, the media draw material from everyday social activities and subject it to a process of alteration that is compelled to accommodate both the limitations of the media as well as commercial and ideological expectations. The selection of items to be covered is directed by editors and producers, respectively. That is, following the selective perception of reporters and cameramen on the site of an event, the final editing process is carried out in such a manner as to fit the expectations of the general public's discourse as well as those of advertisers, politicians, lobbying groups, and social movements. All these efforts transform the original material into an end product that, in most cases, bears little or no resemblance to the social material being reported on and its context. This is precisely the imperceptible process of transforming raw social events into a cultural genre. In other words, the vitality of life occurrences is transformed into codes and expressive objects: a commentary on social events, not objective or true reflections of them. Because media work involves individuals, their actions, and their emotions—in short, everything that combines to create a story — the cultural commentary takes the shape, most often, of a narrative. Barthes (1974) observed with insight that "the classic author is like an artisan bent over the workbench of meaning and selecting the best expression for the concept he has already formed" (p. 173).

Most of the time, this process is subtle, imperceptible, and pulsates under the glossy surface of routine daily work of media corporations. At different times, the process is consciously organized to produce a contrived, cultural commentary on various social aspects by creating seemingly reality-based narratives. The description of the personal experience of a story analyst at American Detective, a prime-time "reality-based" cop show on ABC, is illustrative. Debra Seagal (1993) describes how live material is tampered with to fit the formula, with the effect that this popular show got high ratings and, in turn, brought in rich advertisers:

> There are six of us in the story meetings, the producer, four loggers, and the story-department manager. Each logger plays highlight reels and pitches stories, most of which are rejected by the producer for being "not hot enough," not "sexy." . . . We are to hope for a naturally dramatic climax. But if it does not happen, I understand, we'll work one out. (p. 51)

Seagal goes on to relate how the story analysts are responsible for compiling stock-footage books

> containing every conceivable example of guns, drugs, money, scenics, street signs. This compendium is used to embellish stories when certain images or sounds have not been picked up by a main or secondary camera. Evidently the "reality" of a given episode is subject to enhancement. (p. 52)

Further on, the author describes how the finished episode emerges:

> Once our supervising producer has picked the cases that might work for the show, the "stories" are turned over to an editor. Within a few weeks the finished videos emerge from the editing room with "problems" fixed, chronologies reshuffled, and, when, necessary, images and sound bites clipped and replaced by old filler footage from unrelated cases. (p. 52)

Hence, what contributes to the uncritical surrender to the media is the sense that the textual production communicates in such a manner that no valid distinction is perceived between the social, with its ideological action, and the cultural, with its encoded narratives. It is, thus, the appearance that whatever takes place in the media is only social and that the "objective reality" is what is reported. Yet, in the final analysis, as far as objectivity is concerned, there is no difference between a piece of fiction and a news story.

Western media stories reporting on other cultures or on international events, rather than being objective voices that reflect an emerging global culture, as they claim to be, are instead popular narrative adventures, a new picaresque genre for Western middle-class consumption.

The transformation of international social events into live picaresque genres is often carried out by the volition of the individual participants themselves, who metamorphose themselves into narrative characters once the TV camera is present. Jo Anne Isaak's (1993) observation of the 1991 Communist putsch against Gorbachev's regime and the resistance put up around the barricaded Moscow White House, under the leadership of Yeltsin, is cogent:

The replays of the "barricade tales," as they are now referred to, range in genre from fairy tales to horror movies, or B-grade westerns. In each case there is some overwhelmingly powerful evil that the protagonist, by virtue of having Right on his side, is able to overcome. (p. 39)

Isaak brings up also the comments of the art critic Konstantin Akinsha based on his own personal experiences of the events:

From the first day we watched this revolution on TV, CNN played a key role here. Each person had the possibility of playing a role. We played with all possible stereotypes from Prague in 1968 to Hemingway's Madrid to Santiago. People draw on the stereotypes they received from countless movies. . . . CNN and all international networks capitalise on this. . . . (p. 39)

Existing technology allows both written and electronic media to instantaneously insert international material within their local narratives. The international material enriches the existing local repertoire and even opens up the possibilities for new genres. But again, if there were not a substantial demand for cross-cultural and international programs, Western media, especially American media, would not persist in producing or buying them. Also, one may remark, paraphrasing Marx, that fantasy precedes an approaching reality.

"Global village" is a metaphor for relatively worldwide technological accessibility to media and not for genuine reciprocal familiarity with the intricacy of each others' cultures, let alone the formation of a supra-culture. It is not too difficult to observe that the international media narrative is necessitated by the Western and non-Western middle class in order to make sense of a bewildering world or to reinforce attitudes and lifestyles with the help of familiar categories, simplifying the world's complexity and stripping it of nuances and idiosyncrasies. The latest crisis in Thailand in June 1992 is a good example. When I change from one TV cable station to another, I get the feeling of a small world, a global village, all preoccupied by the same events, with the same heroes. Although all of them reported the same thing, and even the shots were taken from the same spots, I still was not clear what triggered the crisis in Thailand. Gradually, I proceeded to piece together a colorful foreign narrative with the help of relevant categories, borrowed from Western broadcasts during the recent political crisis. Although this story was seemingly logical, it was not only partially false, but also recontextualized, as if it took place in a different Thailand. That is, I made up a story more likely in resemblance to what I thought happens in Thailand than to what really happened. Geertz's (1975) definition of culture is certainly pertinent here: "an ensemble of stories we tell ourselves about ourselves" (p. 448).

The argument that one of the current signs of global culture is the uniformization of cultural codes in various societies can also be disputed. Cultural codes emerge independently in various places, as well as being borrowed, copied, adopted, and appropriated from other social contexts. However, they are recharged by the borrowing culture with new and different connections. Even imitation of external codes of demeanor and employment of similar linguistic codes do not mean that these codes and behaviors carry similar meanings that can interchange with and override their individual social contexts. Although a social context cannot be replicated, cultural codes can be transplanted, but this is an illusory sense of universality.

The following illustration makes the point: In the summer of 1990, the CBC local station in Winnipeg, Canada, broadcast in its *Evening News* a story about local Indians protesting in front of the legislative building, in which they put up tents to repudiate what they believed to be a lack of progress in their affairs with the provincial government. At the same time, in a different and far away country, the newly free national television station of Romania broadcast a story about a sit-in demonstration taking place for a few weeks by students against the new government and their neo-Communist supporters. The students had put up tents in University Square in Bucharest and raised their voices for the first time against the lack of radical reforms by the government. During the same summer, Israeli public television aired a story about the Nurses' Union, which, after finding demands for better working conditions falling on deaf ears, decided to demonstrate in front of the Knesset, the Parliament, by putting up tents and asking for support from the members of Parliament.

The example is illustrative because the three groups, operating in different countries, employed what appears to be the same cultural code to convey discontent with political authorities. Yet the use of tents operated very differently as a metaphor in each situation. For the Indians of Manitoba, putting up tents sent the message that they were the first on that land and were living in tents there long before the building of the provincial legislature. Using tents as part of their protest emphasized the historical difference in the relative claims on the land. For the students in Bucharest, putting up tents in their self-declared "Communism-free zone" was intended to make the point that even after Ceaucescu's regime fell, the Communists were still in the government buildings, whereas the people who made the revolution were still in tents. For the Israeli nurses, putting up tents was intended to make the point that although members of Parliament can afford to live in houses, the nurses can only afford tents.

I assume that the same perspective can be applied to any television format (Fiske, 1989). One would ask whether, for example, someone in Ethiopia or India is as fascinated as a middle-class American by an episode of *The Cosby Show*, in which Mrs. Cosby, a black lawyer from New York, is making a pathetic effort to keep a diet, while her physician husband is teasing her. Will this urban, middle-class concern of Americans make any sense to people who are starving? At a certain basic level the episode surely can make some sense, but in a very different way than it is understood by a middle-class family in the United States.

An interesting pattern is copying a genre that has proven itself successful elsewhere while contextualizing its content and background. This has been the case with the Brazilian soap opera *Isaura* and the French serial *Chateauvallon*, which were explicitly patterned after the American *Dallas* (Mattelart & Mattelart, 1992). The alleged success of *Dallas* outside of the United States can be attributed not only to widespread fascination with American popular culture, but also to its universal formula that permitted, first and foremost, local projections and a reading that accessed the concerns of localities. The polysemic reading of the same media text as well as the recontextualization of it are strong hermeneutical parameters that raise insurmountable obstacles in the transference of media texts from one culture to another, let alone the formation of a universal culture.

Media, in general, and the Western media in particular, are not capable of reforming society, let alone reforming the globe. The perpetual motion of the media, fed by the inexhaustible need for information, establishes a false sense of progress toward global homogeneity. The locus of social change—that is, the place in which signs of change toward a world culture could be observed, if such changes exist—is the social structure of our individual societies as the most fundamental referential system and the collective consciousness of its representation.

MASS MEDIA AND GLOBAL ORIENTATION IN EAST-CENTRAL EUROPE

The second part of this chapter discusses, although briefly, a few changes in the social structure of East-Central Europe vis-à-vis the tasks of the local media. The discussion highlights a new openness toward the integration of this European bloc with Western Europe. The assumption is that an unprecedented openness in one specific global bloc toward integration into a larger geocultural unit could be, although is not necessarily, a sign of a broader global trend. Most of the references of this section refer to the Romanian context; I believe that many of the generalizations in this chapter are valid for the rest of the East-Central European countries.

East-Central Europe—that is, the former Communist European bloc (Poland, Romania, Bulgaria, Hungary, the Czech Republic, Slovakia, and Albania)—has been suddenly catapulted after the 1989 revolutions from xenophobic nationalistic Communism into a condition of anomie characterizing the transition from relatively closed and paranoid societies to democratic political systems that are open and cooperative. This transitory period is full of anguish, confusion, tension, and instability and is experimental in many ways and at all levels, from the individual to the enterprise to the level of government itself.

The anomic condition in which individuals go about their daily affairs is characterized by an acute crisis of normative guidance that also motivates people to search for new rules, new methods, and new norms of behavior to replace the old collapsing structures and paradigms. It is a state of frenzied search for "sacred space" (Cornea, 1990). A state dominated by this condition may be called an *anomic* state.

In such difficult times, it is only natural for many East-Central Europeans to believe that, in opposition to the internal "disorder" in their country, there is an "outside order"; that is, there is a definite special ideal order in Western Europe and North America about which most have only a vague idea, but with which they identify. Furthermore, coming out of long years of political exclusion, many East-Central Europeans feel handicapped, left behind by history and world development. They truly believe that all over the Western world, even in many of the non-Western countries, people have been living better than they do, have accumulated advanced knowledge, enjoyed more of the benefits of wealth, traveled, and have been exposed to rich cross-cultural experiences. In short, coming out of isolation, the sense among East Europeans is that for many years they have been "disconnected" from the West and therefore, as they see it, from the global center.

The sense of disconnection, exacerbated by the frustration of radical changes, chaotic reforms, and the general disorganization of the domestic scene have heightened the orientation of people toward foreign information about world affairs. That is, most Eastern Europeans, especially the educated classes, feel that knowledge and information about what is going on in the West and in the world has become crucial to their own existence; as a result, they are more attuned to international matters. Hence, the local media are expected to be a central source of information about world affairs. However, the national, state-controlled TV and radio monitor much of the flow of information and its interpretation (Radojkovic, 1992). In the anomic state, it is natural to turn to the media to find answers, especially at present when there is an unusual drive among many for being alert to the "new" as an almost eschatological source amid the surrounding bewilderment. Discussing the role of the culture industry, especially the media, just after World War II, Adorno

(1944/1990) succinctly observed: "In a supposedly chaotic world it provides human beings with something like standards for orientation and
that alone seems worthy of approval" (p. 279).

Yet, without an established democratic media culture, the local
media manipulate the anomic crisis toward a partisan political position,
ignoring its role in shaping tolerant and democratic political culture
through the education of public opinion (Totok, 1992). It is also true that
in such times, in which there are unprecedented opportunities to put forward sociopolitical positions, there are very few journalists and newspapers in East-Central Europe that are not tempted to encourage, even to
the point of incitement and making use of vulgar propaganda, the adoption of their political views (Tudoran, 1992).

Under pressures of economic hardship, changes in norms and
morals, as well as the confusion of a multitude of emotional political
positions, many East-Central Europeans, especially the intelligentsia,
look to Western sociopolitical systems for a sustaining governing model.
Inflated fragments of such a "western vision" are eagerly promoted by
local media and by the foreign radio and television stations that broadcast to the region. The desire by many for a vital, modern, and stable
system forms a tacit coalition between consumers (readers and viewers)
and journalists in creating a seemingly coherent Western vision. In other
words, most of the time the West is presented as a beautiful story with
enlightened leaders, strong parliamentarians, masses aware of civic
needs and responsibilities, critical intellectuals, moral policemen, equally
distributed wealth, welfare, and ethical work standards. In contrast, the
villains are, of course, the Communists, local politicians, the Russians,
minorities, and, only recently, the self-made rich.

In such periods of upheaval and anomie, characterized by a lack of
guiding norms and moral standards, there is also an insecure sense of
objective reality. In such circumstances, boundaries between unfamiliar and
unprecedented social events and action, on the one hand, and narrative, on
the other, get blurred. Certainly, when social events are reported by the
news media machine, or worked out into other media narratives, the transformation of the social into the cultural, as in all media practices, not only
passes uncritically (as in many places in the West), but also receives a wel-
comed "collaboration" from the media public. The glorification of the West,
especially the United States, is thus a favored leitmotif in the collective writing of the fairytale. Paraphrasing Emile Durkheim, who insisted that people
do not think, but participate in thinking, one could similarly argue that a collective of people writes its favored narratives as a collective enterprise.

However, there is more in the apparently rosy picture presented
by local East-Central European media. If, during the Communist regime,
most East-Central Europeans were strongly biased toward anything that
originated in the West as a hidden form of protest against the regime

and its propaganda (Bar-Haim, 1989), presently the "Western vision" and the global orientation are promoted by liberal circles in order to counteract the nationalist camps. A global orientation could be subversive and therefore feared by nationalists.

Yet, in spite of the fascination with the sprawling media in their countries and with the new form of power that they exercise, a power very different from the crude propaganda of the Communist regime, the mythology of the media in the eyes of the public is weaker than in the West. The reason that East-Central European media are perceived by the public as less charismatic and more vulnerable than the Western media is because of their direct involvement with politics, both in the past and in the present. Manipulation of the media by the previous regime has been a perennial topic of debate in all the former Communist countries. Furthermore, the debate even extends to former television officials still today in key positions and to the question of how trustworthy various newspapers and even the national television are if they are either officially or unofficially associated with the government or with the various political parties of the opposition (Daskalov, 1992). Because the politicization of media, especially the daily newspapers and weekly magazines, is considered an indisputable reality, and because the turnover of many of the editors and prominent journalists is high, the public's sense of the credibility of most media as independent civic entities is problematic (Fuga, 1992). This is one of the reasons why Western stations and foreign press have more credibility, let alone the enigmatic spell cast by whatever originates from the United States.

Thus, one cannot overlook local consumption demands from the public for Western programs and ways in which local policymakers, in tight cooperation with the major Western international networks, supply relatively cheap programs such as old American movies and documentaries as well as news and current affairs. The international networks available in East-Central Europe include BBC, Radio France International, Voice of America, and CNN. It is evident that in the mass culture void left by Communist propaganda, there is nothing else that can supply the mass media machine as well as public curiosity and excitement better than Western, especially American, programs.

As far as the local press is concerned, again the divisions are based on sharp political identities, almost with no exceptions (Lefter, 1991). If such press as *Romania Mare*, *Natiunea*, and *Europa*, for example—right-wing ultra-nationalistic newspapers in Romania—have rarely dedicated their pages to news or commentaries from the West or elsewhere, such publications as *Revista 22*, *Romania Libera*, *Dilema*, and *Cotidianu*—representing the liberal press—give ample space and prominence to news from the West and elsewhere, as well as to interviews with western intellectuals and political personalities.

If the journalistic discourse of the nationalistic papers throughout East-Central Europe dwell nostalgically on glorious historical events; make extensive use of old rustic, folkloristic, and Christian religious symbolism; and employ traditional imagery such as family, motherhood, virginity, fatherland and other emotional metaphors to draw nationalistic-patriotic images, the journalistic discourse of the liberal papers is altogether different. The latter highlights international events; includes interviews with foreign personalities and investigative stories that uncover corruption; and stresses political-legal commentaries and economic debates. The language is that of educated laymen, whose vocabulary represents a rational attitude toward politics and international affairs as well as openness to other cultures. The liberal press, reflecting the interests of educated non-nationalistic groups, displays a readiness to explore options that assume integration into larger geoeconomic and geopolitical communities such as the European Community, South-East Europe, the Danube Basin countries, and so on.

Up to the end of World War II there were relatively small intellectual groups in each of the East-Central European countries, and many of these intellectuals were nationalists with right-wing inclinations. This situation was particularly characteristic of the most outstanding intellectuals of Romania and Bulgaria. The professional-technical class educated in the universities was very small. The majority of the population was comprised of peasants, small-scale factory workers, and craftsmen, most of them with no more than an elementary education. The present social structure of the former Communist countries is altogether different. There is a large group of young, humanist, critical intellectuals, whose formative period was during the long years of "passive political dissidence." This group, in total contrast to its prewar predecessors, is mostly liberal-democratic in its political orientation and strongly sympathetic with Western political philosophy.

However, the most novel and important factor is a sizeable class of professionals, especially the technically educated. This group has all the potential to develop into a middle class with an urban contemporary style of life and a strong disposition toward work mobility, consumerism, and leisure activities. This class of technical professionals, trained in the scientific technocratic mold, is still to some extent different in its makeup from its western counterparts. Resembling in its embryonic features the Western middle class, this new East-Central European stratum displays some international orientation, although it is still premature and difficult to assess its political and social propensities. It is also difficult to conclude with certitude that this prospectively influential stratum will become similar to its Western counterparts, but it has the potential for concern with surpassing national boundaries as part of redefining its own professional and social prospects.

The liberal media try to rally these two groups, who form the bulk of a liberal and civically aware public, and to strengthen their socio-political disposition. In a sense, the liberal press have become their public voice. However, it seems that the main challenge of the political-liberal media throughout East-Central Europe is presented by their capacity to form public opinion among the working class and those who are either first-generation urban or arrived in the cities during the last decades. This is a large population, with only a basic, or at most a vocational, education. They are insecure about finding permanent employment and still share a semi-rural style of life as well as religious inclinations and nationalist attitudes. Recent political events have shown that this is a volatile and manipulable group that could easily fall prey to the nationalist demagoguery of charismatic leaders. A case in point is the political manipulation of miners in Romania and its devastating repercussions throughout Romanian political culture. Hence, the task of the liberal press to educate this stratum toward a tolerant, civil political culture and toward a wider perspective on local affairs is considerable. It seems that many of the changes that are required and dreamed of in East-Central Europe depend to a large extent on broadening the narrow world of this stratum. It is doubtful whether even the concentrated effort of the democratic, liberal media can form a non-nationalistic pubic opinion in a short period of time (Havel, 1993). However, the task remains to address the public with a discourse that is widely accessible.

The danger of permitting the liberal media to address only the educated public is that, if this should happen, the media would act only to persuade the persuaded, as if all held similar beliefs. It is perhaps easy for liberal intellectuals and journalists to live in an incestuous environment of ideas and creeds and to assume a moral global brotherhood, however fictionalized that world may be. The situation may resemble historically the time during the Weimar Republic when intellectuals and artists throve in a few major cities, in which they exchanged ideas and opinions about world affairs, wrote, argued among themselves, and eventually created around themselves a civilized, tolerant milieu. However, only a few years later they realized that they had no idea about the masses, who were left to the brainwashing of the national-socialism of Hitler and Goebbels. Smith (1990) cogently argues:

> It is one thing to be able to package imagery and diffuse it through world-wide telecommunications networks. It is quite another to ensure that such images retain their power to move and inspire populations, who have for so long been divided by particular histories and cultures which have mirrored and crystallized the experiences of historically separated social groups, whether classes or regions, religious congregations or ethnic communities. (p. 179)

Whether this part of the world succumbs to the burden of local anomie, which, at this stage, is likely to fragment and disintegrate into various types of neonationalism, or starts an accelerated process of closing a historical handicap that will eventually adjust to a postindustrial Western world, remains to be seen. Presently, pressures from the West, in the forms of political-economic reforms, unbalanced trade, and consumer and leisure influences, place a great deal of strain on local societies that are unprepared.

East-Central European societies have a unique historical opportunity to change old institutions, experiment with new civic structures, and explore new models and ideas. International conditions are favorable: the unification of Western Europe, the North American Free Trade Agreement, and the displacement of many regional conflicts from Latin America and the Middle East to the Far East. Nationalism seems to be in retreat in many parts of the world, and the state's authority is undergoing a persistent process of delegitimation, whereas newly constituted international structures and transnational activities (trade, world events, tourism, scientific cooperation, and, of course, mass communication) have become increasingly prevalent. Furthermore, internal conditions of Western postmodern society enable an unprecedented transcultural interplay of ideas and symbolism regarding the nature of civic society that become a definite advantage in the formation of a metaculture. Whether the post-Communist countries will choose the road toward an enlightened, indigenous version of civil society or a primitive, self-destructive nationalism remains to be seen.

However, there are more than favorable external circumstances for a global orientation in East-Central Europe. Both present anomic trends, with their profound effects on the transformation of traditional structures to new capitalist social structures as well as the corollary impulse to question traditional theodicies, could contribute to dissolving old prejudices and rendering ingrained stereotypical categories obsolete. Young people may find that local structures and their rationales, as well as the available range of interpretations and symbolism, are so anachronistic and narrowly defined that only unprecedented changes toward an openness in all aspects of life could generate an emancipatory social environment compatible with their contemporary experience. Such a society may not be subjected to old divisions and demarcations, nor its collective consciousness be any longer subordinated to one singular hegemonic discourse. The individual integrated in a multitude of civil communities will reign supreme as the essence of a newly relevant, non-utopian universality, whereas the immediate surroundings that remain a forceful and yet comforting space will be an extension of a new relationship. That is, a sublime civil space as always should have, but never yet has, been achieved.

7

National Language, Identity Formation, and Broadcasting: The Flemish and German-Swiss Communities*

Hilde Van den Bulck
Luc Van Poecke
Katholieke Universiteit Leuven

In this chapter we show that as a consequence of increasing contacts, interdependence, and globalization, both within and between various states and cultures, national identity and culture have become increasingly problematic. This process is one of the symptoms of the disappearance of the modern organization of society and the rise of postmodern interactions. Analyzing the evolving language policies[1] of Public Service Broadcasters (PSBs) gives a good insight into the (self-)ascribed role of the PSB in the nation-building projects of their communities. Specifically, we show how the evolving language policies of the Flemish and German-Swiss PSB can be explained by looking at their wider socioeconomic, political, cultural, and sociolinguistic contexts.[2]

*This chapter was prepared in the context of *Taal en Omroep*, a research project sponsored by the Belgian F.K.F.O. (Fundamentale Menswetenschappen, nr 2.0070.92).

[1]The "language policy of a broadcasting organization" refers to the institution's choice of a particular variety of language or languages for broadcasting.

[2]Research is based on analysis of documents as well as interviews with experts and privileged witnesses.

Comparative and diachronic research are important because such work allows us to challenge some truisms in media and language studies (e.g., the generally accepted notion that standard language is the "best" variety for use in electronic media), as well as the "short-sightedness" inherent in single-case studies (see Leitner, 1980, 1983, 1985; Wober, 1990). This study compares ways in which the Flemish PSB has stressed standard language use, whereas the German-Swiss[3] PSB has allowed for the Swiss-German dialects to be widely used on radio and television. These quite different policies must be understood as the result of different "accents" in the process of nation building, based on ethnolinguistic identity.

The study is also diachronic. Over time, the Flemish PSB has modified its language policy from strict standard language use to acceptance of a certain degree of variation, whereas the German-Swiss PSB can be seen to have increased the amount of and variation in dialect use in recent decades. These changes must be understood as a symptom of the sociocultural transformation from modernity to postmodernity with its consequent changes in identity formation. In this way, the nation-building projects themselves can be explained as part and parcel of the modern attempt to create a Fordist, stratified, and homogenous society in which citizens have to find their identity. The more recent decrease in some aspects of the importance of national culture and identity can then be situated within the move toward a postmodern society in which there is a decline of contrast and increase in variation, particularly with regard to identities.

BUILDING THE NATION: FLEMISH AND GERMAN-SWISS ETHNOLINGUISTIC IDENTITIES

Collective Identity, Nationhood, and Language

Our starting point, then, is the concept of identity, which does not "express itself as an essence," but is rather produced in a socialization process that includes defining boundaries and establishing a category system (Van Poecke, 1996; Van Poecke & Van den Bulck, 1993). As noted by Morley and Robins (1989), structuralism has taught us that people as well as things do not have an identity or meaning on their own, but obtain these in relation to other people and things, that is, in a

---

[3]*German-Swiss* refers to the German-speaking part of Switzerland (in contrast to the French-, Italian-, and Retho-Roman-speaking Swiss), whereas *Swiss-German* is used to refer to the Swiss variant of the German language (in contrast to German spoken in Germany or Austria).

category system; hence, "difference is constitutive of identity" (p. 12). Or, as Fishman (1972) puts it: "Identity is the result of 'contrastive self-identification': us versus them" (pp. 52-53). In other words, there is no uniqueness without the other(s), no "us" without contact and communication with "them." In order for people and things to find their position vis-à-vis each other in a category system, they need a feature that on the one hand brings them together and, on the other, distinguishes them for the other(s). It is this feature that marks the boundary.

This boundary and communication with the other(s) implies the threat that one can be contaminated or even absorbed by the other. Not only externally, internally too, everything that is experienced as an impermissible deviation form the "us," thus everything "we cannot identify ourselves with" is experienced as a threat and as something that needs to be suppressed. As the work of Levi-Strauss shows (see, e.g., Clement, 1987), communication and identity are always a matter of drawing boundaries and keeping the right distance, implying a fear of pollution or dirt. Following the ideas of Mary Douglas, Leach (1976) speaks of dirt as "matter out of place," arguing that:

> The more sharply we define our boundaries, the more conscious we become of the dirt that has ambiguously got onto the wrong side of the frontier. Boundaries become dirty by definition and we devote a great deal of effort to keeping them clean, just so that we can preserve confidence in our category system. (p. 61)

Collectivities too, according to Levi-Strauss, have a need for classification, for the identification of "us" versus "them" (Schlesinger, 1991). Collective identity formation is a complex process, propelled by a dialectic between internal and external definitions. Schlesinger also stresses the importance of an interactionalist perspective: Collective identity is not a given condition for collective action, but a continuously constructed and reconstructed category. This collective identity is a feeling of identification with a community and/or the institutions by which it is presented, expressed, or symbolized (Schlesinger, 1991). A collective identity may cohere around different elements: class, gender, and nation.

Many authors have stressed the importance of national identity or nationhood in Western-European industrialized countries. On the one hand, the idea of a nation is but an interpretive construct, not an objective structure, making nationhood the result of an ideology. The core argument of nationhood is the underlining of the longevity and antiquity of the collectivity's ties (Smith, 1983). The concept and related ideas of political and cultural sovereignty, though, are in fact relatively recent, born in an era in which Enlightenment and Revolution destroyed the legitimacy of a divine order (Bauman, 1992). Furthermore, the whole debate is ideological in that the integrative relations that nationhood is supposed to secure are often seen in a functionalist perspective (Arnason, 1990), ignoring the fact that national culture is a site of contestation, in which competition over definitions takes place (Schlesinger, 1991). However, we cannot ignore the fact that, particularly in modern, European industrialized societies, nationhood has been a fundamental aspect of an individual's collective identity and of his or her civic and political relations. In that way, there is something of a "lived" reality to national identity (Tomlinson, 1991).

A nation is best understood, then, as an imagined community, conceived as a deep horizontal comradeship, regardless of the actual inequality and exploitation that may prevail; as limited with finite, if elastic, boundaries beyond which lie other nations; and as sovereign, independent from and equal to other nations (Anderson, 1991). Note, however, that a nation is not the equivalent of a state, as the latter is a political, governmental, or administrative collectivity, whereas the former can be a state, federalized, autonomous, or even non-self-governing (Krejci, 1978).

Nationhood, or the identification with a nation, is based on a perceived or ascribed common history (possibly including territory) and culture. The "roots" of the nation are traced back (in some instances even to a sociobiological limit of common descent) by situating the community as a unity throughout the past, stressing the "traditionality" of contemporary aspects of the community that are "handed down" from generation to generation—what Hobsbawm refers to as "invented traditions" (Hobsbawm & Ranger, 1983; Tomlinson, 1991). This also goes for what is seen as the common culture. Culture is here conceived in its materialized, institutionalized, and symbolic aspects. What a people relate to can range from patterns of painting, dance, music, and architecture, to patterns of action (habits and folkways), to patterns of conveying information about other patterns (flags, elections, language; Deutsch, 1966).

Here it is important to note that the creation of a national or ethnocultural identity is always accompanied by a power struggle between elites, both within the collectivity and between the elites of the in and out groups (Brass, 1991). Kellas (1991) distinguishes among three main types of elites: the political elite, encompassing established politicians, civil servants, and the military; the cultural elite, especially teachers, literati, and clergy; and the economic elite, comprising business and trade union leaders. All these groups react differently to national aspirations. Where there is a strong national culture, the cultural elite is likely to be nationalistic, whereas the economic elite is likely to be the least nationalistic. The position of the political elite is crucial, and it is only when it fragments that nationalism is able to make progress.

The importance of language in the process of nationhood is widely acknowledged. In the mobilization of ethnic feelings and longings, and for the creation of the aforementioned contrastive self-identification, use is made of one or other core symbol (Brass, 1991). That language so commonly becomes such a symbol is partially a reflection of the fact that it is the carrier of so many other symbols of nationhood, partially a result of the fact that it is made into a prime symbol by intellectuals and other influential figures who more than any others are adept at its use and manipulation, and partially a result of its infinite interpretability as a symbol that can stand for the entire nation. Thus language often constitutes the most important embodiment of ethnicity, and the means for distinguishing "us" from "them," fulfilling what is called the shibboleth function (Fishman, 1972, 1977).

Language as a symbol can fulfill a double function. It serves as a means of affirming oneself as a group in respect to others, becoming the distinctive characteristic that marks the community from other groups. Via language one tries to distance oneself from and protect against the other communities. As Halliday (1978) puts it: the explicitly formulated "I don't like their vowels" implicitly means "I don't like their values" (p. 179). On the other hand, language is used to strengthen the unity of and bridge the differences within the community.

Contrasting Self-Identifications: The Flemish and the German-Swiss

The Flemish case. Ever since the creation of the Belgian state in 1830, the Flemish have constituted the majority of the population. But the rapid industrialization that Belgium underwent in the 19th century developed chiefly in Wallonia, the French-speaking part of Belgium, and the Flemish community as a consequence declined.[4] The result was a French-speaking dominance in economy and politics, followed by a French linguistic and cultural hegemony (Donaldson, 1983).

The Flemish national identity was formed on the basis of ethnic or ethnolinguistic nationhood. The Flemish nation, being formed in a country on its way to federalization, needed the creation of a national language and culture. Language particularly was put forward as the core element in the contrastive self-identification; on the one hand as a full-fledged symbol and means of identification, and on the other hand as a counterpole to and replacement of French language and culture. Due to historical circumstances, a standard language was not available within the community. That one therefore turned to a standard language that was crafted outside the community, that is, the standard Dutch (or Netherlandic) of the Netherlands, can be explained by looking at the main actors in this process.

---

[4]A situation that lasted until the late 1950s, when the Flemish community started to flourish economically and the Walloon heavy industry died out.

The Flemish movement started off as an elite culture movement (Donaldson, 1983). As Jaspaert and Van Belle (1989) point out, this "cultural group" primarily consisted of literati and philologists, the latter referring to Germanic scholars who had a university education in order to teach the correct language, literature, and culture. They saw (or still see) the Flemish community and the Netherlands as a linguistic and cultural unity that was broken up and that had to be reunited (the Pan-Netherlandic concept and the idea of cultural reintegration) and accepted the Netherlands as the ultimate authority with regard to standard language. This viewpoint was implemented in education, official language policy, and the media.

The creation of an ethnocultural identity can only be successful, though, when supported by social, economic, and political processes. Hence, Jaspaert and Van Belle (1989) refer to a second important group, the growing Flemish middle class, which in its striving for recognition and prestige and in the frustrating realization that learning French was insufficient to achieve this, also turned to a Dutch standard language as a symbol. Only in recent decades, with the decline of French language and cultural hegemony, has this group started to question the "authority" of the North in language matters.

The German-Swiss case. Switzerland's political emergence developed mainly by gradual accretion around the mountain cantons of central Switzerland. Consequently, linguistic diversity was never really an issue within the confederation, which has always underlined its plurality and decentralization (McRae, 1983). The German-Swiss community has always had the dominant position within the country numerically as well as socioeconomically and politically. Nevertheless, German-Switzerland too has developed an ethnolinguistic identity, but—differently from the Flemish case—this was in contrast with the neighboring country Germany.

A Swiss-German standard language never developed due to the lack of an *Eigenkultur* of an urban middle class (Kühn, 1980): The decentralized and ever-shifting political center never allowed for an intellectual center to develop, of which the local dialect could become the standard language (Pap, 1990). Instead, the standard language of Germany (*Hochdeutsch*) was taken as written language. This was mainly due to the economic interests of book publishers and to the contacts between German and German-Swiss literati (Kühn, 1980). However, although in Germany the bourgeoisie took up *Hochdeutsch* as the main oral language, this was unacceptable to their German-Swiss counterparts (Haas, 1990). The German-Swiss middle class accepted *Hochdeutsch* as a supraregional vehicle for communication and as the language for science and art, but not the ideological function it occupied in Germany as a national language. Conversely, it is exactly in the refusal to accept the standard variety as a daily language, and in the retaining of the dialects (*Mundart*) for that purpose, that the Swiss saw the possibility of a national boundary. Therefore, *Mundart* use became a national symbol (Haas, 1990).

The result was that, sociolinguistically speaking, German-Switzerland developed into a diglossia (Ferguson, 1959). In a diglossic language situation there is a sharp and stable distinction between two languages or two varieties of a language according to function and domain. The low variety (in this case, *Mundart*) is used in informal, intimate, and relational domains and is the mother tongue. The high variety (*Hochdeutsch*) is reserved for writing and for formal, institutional, and transitional domains and is only learned later on in life (e.g., in schools).[5]

The industrialization at the end of the 19th century brought a huge influx of German immigrants who occupied important cultural and economic positions. The result was that the oral use of dialect decreased to the benefit of *Hochdeutsch* (Ris, 1979). This led to the first dialect movement, instigated by the intellectual middle class. The *Deutschschweizerische Sprachverein* (German-Swiss Language Society) was founded, which propagated a strict split between standard and dialect according to domain, and praised dialect as a nationalizing force (Sonderegger, 1985). After this buildup in the 1920s of a *Gesamtschweizer heimat* (common Swiss homeland) and cultural awareness, the *Ausbaupolitik* (expansion policy) of Nazi Germany instigated a second dialect movement, *Geistigen Landesverleidigung* (mental defense of the realm), in the 1930s (Ris, 1979). This movement, which lasted until the end of the 1950s, supported the advancement and maintenance of the dialects as the expression of Swiss national character, spiritual *heimat*, stylistically valuable, the daily language of all social strata (democratic idea), a boundary against the outside (useful in foreign policy against the German Reich), and a mirror of the Swiss federal ideal (Sonderegger, 1985).

At the same time, the German-Swiss intellectual middle class strove for a linguistic-cultural distinction between "good" and "bad" language. As the "good" language could not be equated with the standard language, they developed (in accordance with the rise of dialectology) a "doctrine of two purities": one should master both standard and *Mundart*. The worst linguistic-cultural mistake is the mixup of standard and *mundart*, although the mixup of the different *mundarts* was also frowned on (Haas, 1990). This idea remained dominant well into the 1960s.

---

[5]Note that diglossia must be distinguished from the more common situation (such as the Flemish), in which the high variety (standard) and the low variety (dialects) do not have this strict functional distribution, and in which even the high variety is mother tongue to certain segments of society (Deprez, 1981).

PUBLIC SERVICE BROADCASTING
LANGUAGE POLICY AND NATION BUILDING

The Self-Ascribed Role of Public Service Broadcasting

In the establishment and maintenance of such a national ethnocultural identity, the cultural apparatus assigns itself or is assigned a vital role. Virtually all public service broadcasters (PSBs) in modern industrialized countries have contributed substantially to the creation of the aforementioned "imagined community" for the modern nation-state, promoting "an image of the national 'we', an 'us' whose constituent elements are 'ordinary families'" (Morley & Robins, 1989, p. 32). In other words, the community (or parts thereof) attaches great importance to its own "audio-visual space," that is, its own autonomous broadcasting organization that integrates the internal audience and draws the imaginary line that divides that audience from "them," the external audience to whom broadcasts are not aimed (regardless of whether "them" could actually receive the broadcast; Van den Bulck, 1995). The PSBs, according to McQuail, de Mateo, and Tapper (1992), were designed to:

> serve the audiences and social institutions within the national territory, center-peripheral in form of organization, expected to protect national language and culture and (however implicitly) to represent the national interest. As an aspect of their national character, broadcasting institutions were also usually monopolistic or quasi-monopolistic in their form of control. (p. 9)

In all modern industrialized West European countries, according to Desaulniers (1985), television has been given the task of contributing to the creation and development of a national identity and culture, which carried a threefold responsibility: education (to support the national education system), information (to create political consciousness), and entertainment (to articulate a national culture).

This kind of radio and television was marked by a "cultural-educational or cultural-pedagogic logic" (Brants & Siune, 1992, p. 110). Both policymakers and actual broadcasters were strongly influenced by the idea that broadcasting was one of the most powerful weapons in, as Bauman (1992) puts it, the cultural crusade of the modern intellectual: the people had to be educated, emancipated, and liberated from their backwardness, their vulgar pleasures, and, indeed, their linguistic poverty. It should come as no surprise, then, that the PSBs were "colonized by the intellectuals of the professional middle class" (Elliot, 1982, p. 250), who considered themselves as the "viewer's guide to whatever was culturally worthwhile" (Blumler, 1992, p. 11). They were the propagators of what has been called a Reithian ethos (named after the first Director-General of the BBC, Lord Reith), a benign patronizing to "give the public a little more than it wants" (Reith, quoted in Leitner, 1983, p. 58).

So the PSBs were given or gave themselves the task of promoting and educating their audience into a "national bourgeois culture." In this task of social integration and assimilation, which the PSBs shared with other cultural institutions (Collins, 1989), language held a key position.

Flemish and German-Swiss PSB Language Policy

We now turn to how the Flemish and German-Swiss PSBs—colonized by the intellectual middle class—took up their "task" in this ethnolinguistic identity formation.

"Father knows best." As the only (public) medium that reached the entire community, these PSBs—like every West European PSB (Blumler, 1992)—saw themselves to a large extent as the mass medium and virtually as the official mouthpiece of their communities. The language of broadcasting, therefore, was considered to be the "expression of an official, a 'model' institution" (Bal, 1985, p. 26). As the first Director-General of the Flemish PSB put it, as "the only institution where the Flemish manage to be Flemish without a trace of submissiveness," its intention was to propagate the Flemish cultural heritage (Boon, 1962, p. 129). Similarly, the German-Swiss PSB wanted to provide "programs of which the content, worldview, format and atmosphere" were those with which the German-Swiss audience could easily identify (Fricker, 1988, p. 30). In any case, the impression had to be avoided that a German takeover was taking place (Camartin, personal interview, December, 18, 1992).

The PSBs thus had to orient themselves to the language that was used in other public institutions (such as education) and that signified the specificity of the community. Because of the specific context of the respective PSB and the position of each intellectual middle class, this resulted in the Flemish case, in opting for the prestige variety that transcended regional differences, that is standard Dutch, whereas in the German-Swiss case it resulted in the use of the Swiss-German dialect in all its varieties.

This striving for cultural individuality and unity was accompanied by the "Reithian" attempt to "educate" the community. This was very pronounced in the Flemish case, in which the PSB intended to "elevate the Flemish people to an international level" (Peeters, 1962, p. 127). This was seen in terms of providing not only "high" culture and education, but also language programs. The Flemish still had to learn their language, and the PSB assumed a major role in this. As the former head of PSB television, Nic Bal (1989), stated:

> the propagation of standard Dutch was seen in large measure in the light of public education. To us, this was an important task. Some called this pedantic, but we thought that a PSB had the duty to educate its people, certainly as regards the language, in view of the large disadvantages of the Flemings in this area.

A striking illustration of this is programs on language of the 1960s and 1970s on both radio and television.

The German-Swiss PSB, too, was marked by this cultural-educational logic. As Fricker (personal interview, February 13, 1993) stated:

> Broadcasting (first radio, but also television) was seen as a means to inform and entertain but first and foremost as an instrument for the education and cultivation (in terms of "high" culture) of the public. People had to be given ample possibilities for cultural experiences.

In terms of language, this had two implications: First, it meant that, despite the assumed importance of dialect as a language of broadcasting, all "serious" (economic, political, religious) and "high" cultural programs were broadcast in standard German, although clearly a German-Swiss standard (Camartin, 1992). Second, even in the use of dialect it was important that the "official dialects" were used (Fricker, 1993). A good example of the pedagogic logic was the serials produced in different Swiss-German dialects (Fricker, 1988). So, out of the same process of nation-building, two apparently different but basically similar language policies evolved.

The language policy of the Flemish PSB can best be described as a striving for an exclusive and uniform use of standard language, based on the norm formulated in the Netherlands. For broadcasting personnel, this meant the organizing of very language-oriented recruitment examinations and the gradual development of repressive controls. The latter was done initially by external authorities and, from 1961 on, by the secretary of the Director-General.

Because the freelance and casual contributors did not come under this regime, but were nevertheless identified by the public with the institution, measures were also taken in their regard. Thus, in the 1940s and 1950s, people were sought who were not only expert in a particular area, but who also had polished speech. In certain cases, these "outsiders" were even replaced by elocutionists, primarily in the so-called radio chronicles:

> When an expert was not satisfactory in his command of the language or when he spoke a dialect, his text was not only corrected in advance but also read by an elocutionist. On the one hand, one could then be assured of a 'professional' reading, but on the other, the exaggerated, grandiloquent style gave it all an unauthentic character. (Bal, 1989)

In this way, within the broadcasting organization, every nerve was strained to assure a uniform standard language presentation. Of course, in time, almost all successful entertainment series were in dialect. However, it is important to note that these and other examples of the use of nonstandard language were clearly considered tolerated deviations from the norm, resulting from a strategy that aimed to win over the public to better programs.

The German-Swiss PSB's language policy can be defined as diglossic use of standard German and Swiss-German dialects, with the "two purities" as the norm. To achieve this goal, several steps were taken. First, in recruitment, a clear distinction was made between the experts, that is, people preparing the programs, and the actual broadcasting voices. The latter were language specialists: actors, performers, or elocutionists who had had speech training. As Fricker (1993) states: "Even if you did not really have a 'radio voice' if you knew how to present the material linguistically correctly in terms of grammar, vocabulary and pronunciation, you were OK." It was important that candidates did not sound too German, though. As Camartin (1992) puts it:

> A candidate who spoke German in a Germanic, Teutonic fashion, who did not have enough Swiss elements in his speech, was not considered a good speaker. It is interesting to see how the PBS tried to avoid people with a *Buhne-Deutsch*. It might do for say a Goethe-radioplay but not for the Swiss programming in general.

Second, there was a strict hierarchical internal control. Every studio had people who checked what was being broadcast before and during the broadcast (Schmid-Cadalbert, personal interview, December 14, 1992). Freelance workers, for example, had to hand in their texts beforehand for corrections. This was the case for both standard and dialect (Frei, 1985). Finally, this control was very purist as it was based on the doctrine of the "two purities." So, not only the standard but also the dialects had to be pure. As Fricker (1993) points out: "It could be Zurich, Bern, Basel or any *Mundart* as long as it was pure. One was supposed to speak an 'officially existing dialect.' The standard too had to be grammatically correct."

"The customer is always right." In the last 15 years or so, an important shift in these ideas can be seen to have taken place. Language usage on radio and television came under increasing criticism. Thus, in the Flemish case, "silly humor and the use of dialect . . . or an edited variant" (Beheydt, 1984, p. 11) and "the popular dialect speaker . . . together with regional foods, regional beers, and the dialect theater began a successful come-back" (Beheydt, 1987, p. 8). Similarly, language use on the German-Swiss radio and television has been (and still is) the object of fierce debates in public and even academic fora (e.g., Frei, 1985; Ingold, 1985; Schlapfer, Gutzwiller, & Schmid, 1991). On closer analysis it becomes clear that the perceived changes in language usage are the result of changes in the overall language policy of the broadcasters. Developments in the broadcasting domain and accompanying shifts in society seem to be responsible for this.

The successive dismantling of the public service radio and television monopoly starting at the end of the 1970s and continuing throughout the 1980s, combined with societal shifts we discuss later, have contributed to a definitive turnaround in broadcasting objectives. As Saxer (1989) states, due to internationalization, PSB has to find new ways of fulfilling its integration function. The unifying, centralistic point of departure is replaced more and more by decentralization and regionalism in which the propagation of "the Flemish (let alone Pan-Netherlandic)" or "the German-Swiss" message is no longer the prime purpose.

At the same time, the paternalistic "father knows best" philosophy is being replaced by "the customer is always right" approach. The result is that education is increasingly becoming "only" one of the three broadcasting functions. Instead, radio and television are being considered a service to diverse publics that must be treated on equal terms. Programming policy, therefore, is being based ever more on diversity, participation, and smallness of scale. Probably the clearest example of this is the audience segmentation in radio which started in both cases in the 1960s (Feyaerts, 1982; Punter, 1971) and matured during the 1980s. But this shift was also made in television. Frei (1985) observes an increased importance of live-broadcast formats such as interviews, talks, discussions, and so on. More and more, Frei argues, the PSB is trying to get to the *Nahe des Rezipienten*: capturing the audience in the intimacy of its livingroom.

This has been accompanied by a shift in the ideas of the PSB with regard to language use. Indeed, when language standardization and centralization reflect each other, decentralization and regionalization lead—also with respect to language—to a "process that is oriented to the elimination of further unification and therefore is manifested in a trend to democratization and regionalization" (Geerts, 1974, p. 941), and so, too, within radio and television.

In the Flemish case, the original point of departure is reoriented to a striving for what we call (for the time being) a nonuniform standard language policy. First, the need for a standard language usage is being interpreted increasingly from a purely functional and communicational instead of a symbolic and ideological point of view (Berode, personal interview, April 5, 1989). The standard variety is considered the best and the purest "channel" to send media messages with a minimum of noise from "sender" (PSB) to "receiver" (the public). Second, in the area of language policy, the changeover has also been made from a "father knows best" to a "customer is always right" approach. According to Berode (1989), "language education is important . . . but excessive repression leads to psychological resistance with respect to the language both in the speaker and in the listener." Therefore, the attitude toward the norm is being determined ever more from the point of view of the public, for example, in terms of comprehensibility. Finally, the stress has shifted from an absolute demand for uniformity in broadcast language to recognition of the existence of different styles and registers. In this regard, Berode states: "In the past, the stress was placed on pronunciation and purism. The emphasis has now been shifted. . . . When I correct, I will rather say 'bad register' or 'this is as dull as ditch-water.'"

This evolution in normative attitudes has brought about a profound change in measures taken to achieve the norm. Control has not only moved from a more or less exclusively repressive strategy to much wider preventive control, but also from a purist ("don't say . . . do say") to an advisory language policy. The result of this progressive change in language policy is a shift from uniform, standard language use to a language policy that takes greater account of the diversity of the audience.

The German-Swiss PSB can be seen to have altered its language policy in a similar fashion. The demise of the nation-building task to the advantage of decentralization, regionalism, and localism, and the attention to audience diversity, has led to the acceptance of more variation in the Mundart use. As Schmid-Caldalbert (1992) points out:

> Together with the generic programming on radio, we can see that a much larger variety (in terms of registers etc.) is tolerated. Instead of one German-Swiss audience, all different kinds of audience groups are addressed, each in their own "Radiolect."

So, here, too, the ideological and symbolic importance of language is replaced by a functional approach toward broadcasting language.

The end of the Reithian ethos, which brought broadcasters down from their throne to be the *Herzen des Publikums ganz nah* (near the heart of the public), brought about major shifts in language policy (Fricker, 1993). First, this informalization led to an increase in dialect use to the extent that very few programs are still produced in standard language (Ramseier, 1988). What is more, it also led to the end of the doctrine of the two purities. Mixed dialects are used, and the norms for standard language use are much less strictly respected (Fricker, 1993).

These policy changes affected the old regime of control. In recruitment distinction is no longer made between content and presentation, and, as a result, actual broadcasters are no longer people with a background in speech training. As Fricker (1993) puts it: "While previously you mainly had to be able to speak according to the linguistic code, it is now more important that you have a 'radio voice.'" At the same time, hierarchical control is disappearing. Advice (instead of control) is increasingly limited to criteria for choosing between standard and dialect (Burger, 1984) and ways of addressing different subaudiences (Schmid-Cadalbert, 1992).

To account for these changes in the language policy of these (and other) PSBs, the process of nation-building itself has to be examined in a wider framework of changing social structures and formations of identity, in short, the problematic of postmodernity (Van Poecke, 1996; Van Poecke & Van den Bulck, 1993).

THE POSTMODERN ENVIRONMENT

Modernity and the "National Project"

Modernity is associated with the growing stress that capitalism put on a rational control of production: standardization of tasks, division of labor, and standardization of consumption. All this has culminated in what has been called *Fordism* (or *Taylorism*), characterized by

> relative fixity and performance—fixed capital in mass production, stable standardized and homogenous markets, a fixed configuration of political-economic influence and power, easily identifiable authority and meta-theories, secure grounding in materiality and technical-scientific rationality, and the like. (Harvey, 1989, pp. 338-339)

This implies the origin and development of modern abstract, centralized, and bureaucratic states in which linguistic and cultural diversity are suppressed to the benefit of a standardized language and homogenizing culture (Gellner, 1983). This standardized language and national (high) culture, in which the citizen has to find his or her collective identity, must be transmitted via centrally organized national institutions such as education and the media.

It has been pointed out that this Fordist society was dominated by an industrial middle class with its own methods of education, socialization, and social control. According to Bernstein (1971), this (modern) socialization can be characterized as positional and based on an explicit, visible pedagogy. *Positional* refers to the ascription of an identity to the subject that allows him or her to take a position in the predetermined, sharply differentiated, and hierarchical structures. In this way an individual is created who fits into the rigid structure of the Fordist organization of the economy and in the *Gesellschaftliche* organization of society.

This visible pedagogy, according to Bernstein (1975), is marked by strong "classification" and strong "framing." *Framing* concerns the question of control over the communication and socialization processes. In modern socialization, the sender is in control, and the process thus proceeds from the top down; it is paternalistic. *Classification* describes the way in which the division of labor and, more broadly, social reality are organized. It has often been pointed out that modernity is characterized by strong structural and functional differentiation (Crook, Pakulski, & Waters, 1992; Lash, 1990; Lash & Urry, 1987): differentiation into different classes, between the public and private spheres, between work and play, and between the institutional and the everyday world. Each institutional sphere has its own specialized knowledge, rules, criteria of relevance, and value systems on the basis of which the correctness and incorrectness of particular practices are determined.

Modernity, according to Balandier (1988), is obsessed by normalization. In this respect, modernity is simultaneously differentiating and homogenizing. Indeed, if one wants to achieve integration of any communication between the various components of the system, then a unifying language and culture must be propagated (Crook et al., 1992), which are those of the intellectual middle class. Of course, every community or culture classifies, and every classification is hierarchical. It is typical of modernity, however, according to Gellner (1983), that the higher must oust the lower by means of an explicitly educational project, which, in principle, excludes nobody.

Postmodernity and the "Global-Local Nexus"

Already in the mid-1960s, the rigidity of Fordism was unable to resolve the crises that had begun to take shape. Hence, a shift commenced to what Harvey (1989) calls post-Fordist flexible accumulation; flexibility both with regard to the labor process and labor market, and with regard to consumption patterns. From a goods economy there has been a shift to a service economy of which the popular culture form a part; the attempt is no longer to homogenize and standardize consumption, but rather to react flexibly to the divergent personal wishes of the consumer. This occurs by the generalized introduction of rapidly changing styles and fashions (previously style and fashion had been the reserve of the upper classes); by a segmentation of the market "segments," "niches," "lifestyles," and "lifestages" (Willis, 1990), whereby the classic divisions (national, sociodemographic) lose a great deal of their relevance; and by selling not products as such but rather the significance these products have for the individual. What is exchanged and circulated, then, is not wealth but, as Fiske (1987) states, "meanings, pleasures and social identities" (p. 311). The consumer, in other words, is invited to find his or her identity, values, and convictions no longer in predetermined structures, but to construct them by him- or herself (to make him- or herself) on the basis of the consumption of products that are produced increasingly for the global market by companies that are increasingly transnational. In other words, we can observe a shift "from involving people in society as a political citizen of nation states towards involving them as consumption units in a corporate world" (Elliott, 1982, p. 244).

This movement toward post-Fordism has been accompanied by a shift within the middle class, whereby the old ("modern") industrial middle class must give way to a new, rising, postindustrial, post-Fordist ("postmodern") middle class, which is active in the service economy, for example, the media, advertising, higher education, and the world of finance and commerce (Crook et al., 1992), and of which Bourdieu's (1984) "new petite bourgeoisie" is part. Consequently, according to Bernstein (1975), the old, visible, pedagogy or socialization is losing ground to an invisible pedagogy or socialization of the new postindustrial middle class. In this case, socialization is characterized by weak classification or differentiation and weak framing, what Bourdieu (1984) refers to as a "gentle, invisible education" (p. 219). Indeed, it has been pointed out that postmodernism is characterized by de-differentiation and de-hierarchization (Crook et al., 1992; Featherstone, 1991; Lash, 1990): the blurring of the boundaries between high and low culture, between the public and private spheres, and between entertainment and information or education (infotainment, edutainment). Weak framing means that the subject is given the opportunity (demands the right) of educating or socializing him- or herself, has an aversion to being patronized by central authorities, and feels emancipated in everything. Rules and norms are no longer imposed from above but acquired: The subject must choose on the basis of negotiation and communication. This also means that rules and norms remain vague and implicit (Bauman, 1992). Consequently, the educational pattern is no longer positional but personal. "Normalized" individuals are no longer created, but rather the subject is communicated with on the basis of his or her unique social, affective, and cognitive characteristics. In other words, the system produces persons who themselves must fill in their identity. The feeling of having an unambiguous and clearly delineated social identity is weakening (Bernstein, 1971).

This right (in fact, a duty) to constitute one's own identity is fulfilled, as Bourdieu (1984) states, by relating to others, "sharing experiences." In this sense there is a return to the *Gemeinschaftliche* mode, although "rather on the basis of *Wahlverwantschaft* (relationship based on choice) than on the basis of inherited or ascribed characteristics" (Dobbelaere, 1991, p. 221). In this way, society is segmented and fragmented in fleeting, forming, and dissolving "communities," the membership of which implies no long-term commitment and can easily be revoked (Bauman, 1992).

The Dutch sociologist, Wouters (1990), in a similar fashion, speaks of informalization (de-hierarchization), resulting in a "decline of contrasts and an increase in variations" (de-differentiation) (pp. 44-45). Although previously sharp boundaries existed between hierarchically constructed categories of people (of which language was an important indicator and primary symbol), now these boundaries are blurring, and identities become variations of each other. This can clearly be seen to happen with regard to language. Identities become variations of each other, and language is seen more pragmatically as a means of communication (the end of paternalism). The blurring of the differences between the identities and language varieties (and thus also the blurring of the differences in power and status) are precisely what enables people to participate in such postmodern "communities," in which it is more important that one understands, empathizes with, and has contact with others, than that one defines oneself in contrast with the other.

Postmodernity and Language Communities

The current sociolinguistic situation of both the Flemish and German-Swiss communities are good cases in point. In both communities, a linguistic informalization can be observed. More and more the Flemings can be seen to lack the will (and thus the ability) to "talk like the Dutch" (Deprez, 1989a), to the extent that proposals are being put forward to create an independent "frame of reference for Flemish Dutch" (Deprez, 1991, 1992). In German-Switzerland, the informalization has influenced the diglossia situation. Increasingly the low variety (*Mundart*) is taking over domains that used to be the reserve of the high variety (*Hochdeutsh*) to the extent that *Hochdeutsch* is almost entirely pushed back to only written usage (Haas, 1988, 1990; Schlapfer et al., 1991; Sieber & Sitta, 1986). Moreover, the "decrease of contrasts, increase in variations" has led to what Sonderegger (1985) calls the *"Freiheit des*

Ubergriffs" ("freedom to breach the rules"), or the end of the doctrine of the two purities; not only the boundaries between standard and dialect but also between dialects are blurring. Stroop (1991, 1992) observes a similar move of standard and dialect toward each other in a process that should ultimately lead to "middle-languages," that is, varieties that are mixtures of standard and dialect.

Thus the move toward a post-Fordist organization of the economy and the accompanying shift from a "modern" to a postmaterialist or "postmodern" organization of society has been at the expense of national identities and cultures. People are no longer socialized into clearly delineated identities; rather, they constitute their identities themselves to an ever-larger extent through the consumption of cultural and other goods, produced in the increasingly globalized post-Fordist economy. Instead of being given a national identity, people find their collective identities more and more within the "global-local nexus" (Morley & Robins, 1989, p. 12). On the one hand, averse to so-called "modernity," one retreats into small communities. There is a return to the local, the regional, and the small scale (e.g., local radio and regional television)—the everyday world. Balandier (1985) speaks of a "true religion of everyday life" (p. 202). On the other hand, these communities are no longer necessarily place-bound. In this regard, reference has been made to the role of the electronic media in the creation of "media-based proximity" (Balandier, 1988, p. 168), of transnational or cross-cultural "electronic communities" (Ang, 1990, p. 255). As a result of "cultural synchronization" (Hamelink, 1983), the sharpest contrasts decline and we obtain, according to the mechanism described earlier, a process by which national identities and cultures become increasingly mutually accepted variations of each other. People appropriate what is offered and construct in this way their identities within an increasingly integrated world system:

> In other words, in the increasingly integrated world system there is no such thing as an independent cultural identity; every identity must define and position itself in relation to the cultural frames affirmed by the world system. (Ang, 1990, p. 253)

According to Wouters (1990), no single state can still withdraw from the "increasing interwovenness within a network of political, economic and cultural ties. All have become integral components of one world process" (p. 281).

THE RISE AND FALL OF PUBLIC SERVICE BROADCASTING LANGUAGE POLICY

It now becomes possible to understand the shift in the language policy of public service broadcasters as part and parcel of these wider societal changes. The original setup of the PSB fitted the modernist organization of society. These broadcasting systems went along with the principles of the Fordist economy and strong, centralized states. These organizations were staffed to a large extent by members of the "modern" middle class (e.g., the Flemish PSB was dominated by the above-mentioned Germanic scholars; Hemmerechts, 1984) and hence reflected the habits of this class. In other words, both the nation-building project and the paternalistic ethos can be seen as elements of the sharp boundary maintenance and framing of visible pedagogy, or socialization.

Together with the rest of the cultural apparatus, public service broadcasters, by means of education, information and entertainment—which were segregated from each other—had to promote social integration, homogeneity, and assimilation into the dominant, high culture. The strict standard language policy of the Flemish PSB is a clear example. But this does not mean that modern broadcasting offered no diversity or was not pluralistic. On the contrary, diversity and pluralism were values modern broadcasting put strongly to the fore but were seen as licensed differences, or licensed pluralism (the "pure-dialects" policy of the German-Swiss PSB is one example of this). Modern broadcasting followed in this respect the double movement that marks modern society: on the one hand, a strong differentiation between groups and categories of people, whereas on the other hand, the need to bind these groups together, to bring them into contact with each other and thus to integrate them into a structured whole of which the nation—as "imagined community"—was the point of reference.

At the same time, modern broadcasting was marked by a "cultural-educational logic" (Brants & Siune, 1992, p. 110), a benevolent paternalism that expresses the strong framing of visible pedagogy. As the first Director-General of the BBC—mother of all public service broadcasters—Lord Reith stated, "We are apparently setting out to give the public what we think they need—and not what they want, but few know what they want, and very few what they need" (quoted in Murdock, 1992, p. 28). Control over communication was thus clearly considered to lie with the sender. As such, modern broadcasting functioned on the basis of what Casetti and Odin (1990) call a "vectorised pedagogical contract," whereby the audience constitutes one large class, as it were, with the broadcaster as their schoolmaster, teaching them, among other things, the correct language and language use. Although this paternalism gradually lost its sharp Reithian edges, it remained the case that "despite the greater pluralism of public broadcasting in the 1960s and 1970s 'ordinary people' were still spoken about far more often than they spoke for themselves'" (Murdock, 1992, p. 31).

In the last 15 to 20 years, a new broadcasting marketplace appeared to have developed: The rise of multichannel broadcasting has produced a "new and hectic competitive environment" (Blumler, 1991, p. 195). Together with multiple televisions in one home and the introduction of new technologies, it made broadcasting go through an evolution comparable to the shift from a Fordist to a post-Fordist economy. Increasingly, PSB no longer is assured of a stable and loyal audience that it can divide along the customary category system, but rather has to deal with a public that segments itself on the basis of personal taste and preference (McQuail, 1992). There is, in other words, a shift in control over the communication process (framing) from producer to consumer. What is more, public service broadcasters—which had a strong entanglement of culture and politics, but were free of commercial influences— are now confronted with generalized postmodern commercialization and commodification of culture. More and more the idea takes hold that broadcasting is a business, more or less like any other, in which a broadcasting market, shaped by consumers' viewing decisions arises, characterized by a pressure to gain as large a part of the audience as possible. As a result, the national character of public service broadcasting is threatened.

With the disappearance of a community's own audiovisual space, the term *national culture* fits the reality of broadcasting, particularly television, less and less (Collins, 1990). Combined with the drive to gain large audiences, PSB is also forced to make programs that are acceptable in multiple markets, both domestic and global (Blumler, 1991), and that are aimed at everyone irrespective of age, sex, class, ethnicity, nationality, or culture. In this way, broadcasting follows the trend toward a reduction of contrasts and an increase of variations, at the expense of the strong classifications of modernity. Changes in the respective language policies are clear indications of this: both the Flemish and German-Swiss PSB allow for different "radio- and television-lects" to be used. Simultaneously, PSB is forced to let go of its Reithian ethos, no longer trying to "teach" its audience the correct language (be it standard Dutch or "pure" dialect). Its function is thus shifting to "producing and reproducing skillful and eager consumers, rather than obedient and willing subjects of the state" (Bauman, 1992, p. 17). In other words, there is a shift of the center of gravity from sender to receiver in the communication process of postmodern broadcasting, comparable to the wider societal shift from strong to weak framing.

The net result of this double movement within broadcasting is that the contrasts between programs and between audiences blur and that, on both levels—programs and audiences (or collective identities)—one can speak instead of variations. It is on the basis of this blurred, but not eliminated, group identity that the public now chooses from the large supply of programs that differ very little from each other, and, in this way, segments itself. It should come as no surprise, then, that in this new framework the original nation-building projects of the PSBs examined here—in which language policy was a core aspect—could not retain their importance.

8

Globalization and the Music of the Public Spheres*

Keith Negus
University of Leicester

In this chapter I trace the movement of sound across various global spaces and public spheres and pinpoint some of the ways that music moves beyond simply being a form of aesthetic expression or commodity to become a medium of transnational communication and affective knowledge. My point of departure is with the self-proclaimed "global" strategies of the recording industry and the responses that these have aroused, both inside and outside the music business in Europe. I take this as a concrete focus to begin interrogating some of the abstractions and universalisms of arguments about globalization. I argue that what has so often been labeled as "globalization" is, when examined more closely, a series of very *particular* cultural movements, corporate strategies, and political struggles. These are certainly occurring over space and time and across nation-state boundaries, but they are not quite as "global" as many corporate commentators and academic theorists have suggested.

*I thank Annabelle Sreberny-Mohammadi, Patria Román Velázquez, and Philip Tagg for their encouraging comments, constructive criticisms, and useful suggestions in response to an earlier draft of this chapter.

My argument here is that the "global" repertoire policies initiated by the major entertainment companies do not produce dynamics that can be neatly explained by reference to theories of globalization as an abstract dichotomous homogenizing or fracturing universal force or a "dialectic" of the global and local (and in making this argument, I critique the work of Anthony Giddens who has proposed such a theoretical model). Instead, in this context, globalization involves untidy human struggles over a series of quite specific practices through which attempts are being made to impose and assert a "dominant particular" (Hall, 1991b, p. 67) as a "global" universal. As a consequence, the entertainment companies that are pursuing "global" policies are continually confronting the active responses of different producers and audience groups who are attempting to resist these narrow particulars and generate alternative routes of cultural expression. Research into the particularities and power relations of such struggles might contribute far more to our understanding of specific changes that are happening in the world than the grand universalisms of theories of "globalization."

In the second part of this chapter I move on from this argument and follow some of the tracks as music moves out from the commercial direction of the corporations and its status as commodity and becomes an important medium of transnational communication and a significant form of affective knowledge. In doing this I highlight how music is frequently central to individual lives and collective political struggles and how it is an important element in the creation of distinctive and identifiable public spaces of communicative activity. I do this not only to indicate the power of music as an expressive form of communication, but also to indicate the disjunctures and dislocations between the "globalization" of music within production and its "global" uses as a form of affective knowledge and media of communication in the field of consumption (a lack of fit that indicates that the conventional designations of production/consumption and their assumed theoretical relations are becoming increasingly inadequate for referring to the distribution and social use of musical styles around the world). I introduce these themes in order to contribute to a critique of concepts of the public sphere derived from Habermas (1974, 1989). In particular, I am concerned about the way in which theories of the public sphere neglect significant nonlinguistic areas of contemporary communication while privileging a logocentric view of knowledge and political communicative action. Particularly neglected is popular music, which I suggest can be used to contribute to the formation of spheres of public knowledge that have the potential to be independent of the interests of individual states and irreducible to the boundaries of constructed commercial markets.

GLOBALIZATION AND THE MUSIC INDUSTRY

The term *globalization* has been used in a number of different ways and has been incorporated into various discourses both inside and outside the academy. There are two articulations of the concept that are relevant to my discussion here. First, there is the way that processes of "globalization" have been theorized by Anthony Giddens, who offers important and influential interventions within contemporary social theory that are relevant to my account of how popular music might be an outernational form of communicative cultural expression. Second, there is the way that "globalization" has been adopted as a description of a set of business strategies by entertainment corporations as they pursue ever more consumer markets across the world. What I emphasize here are the similarities in the way that globalization is employed in both discourses, and also the particularities that are elided when this term is used in a rather benign universalistic manner.

In his brief and schematic discussion of processes of globalization in *The Consequences of Modernity* (1990), Giddens notes that this concept indicates a shift away from ideas about a bounded society toward conceptions of how social life is ordered across space and time; distant events are lifted out of their immediate local context and relayed, by the communication media, across the surface of the world to other localities. Giddens, like other writers who have written on this subject (see Featherstone, 1990), has stressed this movement across borders and the concomitant trends toward "cultural globalization" as events are experienced simultaneously across the world and as cultural forms and commodities are consumed concurrently in a variety of geographical locations. With little reference to empirical research, Giddens (1990) presents an abstract and frequently impressionistic account based on the idea of a "dialectic" of globalization moving across the planet. There is little concrete sense of the humans involved in this dialectic. There is no real sense of any disruption to or discontinuities occurring within this process; driven as it is by the "diffusion of machine technologies . . . the global extension of the institutions of modernity . . . [and] . . . the global money markets" (pp. 76-78). Giddens is on spaceship earth, bearing witness as the planet is becoming "one world" (p. 77).

Very similar ideas inform the outlook of senior executives within the music and entertainment industry. Trade magazines and company reports regularly feature discussions of globalization and "global-local" relationships. The industry's own magazine, *Music Business International*, regularly employs the term and spends much space commenting on the "global reality that is changing the face of music" (*Music Business International*, 1993, p. 3). However, for the people actually working in the music business, such abstract ideas about globalization can only have any concrete meaning if they are translated into a series of quite specific working practices and repertoire policies by the corporations involved. I have described some of the "global" operations of the music industry in more detail elsewhere (Negus, 1992, 1993). Here I very briefly summarize what *globalization* concretely involves.

Two distinct but interrelated general practices can be identified: First, the world has been divided into a series of discrete regional territories or market blocs and a number of judgments made about which areas are to be accorded top priority. Such judgments are informed by very particular considerations, the most important being the size of the market (the number of potential consumers and revenue that can be generated), the "penetration" of the technologies of musical reproduction (tape machines and record and CD players), the media systems that can be used for promotion (television, radio, printed word), and the existence of copyright legislation that will ensure that recordings broadcast by the media and played in public will generate rights revenue that will accrue to the corporation. The markets being accorded top priority at the moment are in North America and Europe, with the latter rapidly becoming equally as important as the United States, which has been the industry's main focus of attention for many years.[1]

The second global strategy involves personnel in the central marketing divisions of the corporations assessing the music being produced by the different company labels and subdivisions and drawing up a priority list of "international" repertoire. The term, *international repertoire*, is regularly used by personnel within the record industry, reported in trade reports and corporate publications, and can frequently be found employed in record stores in non-English-speaking countries.[2]

---

[1]For over 30 years the United States has been the most important source of revenue and repertoire for the international recording industry. However, since 1988, the income generated from the sales of recorded music in the European Community (EC) taken as a whole has been creeping above that of the United States. At the time of writing, the most recent figures indicate that retail sales in the EC account for approximately 34%-35%, whereas those of the United States are 31% of the world total (IFPI, 1989, 1991, 1992, 1993a). In a similar way, between 1989-1990, revenues derived from the exploitation of music publishing rights within the EC member states accounted for 55% of the world total, whereas those of the United States were considerably less at 28% (Lightman, 1992). The importance of Europe has also increased since the collapse of the Stalinist regimes of Central and Eastern Europe.

[2]International repertoire does not refer to the same thing as world music, a term that emerged in the 1980s and that was mainly used in the United Kingdom, United States, Canada, Australia, and Japan to refer to an eclectic mixture of non-Anglo-American styles, rhythms, and sounds (initially emerging as a sales category to resolve a marketing dilemma within the entertainment industries— how to construct a market space to place such a diversity of music).

International repertoire signifies a music that is predominantly (but, by no means necessarily) composed of Anglo-American artists who perform pop-rock music that is sung in English. In theory, as long as they fit the criteria, an "international" artist can be drawn from anyplace. As an international marketing director for a major musical entertainment group remarked, anyone can be prioritized as international repertoire "as long as they sing in English without an accent."[3] These are the artists that will be accorded the most investment and have their recordings released simultaneously in all of the major territories of the world. This can be contrasted with "regional repertoire," a secondary list that will contain artists who will be promoted to other more regional audiences (such as Latin America or Southeast Asia), and "domestic repertoire," the lowest priority of recordings that are judged to be suitable for one national territory.[4]

Like the term *global, international repertoire* has come to refer to something that is "international" in one specific sense. It has become a music business euphemism for the recordings of Anglo-American artists singing conventional rock/pop songs in English. The record industry's own statistics and a number of media scholars have highlighted how this Anglo-international repertoire has dominated sales charts and radio playlists throughout the world for a number of years (Hung & Morencos, 1990; IFPI, 1993b; Laing, 1992; Negus, 1993; Robinson, Buck, & Cuthbert, 1991; Wallis & Malm, 1984). This has been particularly so in Europe, in which the introduction of pan-European repertoire policies provides an illustration of the particularity of the global commercial music strategies that are reinforcing this dominance.

CORPORATE COMPOSITIONS: GLOBAL STRATEGIES IN EUROPE

Since the end of the 1980s, the major record companies have been establishing pan-European marketing and repertoire divisions (moving away from a system of semi-autonomous offices in each national territory). The aim is to acquire artists and coordinate the simultaneous release of prioritized recordings across the entire continent. Despite vari-

[3]Personal interview with Mike Allen, International Director, Polygram International, May 11, 1993.

[4]This is a very condensed and simplified summary of record company strategies, drawn from information reported in Music Business International during 1993 and IFPI's Annual Review (1993b), and supported by personal interviews with Stuart Watson, Senior Vice President, MCA Records International (June 9, 1993); Mike Allen, International Director, Polygram International (May 11, 1993); Jonathan Morrish, Director, Corporate Public Relations, Sony Music Entertainment (April 28, 1993); and Hiroshi Kato, Managing Director, LOE Entertainment (June 18, 1993).

ous platitudes about supporting "local" talent, the European continent is increasingly being viewed as one big potential market for the international repertoire of the major entertainment companies. As a result, patterns of investment have shifted in two important ways: first, from signing and producing the music of a large number of local artists to marketing the music of a small number of international stars (Rutten, 1991); and second, from financial decision making distributed across a series of local companies and corporate subdivisions to investment centralized in one regional operations center.

To give just one example of this, in 1991 Sony Music introduced a label called Sony Music Soho Square, which was to operate as the industry's "first ever pan-European repertoire source" (*Music Week*, 1991, p. 1). Not only was the chosen title decidedly English, being named after the company's base in London, the brief of this "pan-European" label was restricted to signing only English-speaking artists in Europe. Although having scouts seeking artists in various European countries, the label was firmly based in London. The label's director explained that when artists were found they would be brought "over to the UK" and developed in London ("A & R World," 1992, p. 22). This is by no means an isolated example; most of the major record companies began to follow suit and started implementing very similar schemes (see Negus, 1993). By the beginning of 1994, for example, Virgin's Spanish subsidiary had no local artists signed to its roster.

What I am outlining here is a process by which the major record companies have been rationalizing in order to set agendas and priorities across existing national divisions and to coordinate the placement of a small number of acts on a panregional (European) scale. Such "global" policies undoubtedly involve the relaying of music and images to distant places and the simultaneous crossing of boundaries (particularly via radio and video)—as globalization theorists like Giddens suggest. However, what I am describing here is a very particular attempt to regulate, order, and control the regional organization of popular music production and consumption. One of the most immediate impacts of such policies is that they impede the prospects for local performers who do not sing in English and privilege artists from Britain and the United States, reinforcing and maintaining the cultural dominance of Anglo-American pop (Wallis & Malm, 1984, 1992). To simply describe such a process as "globalization" (whether as homogenization or as a dialectic between the global and local) is to partially mask or simply ignore the unequal relationships being actively formed across the European continent and beyond. In the first instant, these are quite specific transnational practices (Sklair, 1991) arising from the motivations of transnational corporations.

Such transnational practices have not simply been imposed on hapless producers and consumers, and I do not mean to suggest that the popularity of Anglo-American pop music can be explained simply by reference to the international marketing mechanisms of the entertainment industry. However, musicians are not doing as they please, audiences are not simply getting what they want, and there have been a number of reactions from those who feel excluded by the dominant particular that is being distributed as the "international" in music. First, there have been responses within the music industry. This has often taken the guise of alliances between personnel and groups in different national territories. For example, in 1992, record industry agencies from France, Germany, Ireland, Belgium, The Netherlands, and Denmark formed The European Music Network, with the aim of "maximising cross border exposure" for their national artists (Clark-Meads, 1992, p. 33). In a similar way, the Latin American Federation of Societies of Authors and Composers was formed in 1993 as an alliance of music rights societies from Latin America, Spain, and Portugal, with the explicit aim of challenging the Anglo-American hegemony that permeates the record industry (Llewellyn, 1992).

These two examples are an indication of a struggle that is occurring within the webs of the entertainment industry, a struggle about "global" policies and priorities, about the distribution of investment, about the formation of promotional agendas, and about which genres and artists will ultimately receive the push to become commercially successful. Such struggles are not simply confined to the "local," but are occurring across national boundaries, and, inevitably, they do not stop at the edge of Europe.

These untidy movements within the music industry are occurring at the same time as further series of reactions to such "global" policies are being generated outside (but in relation to) the commercial entertainment industry. In recent years a number of European governments have attempted to support their musicians and music industry. State organizations in France, Denmark, Sweden, and The Netherlands (and, further afield, similar bodies in New Zealand, Australia, and Canada) have been implementing various popular music policies and assisting musicians and bands in producing, distributing, and performing, both nationally and internationally (Bennett, Frith, Grossberg, Shepherd, & Turner, 1993; Malm, 1982; Van Elderen, 1985). Such state initiatives have not simply involved local responses to global movements, although they are certainly part of a process in which vague global strategies are directly confronted and translated into particular practices in specific localities (Negus, 1993). Instead, such responses involve a local, national, and transnational element. That is, state representatives are working locally by providing facilities in specific areas; acting nationally by supporting the development and distribution of national music (whether defined by language or the legal citizenship of its producers) against imported forms of music and "international repertoire"; and operating transnationally by contributing the internationalization of their own nations' repertoires into overseas markets.[5]

What I am referring to here are particular transnational practices. These may well involve the "re-ordering of social life across space and time" and the intensification of worldwide social relations which, as Giddens (1990, p. 64) argues, link distant localities in such a way that local happenings are shaped by events occurring many miles away, and vice versa. However, far from this being due to the "dialectical character of globalization" (p. 67), driven by the abstract forces of modernity, this is an asymmetrical conflict-ridden process that involves quite specific power struggles that arise due to corporate attempts to construct and pursue quite partial "global" practices that then result in opposition both within and without the corporation. The way that the dominant particulars of globalization are being resisted and contested, and the way in which a phenomenological experience of cultural subordination is frequently articulated during such struggles, suggests that these practices involve more than residual or rhetorical elements of a struggle over "cultural imperialism"; it is, perhaps, "not yet the post-imperialist era" (Schiller, 1991). It may well be a difficult job to identify whose or which culture is involved and to untangle the threads that become woven together when these cultural forms are received, interpreted, and appropriated during the exchanges between different companies, audiences, and musicians. It seems premature, however, to avoid this difficult task by making a conceptual shift to the abstract dialectal forces of modernity and globalization, as Giddens (1990) and Tomlinson (1991) do, and a shift away from an analysis of forms of cultural domination that are directly connected to (but not reducible to or simply determined by) the changing organizations of contemporary capitalism.

Further questions about the simplicity of the dialectical abstractions of globalization theory can be raised by reference to two of the central conceptual terms employed by Giddens (1990) in his discussion of this process: disembedding and reembedding. *Disembedding* refers to "the lifting out of social relations from local contexts of interaction and their restructuring across indefinite spans of time-space" (p. 21). In contrast, *reembedding* refers to "the reappropriation or recasting of disembedded social relations so as to pin them down (however partially or transitorily) to local conditions of time and place" (pp. 79-80).

Some aspects of the processes I have been describing could be viewed as processes of disembedding and reembedding, that is, entertainment corporations seek to commandeer and generate revenue from

[5]The French Music Office has been doing this in the United States; and Australian government bodies have been assisting their artists in the United States and in Southeast Asia, for example.

particular forms of music and promote it as international repertoire across time and space (disembedding), whereas local audiences and musicians respond by "pinning down" their own music, and in doing so emphasize the local and the particular in opposition to the global, the international, and the disembedded. Therefore, these metaphors do provide a way of characterizing actual processes that are occurring, and I do not dismiss Giddens' work in toto on the basis of my own partial critique here.

However, these metaphors provide little explanation of the particular human dynamics and power relationships involved. Giddens's (1990) largely abstract discussion of "disembedding mechanisms" (operating in conjunction with "expert systems" and "abstract systems") gives the process a rather mechanical quality, with any sense of real human struggles rather absent. When he refers to nation-states as "actors" and corporations as "agents" (p. 71), it gives the impression that they are mysteriously moving and thinking with one undivided "body." One of the main points I have sought to make here is that it is within the webs of the corporation where the struggles and negotiations occur, as capitalistic corporations adopt, implement, and struggle to impose very particular "global" practices in very specific regional contexts. It at this point that a whole range of individuals and groups challenge or oppose such activities. It is these struggles that lead corporations to become agents in any meaningful manner. It is these practical activities and not the abstract movement of modernity that are "globalizing" the world. It is here that detailed research into such struggles could contribute much to our understanding of the very particular, concrete, and clumsy ways in which the "dialectic of globalization" is being moved across the planet and raise questions about just who is doing the pushing. Such research might reveal that the dialectic of disembedding and reembedding is not quite so symmetrical and that there is more than an interaction between yet another new binary opposition (the global and the local) at work here.

Those who have been trying to keep track of the movement of music have had difficulty confining music to particular localities and have been confronted with the way that music is continually on the move (Chambers, 1993; Lipsitz, 1994). No sooner has a music emerged from a subcultural group (Hebdige, 1979) to be coopted by the entertainment corporations (Chapple & Garofalo, 1977) than it is turned into part of the national heritage and used to promote tourism, and then it escapes and becomes part of the vernacular fabric of everyday life.[6] It is this shift that

---

[6]I am thinking here of the Beatles, whose music moved, in the space of 30 years, from leather-clad rockers in the clubs of Hamburg's red-light district to the executive suites of EMI and the corridors of Buckingham Palace, and now accompanies wax works dummies on Liverpool's heritage dockside. The Beatles' songs, meanwhile, have become part of British everyday vernacular, played in pubs and at children's birthday parties and whistled by window cleaners.

provides clues as to how popular music might escape from the regimes of corporate "globalization" and provide intimations of possibilities for the creation of alternative transnational public spheres.

POPULAR MUSIC AS TRANSNATIONAL KNOWLEDGE AND AFFECTIVE COMMUNICATION

In their studies of music making in various countries around the world, Wallis and Malm (1992) have indicated how vast amounts of music are produced and consumed "below the national level of government and corporate activities" (p. 22). Such everyday musical activities do not confine themselves to specific localities, but carve out and follow a number of "pathways" (Finnegan, 1989). Some of these have been traced by Michael Pickering (1987) when following the movement of specific songs through time and across the spaces of everyday life between the 17th and 19th centuries in Britain. Hints of the variety of contemporary routes being taken by music are registered as the sounds of a collective of amateur musicians from the small English city of St. Albans were exchanged in solidarity with Romanian musicians immediately after the fall of Ceaucescu during 1990 (Johnson, personal interview, December 3, 1990). These hints are also are apparent in the mutual visits, exchanges of recordings, and combined performances involving musicians from Ireland and Turkey exploring the Arabic influences on both musics (Stokes, 1991); and manifested in the way in which Welsh musical enthusiasts have been distributing recordings, paying visits, and forming links with other Celtic regions across Europe for a number of years (Wallis & Malm, 1992).

Such examples provide only the merest hint of the "invisible" activities engaged in by "amateur" singers, musicians, and their audiences. Such practices frequently do not correspond to the interests of the entertainment industry. For this reason, they often remain hidden— invisible and inaudible (see Finnegan, 1989; Fornäs, 1993). This is an important but under-researched and theoretically neglected area of communicative activity and social practice. It is here, in the "hidden" world of everyday music making, where sounds move beyond their commercial commodity status and slide between the spaces that open up between the local, the national, and the global. Here music is continually being used to create a series of "affective alliances" (Grossberg, 1992). These alliances constitute pan-regional spheres of communication that are outside of nation-state regimes and not reducible to the commercial marketing categories of the music business. Such alliances have the potential to have a direct impact on politics and culture.

To argue that music is powerful—politically and culturally—is not particularly new; a recognition of the political power of music goes back at least to Plato, and the 20th century has witnessed the banning of music by political regimes in Stalin's USSR, Nazi Germany, and Pinochet's Chile (Tagg, 1990). In Anglo-American theorizing since the 1960s, much has been written about the potential political and cultural influence of rock music, whether used by hippy radicals (Street, 1986), youth subcultures during the 1970s (Willis, 1978), or by those seeking to impose censorship on music during the 1980s (Cloonan, 1991; Grossberg, 1992). Much of this has concerned the symbolic role of music. Here I wish to emphasize the explicitly material way in which music can operate as an "affective" form of political communication and knowledge. In pursuing this line of thought, I draw on Lawrence Grossberg's (1992) argument that music works at the intersection of the body and emotions, generating affective alliances between people that in turn create the energy for social change. Such affective alliances do not operate according to liberal bourgeois democratic political theory, nor do they correspond to the rationale of conventional political movements. But the affective empowerment that is generated does provide the potential for optimism and political change. Grossberg argues that such alliances are increasingly important in a world in which pessimism has

> become common sense, in which people increasingly feel incapable of making a difference . . . affective relations are, at least potentially, the condition of possibility for the optimism, invigoration and passion which are necessary for any struggle to change the world. (p. 86)

A number of writers have identified this potential energy emerging on an everyday level, as music escapes its narrow definition as a commodity and provides forms of empowerment (Chambers, 1985; Gilroy, 1993b). It has also been apparent in more dramatic and revolutionary political struggles and social changes. An indication of music being used in this way was apparent during the events in the former German Democratic Republic (East Germany) that led to the breaking down of the Berlin Wall.

In the GDR, under the previous Stalinist regimes, music was heavily censored and regulated. In 1965, Erich Honecker, then Chief of National Security, had deemed that rock music was not compatible with the goals of a socialist society, as part of a general regime of cultural repression particular sounds were effectively banned.[7] As a result, the performance and transmission of specific musical sounds became a non-linguistic, nonrepresentational way of communicating opposition to the

---

[7]It should be noted that this policy was implemented with varying degrees of ambiguity, with the state providing and then withdrawing organizational support for various forms of rock music at certain periods during the 1970s.

system. Peter Wicke's (1991, 1992a, 1992b) illuminating work on the role of rock music in the former GDR indicates that the music that was created by musicians and shared by their audiences played a vital role in communicating ideas of solidarity and building resistance. By being a central element in the organization of private, underground, and public events, music became integral to the articulation of opposition and generated an affective sense of solidarity, the solidarity that was so visible in the broadcast scenes that accompanied the breaking-down of the Wall. By improvising performances on trailers or trucks in public places and by distributing sonorial material within the state and across its borders into surrounding territories (via illegally produced recordings and broadcasts), rock musicians were able to operate as cultural catalysts, mediating cultural values that symbolically and materially challenged the system. Rock music did not "smash the wall" (Pekacz, 1994), but it did provide an important means of communicating dissent and forming alliances that in turn connected with broader political struggles at the time.

Much more could be written about the role of music in the changes in the GDR. In my brief reference to these events here, however, I want to draw two points from Wicke's (1992a) observations: My first point concerns the way that music communicates. Wicke observes that:

> Music is a medium which is able to convey meaning and values which—even (or, perhaps, particularly) if hidden within the indecipherable world of sound—can shape patterns of behaviour imperceptibly over time until they become the visible background of real political activity. (p. 81)

It is this "intangible" presence of music as a form of affective communication that has so often been acknowledged in everyday discourse, but frequently neglected in studies of the media due to the apparent nonreferentiality of music and the way it seems to operate at the level of the "phatic and the ineffable" (Gilroy, 1993a).[8] It is partly this aspect that makes music difficult to tie down—to embed, in Gidden's language—and contributes to its ability to keep on the move.

Wicke (1992b) also describes how cheap radio receivers were used as amplifiers in order to create a form of "publicity" that was outside of the control of the state. Here Wicke's reference to publicity need not simply be understood in the same way as product promotion or marketing. Instead, it bears a relation to a conception of publicity as employed in Enlightenment thought from Kant to Habermas. This is publicity as a critical principle that can make a direct contribution to public knowledge.

---

[8]For an analysis of how music encodes and communicates quite specific cultural meanings, see Tagg (1990).

As John Thompson (1993) observed, "The critical principle of publicity is the idea that the personal opinions of private individuals could evolve into a public opinion through a process of rational-critical debate which was open to all and free from domination" (p. 178). Wicke does not make this connection overtly, but this principle of publicity is of direct relevance to discussions that have derived from Jürgen Habermas's concept of the public sphere as a space in which dialogic communication can be conducted that is free from both state and commercial interests. This seems particularly relevant to the way that music is continually used for mediating public communication and private experience outside of and across the strictures of the state and constructions of the commercial markets. Music generates a public form of knowledge and a mode of understanding that is shared by vast numbers of people; these are people who know that the meanings of music are not *that* indecipherable.

Throughout this chapter I have been drawing on Paul Gilroy's evocative arguments about the importance of music within the counter-discourses that have opposed the particular forms of communication privileged by modern bourgeois rationality. This is vividly illustrated in his work on the formation of identities within the Black diaspora. Tracing the enduring resonances of the terror of slavery within the Black diaspora of the Atlantic world, Gilroy (1993a) has made the important point that:

> Access to literacy was often denied on the point of death and only a few opportunities were offered as a poor surrogate for the other forms of individual autonomy denied by life on the plantations and in the barracoons. Music becomes vital at the point at which linguistic and semantic indeterminacy/polyphony arise amidst the protracted battle between masters, mistresses and slaves. . . . Music, the grudging gift that supposedly compensated slaves not only for their exile from the ambiguous legacies of practical reason but for their complete exclusion from modern political society, has been refined and developed so that it provides an enhanced mode of communication beyond the petty power of words—spoken or written. (pp. 74-76)

Gilroy has traced how, for many years, music has operated beyond the boundaries of the nation state as a transnational, pan-regional form of cultural communication. It has provided diverse populations of Black people with a vision of the future based on the "politics of fulfillment" (rather than the "rational" teleologies of liberal bourgeois politics). It has provided an affective form of communication that is not simply subjective, intuitive, and irrational, but that generates forms of "counterrationality," which in turn create affiliations, alliances, and understanding among dispersed and diverse groups of people. Gilroy has shown that within the Atlantic triangle of Africa, the Americas, the Caribbean, and

Europe, music has been a significant means of articulating and communicating experiences, and that in the process it has transformed the cultural life of both Black and White citizens of Europe. Gilroy's work is suggestive of the way that musical forms directly contribute to "intercultural conversations," yet such dialogues have received little acknowledgment in contemporary debates about the public sphere. It is to this point that I now turn.

POPULAR MUSIC AND THE POSSIBILITY
OF A TRANSNATIONAL PUBLIC SPHERE

Contemporary theories of globalization and the public sphere are based on a number of assumptions and claims about contemporary culture and the modern communication media. My focus here is inevitably only on one particular aspect of these assumptions, and to pursue this I return to Giddens (1990), who in discussing the globalizing impact of modernity, identifies culture as fundamental and the mass media as central. However, in his brief allusion to the "cultural globalization" generated by the mass media, he refers only to the print media, the growth of mass circulation newspapers, and "the pooling of knowledge which is represented by the 'news'" (p. 78). This is a narrow definition of public knowledge, but it is one that can be found frequently among those writers who have drawn on Habermas's concept of the public sphere to develop a prescriptive politics for the communications media.

In Habermas's (1974, 1989) formulation, the public sphere is an area of social life in which "something approaching public opinion can be formed" (1974); access is guaranteed to all citizens, the freedom of assembly and the freedom to express opinions is guaranteed, and all citizens are able to engage in communication and dialogue without coercion or constraint. Habermas's concept has taken on a particular relevance for communication researchers because the public sphere is explicitly about communication and the media: "Newspapers and magazines, radio and television are the media of the public sphere" (1974, p. 49).

Although acknowledging the limitations of this approach and the need for "reconstruction,"[9] a number of writers agree that the concept of the public sphere is useful for developing a democratic politics that might

---

[9]The concept of the public sphere has been subject to a number of criticisms: the accuracy of Habermas's version of the historical emergence and subsequent decay of a public sphere has been questioned and the concept has been criticized for its gender bias, its privileging of public discourse over private, and its lack of attention to nonbourgeois public spheres (see Calhoun, 1992; Dahlgren & Sparks, 1991; Hohendahl, 1979).

be exercised through media that are free from the constraints of both the state and the market (Calhoun, 1992; Dahlgren & Sparks, 1991; Garnham, 1990; Hjarvard, 1993).

Yet, in referring to a media permeated with nonlinguistic images and sounds, there has been a tendency to uncritically follow Habermas's emphasis on speech and language as the means of communication for reaching an understanding through dialogue. As a result, what is continually emphasized and predominates in such arguments is a logocentric model of communication based on rational discourse that in turn explicitly privileges the work of journalists in the print media and broadcast news (Curran, 1991a; Dahlgren, 1991; Garnham, 1990).

Such an orientation involves a very narrow conception of contemporary knowledge, information and communication. As John Durham Peters (1993) has pointed out, "Habermas prizes conversation, reading and plain speech as worthy forms of discourse for a democratic culture and is frankly hostile to theatre, courtly forms, ceremony, the visual and to rhetoric more generally" (p. 562).

Musicologist Philip Tagg (1990, 1992) has made a similar point about the historical neglect of musical knowledge and music as communication. Tagg has highlighted how, within the European enlightenment tradition of Western thought, a conception of knowledge has developed that is logocentric and excludes major aspects of nonverbal (gestural, sonic, and visual) communication. Taking television as a favorite site for studies of the media, Tagg notes how television has been identified as one of the most important mediums providing messages influencing political, economic, and cultural activity. Yet what is so often ignored when television broadcasts are analyzed by media scholars is the music.[10]

Music is pervasive in everyday lives across the world. Its sounds range from the subtle and carefully researched use of tones in shopping malls to the improvised appropriations of melodies and songs that are collectively chanted at sporting events. For many years, election rallies, party broadcasts, and political events have had their associated imagery and music, songs, and anthems (whether broadcast or not). Yet, communication researchers have often merely focused on the verbal delivery of the words and the reporting of the "issues." As Peters (1993) has argued, what is frequently missing is a "conception of communication, appreciative of its gloriously raucous as well as its soberly informative qualities" (p. 567). Such elements remain underintegrated into arguments about contemporary communication due to residues of an anachronistic and elitist model of knowledge that continues to make a distinction between "information" and "entertainment" (Garnham, 1992),

---

[10]P. Tagg & R. Clarida (n.d.). For details contact P. Tagg, Institute of Popular Music, PO Box 147, University of Liverpool, Liverpool L69 3BX, UK.

with the consequence of privileging the institutionalized "rational" public discourse of the liberal bourgeois classes of the industrialized West.

The producers and consumers of pop music, however, have frequently recognized the communicative power of the "gloriously raucous," particularly when harnessed to global mass-mediated events such as the Live Aid concerts that raised awareness about famine in Ethiopia and similar broadcast events that helped change the political climate that resulted in the release of Nelson Mandela. Such mega-events are certainly not autonomous from states or markets and have to be created between the contours of multiple state broadcasting organizations and political systems of government. They also have to continually negotiate the attempts at incorporation posed by the music and entertainment industry (Garofalo, 1992). But the creation and impact of these events cannot simply be reduced to the influence of either state or commercial interests. It is at such moments when the potentials for a gloriously raucous transnational space of communication are vividly apparent, but underrealized.

In his introduction to a collection of readings on the public sphere, Dahlgren (1991) has called for a more "nuanced understanding of the limits and possibilities of meaning production and circulation . . . [to] avoid such pitfalls as assuming cardboard cut-out versions of 'rational man' (p. 9). My concluding call is for such a nuanced view to incorporate an understanding of the way in which a variety of musics communicate within and across a transnational public space or multiple overlapping and interacting public and private spheres. Of course, the spaces created by the movement of music are not simply "public." The transnational movement of music continually connects the private politics of affective emotional communication with the public declarations of collective desire. And, as Nancy Fraser (1992) has observed, the terms *private* and *public* are not transparent categories of social life, but culturally constructed rhetorical labels.

A more nuanced approach to such affective communication would also need to acknowledge that music is significantly different from other forms of mass communication such as the newspaper, book, film, and television broadcast. Not only is music less dependent on language[11] or reliant on formal education and the acquisition of a sophisticated body of knowledge, but it is based on forms of affective expression and communication (antiphony, rhythm, timbre, paralinguistic vocal expressions, etc.) that have been shaped by musical technologies, techniques, and cultural (ex)changes that have occurred as a result of the movement and meeting of various diasporas long before it became an electronically

---

[11]Lyrics are always performances and affective utterances that do not simply communicate as words (see Frith, 1987).

reproduced and commodified media form associated with the entertainment media of the "West" (Goodwin & Gore, 1990). These elements have not simply disappeared, but too often they are not heard or are forced from earshot by dismissive condemnations of "Western" pop music. Noisily offensive to the rather genteel version of communicative discourse advocated by Habermas and those who follow his line, it may perhaps be these very elements that allow popular music to communicate across cultural, political, and geographical boundaries so effectively.

If a less culturally encoded (Peters, 1993) and less politically exclusive praxis of knowledge creation and public communication is needed, then perhaps it is time we started listening more closely to the music of the public spheres.

9

International News Agency Coverage of the Rio Earth Summit

C. Anthony Giffard
University of Washington

The United Nations Conference on Environment and Development (UNCED) that took place in Rio de Janeiro in June 1992 was the largest international conference ever held. The meeting had two broad goals: to focus the world's attention on environmental concerns, and to set forth an agenda to achieve sustainable development. It was attended by more than 100 heads of state from developed and developing nations. Tens of thousands of people attended the Earth Summit itself, or the parallel non-governmental organization (NGO) conference called Global Forum. Hundreds of NGOs were represented, ranging from well-known international organizations like Greenpeace to little-known local groups in Third World countries. An estimated 8,000 journalists reported on the event for individual media organizations or for the news agencies that provided the bulk of the coverage (USIA World, 1993).

This was the first major international conference since the end of the Cold War. East-West tensions had largely faded into history; the former Soviet Union, preoccupied with its own internal problems, was not a major player. The conference was one of the first to articulate the concept that many problems facing mankind are planetary in scope and cannot be solved by traditional diplomacy that pits nations or regions against one another. Despite the realization that cooperation rather than competition was required, however, a new concern was about North-South tensions, between the wealthy industrialized countries and the relatively poor nations of the developing world.

Central to the concept of what Hamelink calls the "global civil society" (Hamelink, 1991) is the belief that problematic issues such as human rights, peace, social justice, and the global environment affect everyone. With the end of the Cold War, the environment emerged as a potential lever for developing countries seeking to obtain the levels of aid, investment, and access to rich-country markets to which they felt entitled. For the North, protection of the environment—particularly saving tropical rain forests to absorb carbon dioxide produced mainly in the industrialized countries, and as a genetic reservoir—was the major goal. The South, however, asserted it had a right to make economic use of its resources and should not have to make sacrifices to compensate for excessive growth and consumption in the North (Petesch, 1992). Its concern was development and the extent to which the North was willing to pay for measures taken in the South to mitigate global environmental degradation (Hurrell & Kingsbury, 1992).

The environmental movement is convinced that "the world's resources are limited, that gross inequalities and injustice bring not only suffering to millions of human beings, but catastrophe to the environment. It recognizes that environmental depletion in one part of the world inevitably takes its toll in other parts. In short, it pictures the world as one" (Paul & Savio, 1993, p. 1). Inevitably, however, the issues were also seen in terms of nationalistic interests. "This is about sharing power," said Rizali Ismail, Malaysia's ambassador to the United Nations and a leading spokesman for the Third World perspective:

> When it was East versus West, our development needs were ignored unless you were a marionette of the Soviet Union or the United States. Now with the environment seriously frightening many people in comfortable paradise areas, for the first time people are taking us seriously. That is leverage, and we are not bashful about using this. ("North and South," 1992, p. A3)

These issues have drawn the attention of concerned citizens, often banded into nongovernmental organizations, who are using new communications technologies to set up worldwide networks for the exchange of information and ideas. Foremost among the organizations facilitating this interchange is the Association for Progressive Communications (APC), which connects community leaders, activists and opinion shapers in almost 100 nations through a network of computers. Prior to and during the Rio Earth Summit, dozens of environmental groups used APC to share information about the preparatory meetings, the Earth Summit itself and the Global Forum. The focus of much of this information exchange was on cooperative, multinational efforts to alleviate global environmental problems.

The discussions on the computer networks tended to downplay regional differences and focused instead on cooperative solutions. For the general public, however, news about the conference came not from computer networks but from the news media. Furthermore, traditional news values typically dictate an emphasis on conflict rather than collaboration. This study examines news agency coverage to determine whether there were significant differences in reporting on the Earth Summit by major agencies based in different regions and, more specifically:

1. Did the agencies generally present environmental issues as global problems needing global solutions, or did their reports reflect the traditional news values of conflict?
2. Which geographic regions received the bulk of the coverage, and which individual nations featured most prominently?
3. Were both Western and Third World actors and sources covered?
4. Which issues, documents, and treaties received the most attention?

These questions are particularly germane in light of a recent national survey of journalists in the United States, which found that despite the public's growing concern with the environment, most journalists admit that they do not do a good job of covering it. The study reported that fewer than 1 in 10 journalists say the press is perceived by the general public as a "very good" source of unbiased environmental information (Foundation for American Communications, 1993).

MEDIA AND THE ENVIRONMENT

Media interest in the environment is a relatively recent phenomenon. Schoenfeld, Meier, and Griffin (1979) argue that, before 1969, newspapers were slow to recognize "environmentalism"—a contention supported by the findings of Brookes, Jordan, Kimber, and Richardson (1976). Einsiedel and Coughlan (1993) pointed out that there has been a noticeable oscillation of media interest in the environment over the past 35 years, but that coverage generally has shifted from local issues to a more global orientation. After the heightened attention during the late

1960s and early 1970s, interest in the environment leveled off, and the issue lay fallow until the late 1980s (Hansen, 1991, 1993; Lowe & Morrison, 1984). Interest in the environment picked up again after the "dark years" of the Reagan presidency, and then, in the early 1990s, media attention seemed to be falling off again (Hansen, 1993; McClellan, 1992; Stocking & Leonard, 1990).

Although media interest may have been sporadic over the last three decades, there have been notable—although not necessarily laudable—trends in the nature of the environmental coverage. Examining the relationship between social movements and the press, Kielbowicz and Scherer (1986) found that the relationship was influenced by elements of the newsmaking process: the media's preference for dramatic events, the journalists' reliance on authoritative sources, the deployment of media resources and the rhythms of news, the values of the journalism profession, and media competition. Similarly, some argue that environmental coverage is "guided more by the traditional determinants of news and the availability of dramatic visual images than by the scientific degree of risk of the situation involved" (Greenberg, Sachsman, Sandman, & Salomone, 1989).

Reporting on the environment tends to be dramatic and event focused (Einsiedel & Coughlan, 1993; Friedman, 1991; Wilkins & Patterson, 1987). Journalists covering the topic rely on authoritative sources, focusing their attentions on organized bases of environmental activity (Corbett, 1992; Cottle, 1993; Hungerford & Lemert, 1973). The rhythms of the news (Schoenfeld et al., 1979; Stocking & Leonard, 1990) and the demands of "objectivity" (Dennis, 1991) put constraints on both the choice of stories as well as the manner in which they are covered.

Proximity may also play a role. Hungerford and Lemert (1973) contend that journalists generally write about environmental problems "just up the road apiece," and Cottle (1993) found a direct relationship between spatial distance and the amount of coverage. The further a story moved from the local setting, the less coverage it received from television news. However, Einsiedel and Coughlan (1993) argue that there has been an increase in the use of the global context with regard to environmental problems, and Gersh (1992) points out that global issues are diverting attention from more pressing local environmental problems.

Environmental coverage, like other types of reporting, is often characterized by conflict between nations or individuals. Because "the media still value people and ideas in conflict more than conditions and trends that are omnipresent" (Dennis, 1991, p. 60), environmental coverage often is reduced to "a conflict of authorities and even personalities quoted in the media" (Burnham, 1991, p. 40). Unable to explain the scientific and political complexities associated with a given environmental problem (Wilkins & Patterson, 1987), and similarly unable to investigate the interconnections between issues (Stocking & Leonard, 1990), the environment becomes a personality conflict, and environmental stories "little more than informational dumps into which the reporter unloads quotes" (Stocking & Leonard, 1990, p. 37).

Environmental journalism contains little science (Dunwoody & Griffin, 1993), little information concerning the costs and benefits associated with a given issue (Wilkins & Patterson, 1990), and little of the information necessary to mobilize against a problem (Hungerford & Lemert, 1973). Furthermore, although environmental stories are often reduced to personal conflict—tree huggers versus loggers—the framing of those conflicts generally supports the status quo. On the coverage of wildlife issues, Corbett (1992) found the newspaper reader receives "an extremely one-sided viewpoint that strongly reinforces the current wildlife management system" (p. 936). Similarly, coverage of the Superfund sites was framed according to the "interpretation championed by the prevailing power structure" (Dunwoody & Griffin, 1993, p. 48). More generally, Stocking and Leonard (1990) argue that coverage of the environment simply fails to challenge the conventional wisdom: Recycling, not reduced consumption, is "the answer."

Anders Hansen (1993) holds that the importance of the media's coverage of environmental issues lies not in its (questionable) ability to describe the reality of current environmental circumstance, but rather in the "insights into the power of different groupings in society to define what should be the focus of public concern" (p. xvi).

Finally, some scholars argue that by focusing their attentions on the established power structure, "the media have failed to notice the environmental problems that are of particular consequence to poor and minority communities" (LeMay & Dennis, 1991, p. xviii). In international terms, they have ignored the issues of concern to the developing nations of the Third World (Bendix & Liebler, 1991; Hansen, 1993). Coverage of these concerns is a major focus of this paper.

Environmental Issues in Rio

Among the issues on the table in Rio was Agenda 21, a blueprint for financial resources and methods to implement the Rio Declaration. The nonbinding proclamation on environmental rights and responsibilities is intended to guide environmental policy. Agenda 21 is a plan of action for protecting the environment while encouraging development through the 21st century. The 800-page document includes chapters on biodiversity, global warming, population growth, toxic waste, ocean pollution, desertification, women's rights, energy efficiency, and funding mechanisms that would enable poorer nations to promote development without damaging the environment. At issue here was how much aid developed countries should provide, and who should decide how it should be allocated.

Another issue that was discussed was the Convention on Biological Diversity, a binding pact to address the high rate of extinction of plants and animals and maintain the diversity of species. It also stipulates that countries of origin of genetic materials used in industry should share in the profits. To the Third World, this represented the possibility of being paid for conserving their resources. The U.S. refused to sign at the time on the grounds that the treaty would hurt U.S. industry and cost American jobs.

A further issue discussed was the Convention on Climate Change, a treaty urging a reduction in the emission of carbon dioxide and other "greenhouse" gases that are thought to be responsible for global warming. The U.S. signed the treaty, but only after ensuring that its language did not commit industrialized nations to measures that could hurt their economies while reducing greenhouse gas emissions.

Also discussed was a statement on forest principles, an outline of principles and methods aimed at encouraging conservation in tropical, temperate, and northern forests. The industrialized countries focused on preservation of tropical rain forests, whereas developing nations wanted regeneration of temperate forests. To developing nations, forests are resources ripe for exploitation as potential farm land and sources of fuel and exotic timber that can command high prices as exports. To the industrial countries, they are a treasure trove of biodiversity and greenhouse gas sinks.

A major concern in each instance was money. Third World nations wanted a commitment from the West to provide 0.7% of their GNP for foreign development aid by the year 2000. The industrialized nations rejected a specific figure and deadline. Also at issue was the amount of money to be donated to two World Bank organs: the International Development Association and the Global Environmental Facility (GEF). Third World nations resented the GEF—a special fund set up in 1990 for financing biological diversity, water quality, and climactic stability—because of a perception that it was controlled by the World Bank, which in turn was dominated by industrialized countries (Hawkins, 1993). They wanted democratization of the operating and decision-making practices of the GEF, and insisted that it not place political or other conditions on development aid.

METHOD

The study covers the period May 13 through June 14, 1992, that is, two weeks prior to the Summit and the conference itself. Before mid-May there was very little coverage by the major news agencies. Interest dropped off sharply once the talks ended and the world leaders went home. We examined every report that mentioned the Summit in its lead paragraph and ran during that four-week period on four international news agencies. They were the New York-based Associated Press (AP), the New York Times News Service, the London-based Reuters news agency World Wire, and the English-language world service of Inter Press Service (IPS). IPS, which specializes in news about the developing world, is widely used in parts of Africa, Asia, Europe, and Latin America. The texts were studied using TEXTPACK, a computerized content analysis package, and the Statistical Package for the Social Sciences (SPSS).

The wire services carried a large number of reports. Over the period we examined, Reuters ran 167 reports (70,111 words) about the conference, the New York Times News Service ran 69 reports (59,526 words), and the AP ran 102 reports (48,990 words). The IPS English Service carried 85 reports (46,394 words). IPS had a major role at the conference in addition to its news agency function. It published a daily newspaper for delegates about conference proceedings called *Terra Viva*, with a circulation of 40,000 copies in English and Spanish. Much of the material in the paper was distributed to IPS subscribers over the daily wire services.

FINDINGS

Agreement or Conflict

To determine whether the agencies saw the conference in terms of a collaborative effort in solving environmental problems or a zero-sum game in which gains by one side would have to be made at the expense of the other, we examined the proportions of words that expressed either agreement or conflict. We calculated the frequencies of all words used in the texts and compiled from those a thesaurus of the 30 most frequently used words indicative of cooperation and a corresponding number indicating disagreement. Those suggesting agreement included such verb forms as *accepted, adopted, negotiated, promised, shared, solved,* and *succeeded.* Those indicating disagreement included such words as *accused, argued, attacked, criticized, demanded, opposed,* and *warned.* The total number of occurrences of these words was 1,107.

The results showed some significant differences among the agencies. IPS had the highest proportion of "positive" verbs (61.2%). The New York Times News Service was the second most positive, at 55.6%. Both the AP (43.7% positive) and Reuters (44.8% positive) put more emphasis on conflict than cooperation. The positive verbs that occurred most frequently were *adopted, agreed, approved,* and *signed.* Most of these occurred in the context of nations ratifying the various treaties. The most frequent negative verbs were *criticized, opposed, refused,* and *warned.* Much of the conflict had to do with funding. According to Reuters, for example, the Third World "demanded" $600 billion a year to implement environmental programs that would curb tropical deforestation and preserve biodiversity. The West, Reuters reported, was "horrified" by these numbers. There was, said the AP, a "fierce battle" when the industrialized nations wanted to channel all environmental aid through the Global Environment Facility, whereas developing nations wanted a vehicle more responsive to their needs.

Individual nations and regions often were depicted as being either supportive or hostile to the conference's aims. Germany, Denmark, the Netherlands and Japan, in particular, were praised for their pledges to increase development aid and to curb emissions of greenhouse gases. The United States was singled out as being obstructive and isolated (even by sources quoted on the AP and New York Times services) for resisting specific limits on carbon dioxide emissions and for refusing to sign the biodiversity treaty. Malaysia, India, Brazil, and China were reported as being the most obdurate in opposing any curbs on logging in tropical forests without adequate compensation from the industrialized world.

Coverage of Developed and Developing Areas

As can be seen in Figure 9.1, IPS had the most balanced coverage of developed and developing areas. This was determined by having the computer count each mention of a country in the entire file, and code countries into developmental categories. Thus, nations in Europe, North America and Japan were coded as developed; the rest of Asia, Africa, the Middle East, Latin America and the Caribbean as developing.

IPS was the only one of the four agencies to refer more often to developing than developed nations. It also had the highest proportion of references to the United Nations system.

Nongovernment Organizations

NGOs based in the developed world, and particularly the United States, were referred to far more often than those in developing nations. Greenpeace drew the most attention with a string of press releases and confrontational stunts. Other U.S.-based groups, such as the World

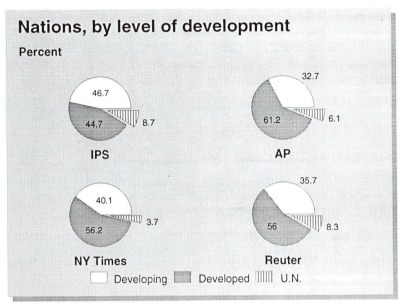

Figure 9.1. Nations, by level of development

Wildlife Fund, Friends of the Earth, and Conservation International, also attracted a lot more agency coverage than Brazil's Planeta Famea, the Philippine Green Forum, or the Third World Network. Most references to these organizations were in the context of the Global Forum, which attracted significantly less attention than the official, intergovernmental Earth Summit itself. Little attempt was made to analyze the significance of these NGOs in articulating and agitating for ecological reform. The best coverage of the NGO activities appeared in two publications put out for the benefit of conference delegates: *Earth Summit Times*, a foundation-sponsored venture; and *Terra Viva*, a daily newspaper produced by IPS. The concept of a global civil society was not mentioned in the agency reports we studied.

Regional Coverage

In terms of specific geographic regions covered, there again was a clear difference between the agencies, as shown in Figure 9.2. Whereas the AP and New York Times mentioned North America (the United States and to a much lesser extent Canada) more often than any other region, and Reuters paid the most attention to European nations, IPS paid less attention to Europe and North America, and more to Africa, Asia and to the United Nations. More specifically, Table 9.1 lists the nations that were mentioned most frequently. Among the top dozen nations on the AP and Reuters services, seven are developed countries. Only three developed countries—the United States, Japan, and Britain—appear among the top dozen nations on IPS. The figures in parentheses are the number of references.

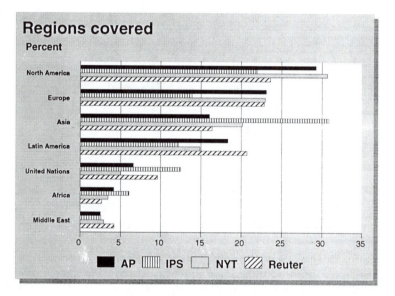

Figure 9.2. Regions covered

Table 9.1.

IPS		AP		Reuters	
U.S.	(224)	U.S.	(366)	U.S.	(347)
U.N.	(136)	Brazil	(135)	Brazil	(194)
Japan	(81)	U.N.	(89)	U.N.	(163)
China	(33)	Japan	(64)	Japan	(76)
Brazil	(25)	Germany	(29)	Britain	(60)
Britain	(21)	Switzerland	(21)	Germany	(51)
India	(20)	Britain	(32)	Israel	(22)
Philippines	(16)	France	(22)	Malaysia	(18)
Caribbean	(15)	India	(10)	China	(15)
Pakistan	(15)	Netherlands	(99)	Colombia	(12)
Venezuela	(12)	Austria	(8)	France	(12)

Actors and Sources

Only named individuals were coded as actors and sources in this study, not nations or organizations. Altogether, more than 500 different names of people appeared in the combined files of the four agencies as actors or sources or commonly both. Most of these, however, were people who were mentioned once or twice in a single story—"person-on-the-street" interviews, quotations from individual ecologists, economists, indigenous people such as rain forest Indians, and assorted academics and spokesmen for various groups. We counted the number of times each individual was mentioned by name. A handful of actors accounted for by far the majority of the references.

The most frequently mentioned newsmaker was U.S. President George Bush, whose name appeared 664 times on the combined files. Second was William Reilly, administrator of the U.S. Environment Protection Agency and head of the U.S. delegation in Rio. He was mentioned 237 times, not only as spokesman for the U.S. delegation, but because of a dispute he had with the White House over U.S. policy at the Summit—a confirmation of earlier research in which it was cited that environmental coverage is often characterized by conflict between groups or individuals (Dennis, 1991). Third was Maurice Strong, chairman of the Earth Summit, who had 132 mentions, followed by then Sen. Al Gore, who led a U.S. congressional delegation to the summit and was highly critical of the Bush administration's environmental policies there (Gore was mentioned 57 times).

The top dozen was rounded out by British Prime Minister John Major (49); Brazilian President Fernando Collor (48); Stephan Schmidtheiny, head of the Swiss Business Council for Sustainable Development (40); Cuban President Fidel Castro (whose 40 mentions were usually in the context of his giving a speech with arch-enemy George Bush in the audience), Japanese Prime Minister Kiichi Miyazawa (35); German Chancellor Helmut Kohl (33); Norwegian Prime Minister Gro Harlem Brundtland, author of the Brundtland report on environment and development (29); and the Dalai Lama (28). The emphasis clearly was on political and economic elites from the industrialized world.

It is observed that only two Third World leaders appear among the top dozen individuals—Collor (as leader of the host country) and Castro. The top 20 include only three more Third World figures: India's environmental minister Kamal Nath (27); Tommy Koh of Singapore, chairman of the main committee for the Summit (23); and Jamsheed Marker, Pakistan's ambassador to the U.N. and spokesman for the G-77 group of nonaligned nations. If one counts the total number of mentions of the top 50 individuals on the combined files of the four agencies, Third World personalities account for just 6.4% of all references.

Figure 9.3 illustrates two main points. First, every agency referred more often to actors and sources from the developed than from the developing world. Second, there is a very clear distinction between the kinds of people reported on by IPS than by the other agencies. IPS came closest to a balance. Forty percent of its reference to individuals were from the Third World. IPS also had the highest proportion of mentions of individuals representing the United Nations system.

As Figure 9.4 shows, the news agencies referred to developing nations (mentions of U.N. personalities are excluded here) more often than to people from those nations. The AP, New York Times, and Reuters mentioned or quoted Third World actors only a quarter to a third as many times as they mentioned Third World countries. They appear to have felt more comfortable quoting U.S. or European sources about developing countries than spokesmen from the developing world themselves. One reason for this disparity was the disproportionate amount of attention paid to George Bush. IPS again was an exception, with almost as many references to people from developing nations as to the nations themselves.

Figure 9.5 illustrates the heavy emphasis that the AP, New York Times and Reuters put on American personalities. Almost all people mentioned by name by the AP were North Americans; for the New York Times the figure was almost 60%. Reuters paid proportionately more

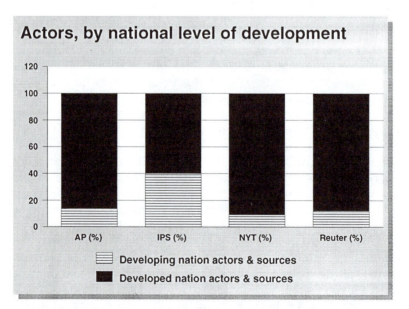

Figure 9.3. Actors, by national level of development

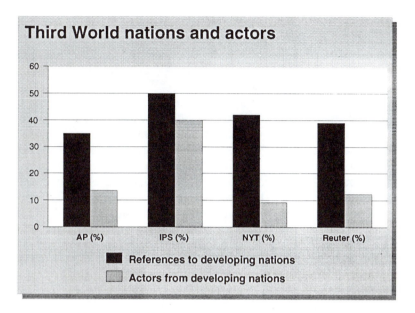

Figure 9.4. Third World nations and actors

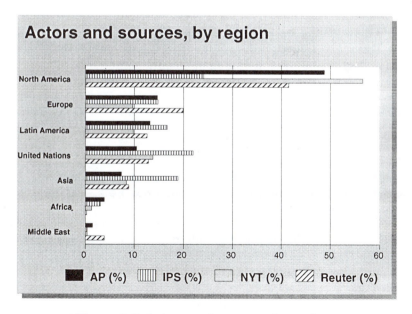

Figure 9.5. Actors and sources, by region

attention to Europeans than did the others. IPS has a more even distribution among people from Asia, North America, Europe, South America, and various U.N. organizations. Both Africa and the Middle East appear underrepresented on all four agencies—but these regions were not significant players at the summit.

Every agency, including IPS, mentioned George Bush and William Reilly most frequently. Maurice Strong was usually in third place. After that, however, the order varied considerably. One reason for the attention paid to Bush and Reilly was that, for the AP and New York Times at least, the coverage was heavily influenced by domestic politics in the United States. The New York Times leaked the fact that Reilly had written a memorandum urging that the United States sign the Biodiversity Treaty.

The convention was opposed by Bush because of concerns about its impact on the American biotechnology industry. The United States was isolated on the issue, and the political storm this raised in the midst of the 1992 presidential election campaign accounted for the coverage. For the AP and New York Times, the Rio Summit was in part a domestic political story that happened to be taking place in a foreign country.

Individuals mentioned by each service

Table 9.2 shows the top 25 individuals mentioned by the four news services. The list of 25 people the AP mentioned most frequently by name includes only 6 Third World figures. If all references to individuals are counted, including repetitions, mentions of Third World people account for just 24% of actors and sources on the AP. Fidel Castro appeared in several reports about his appearance at the same venue as George Bush. Fernando Collor was mentioned in his role as president of the host nation—and in some reports because of his impending impeachment. There also were various celebrities who had little to do with the environmental issues at stake, but nevertheless attracted attention. They included the Dalai Lama, Brazilian soccer star Pele, and American actress Shirley MacLaine.

For IPS, the 25 people mentioned most frequently include at least a dozen Third World leaders. Individuals from developing nations accounted for 40% of all references to people, including multiple mentions. The New York Times News Service, like the AP, had only a half dozen people representing the Third World in a list dominated by Western government officials. Individuals from developing nations accounted for a scant 9.2% of all references to people. The Reuters top-25 list differed somewhat from the AP and New York Times in that, whereas Bush and Reilly were still the most frequently mentioned

Table 9.2. Top 25 Individuals in the News.

AP	IPS	NYT	Reuters
George Bush[1]	George Bush	George Bush	George Bush
William Reilly[2]	William Reilly	William Reilly	William Reilly
Maurice Strong[3]	Tommy Koh[4]	Maurice Strong	Maurice Strong
Fidel Castro[5]	Maurice Strong	Stephen Schmidheiny[6]	John Major[7]
Fernando Collor[8]	Al Gore[9]	Dan Quayle[1]	Carlo Ripa Di Meana[11]
Al Gore	P.J. Patterson[12]	Kiichi Miyazawa[13]	Al Gore
Stephen Schmidheiny	John Major	Kamal Nath[14]	Fidel Castro
Dalai Lama[15]	Gro harlem Brundtland[16]	Curtis Bohlen	Jacques Cousteau[18]
Russel Mittermeier[19]	Kamal Noth	Fernando Collor	Helmut Kohl[20]
Jacques Cousteau	Laurens Jan Brinkhorst[21]	Gro Harlem Brundtland	Subroto[22]
T.J. Glauthier[23]	Jamsheed Marker[24]	Helmut Kohl	Dalai Lama
Helmut Kohl	Kiichi Miyazawa	Marcos Azambujas[25]	Jane Fonda[26]
Maumoon Abdul Gayoom[27]	Nafis Saidk[28]	Al Gore	Fernando Collor
Mikhail Gorbachev[29]	Gawin Chutima[30]	Robert Hahn[31]	Lewis Preston[32]
Chico Mendes[33]	Fernando Collor	John Major	Dixy Lee Ray[34]
Kiichi Miyazawa	Julius Nyerere[35]	Boutros Boutros-Ghaili[36]	John Denver[37]
Timothy Wirth[38]	Mostafa Tolba[39]	John Denver	Pele[40]
Scott Hajost[41]	Martin Khor[42]	Jose Goldemberg[43]	Jacques Attali[44]

Table 9.2. Top 25 Individuals in the News (cont.).

Shirley MacLaine[45]	William Draper[46]	Tommy Koch	Bill Clinton
Pele	Hugh Desmond Hoyte[48]	Richard Mott[49]	Michael Howard[50]
Dan Quayle	Enrique Iglesias[51]	Mostafa Tolba	Stephen Schmidheiny
Richard Benedick[52]	Richard Mott	Ting Wen Lian[53]	Boutros Boutros-Ghali
Jan Laurens Brinkhorst	Michael Cutajar[54]	Russell Train[55]	Brian Mulroney[56]
Robert Grady[57]	Dan Quayle	Clayton Yeutter[58]	Klaus Toepfer[59]
John Major	Emil Salim[60]		Ribtii Awad[61]

1. U.S. President
2. EPA Administrator and Head of U.S. Delegation
3. Chairman of the Earth Summit Conference
4. Chairman of the main committee for UNCED
5. President of Cuba
6. Business Council for Sustainable Development
7. British Prime Minister
8. President of Brazil
9. U.S. Senator
10. U.S. Vice President
11. European Community Environment Chief
12. Prime Minister for Jamaica
13. Japanese Prime Minister
14. Indian Environment Minister
15. Tibetan Spiritual Leader
16. Norwegian Prime Minister
17. U.S. Assistant Secretary of State for Environment
18. French undersea explorer
19. President of Conservation International
20. Chancellor of Germany
21. Head of European Community Delegation
22. Secretary-General of OPEC
23. World Wildlife Fund Representative
24. Spokesman for G-77 and Pakistan's Ambassador to the UN
25. Of Brazil, Chief Negotiator for the Summit
26. U.S. Entertainer
27. President of the Maldives
28. Director of UNFPA
29. Former President of the Soviet Union
30. NGO Coordinating Committee on Rural Development
31. Economist with American Enterprise Institute
32. World Bank President
33. Brazilian rain forest martyr
34. Former Head of U.S. Atomic Energy Commission
35. Former President of Tanzania
36. United Nations Secretary-General
37. U.S. Entertainer
38. U.S. Senator
39. Executive Director of U.N. Environment Programme
40. Brazilian soccer star

Table 9.2. Top 25 Individuals in the News (cont.).

41.	Environmental Defense Fund Representative
42.	Malaysia-based Third World Network
43.	Brazilian Education and Environment Minister
44.	President of European Bank for Reconstruction
45.	U.S. Entertainer
46.	Administrator of UNDP
47.	Then-Governor of Arkansas and Presidential Candidate
48.	President of Guyana
49.	World Wildlife Fund
50.	Britain's Secretary of State for the Environment
51.	President of Interamerican Development Bank
52.	U.S. State Department of negotiator
53.	Malaysian Diplomat
54.	Head of UN team that negotiated climate treaty
55.	World Wildlife Fund
56.	Canadian Prime Minister
57.	Environment Policy Planner at the White House
58.	Bush's Domestic Policy Coordinator
59.	German Environment Minister
60.	Indonesian Environment Minister
61.	Head of the Palestinian delegation

names, European leaders such as British Premier John Major, European Community environment chief Carlo Ripa di Meana and German Chancellor Helmut Kohl were accorded more prominence. Individuals from developing nations accounted for 12.3% of all references to people on the Reuters list.

Topics

Analysis of the emphasis that the news agencies put on different topics shows that South and North had very different agendas, and that these were reflected in the coverage provided by IPS and the Western agencies. To determine the news agendas, computers were programmed to look for key words relating to each major topic—Agenda 21, Biodiversity, Climate, and Forests—and to count the frequency of words in each category. We also constructed a thesaurus of words that dealt with funding—how much money the industrialized nations would commit for protection of the environment, and who would decide how the money should be spent.

For the AP, Reuters, and New York Times, the most important topic was forests, and specifically the need to preserve tropical forests in Brazil and elsewhere (Figure 9.6). This was the line pressed by the Bush Administration, which promoted a global forest protection plan called Forests for the Future. The plan failed to get support from the developing countries, who pointed out that temperate ancient forests—including those in the Pacific Northwest—would be logged off in the next 20 years if they were not protected. The U.S. interest in this issue is reflected in the large amount of coverage by the AP in particular. Forests were only the third highest priority for IPS. The Climate Treaty, and especially global warming, also was high on the agenda of the Western nations, and of somewhat lesser interest to the developing world—except for those low-lying and island nations whose territories could be inundated if melting ice caps raised the level of the oceans.

For IPS, the topic that the commanded most attention was Agenda 21, the overall blueprint for action to protect the environment while encouraging development. IPS devoted nearly 40% of its coverage of specific topics to Agenda 21, or twice as much as the average for the Western agencies. The main reason for IPS's focus on Agenda 21 was that this document encompassed most of the themes relating to development. (The word *development* occurs more than 200 times in the IPS file we sampled, compared to 45 mentions in the AP, 107 in the New York Times, and 115 in Reuters.) Also covered in chapters of the voluminous Agenda 21 document were other issues of central concern to the Third World, including environmental problems resulting from rapid industrialization, pollution control and waste management, and inade-

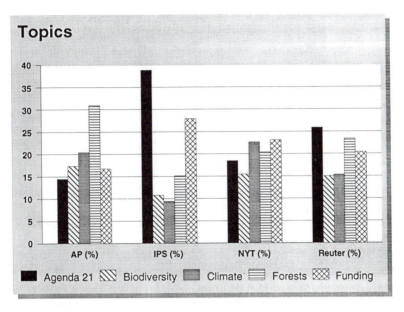

Figure 9.6. Topics

quate supplies and quality of drinking water. IPS referred to the document itself (Agenda 21) 72 times, which was twice as often as any other agency. Other high-frequency words and phrases in this category on IPS were *population* and *sustainable development*—often references to the creation of a new U.N. body—the Commission on Sustainable Development—that would monitor compliance with the summit meeting's environmental goals.

The second highest priority for IPS had to do with funding. Here, too, IPS had a larger proportion of coverage (28% of its total) than the Western agencies. The most frequent key words on the IPS file in this category were *aid, loans, funding, GEF,* and *World Bank.* For the Western agencies, the most frequent key words related to funding included *money, price,* and *cost;* they showed very little interest in the GEF or the Commission on Sustainable Development.

A question that arises from this study is how well the various agencies performed in covering the Earth Summit. The media coverage as a whole had its critics. A Third World perspective came from Everton Vargas (1992) of the Brazilian mission to the United Nations. He writes that "what was striking to diplomats was the superficial treatment of UNCED by the American press, both print and television, and the relative failure to provide accurate reporting. The media were very much dependent on the sources they consulted, embracing the bias these represented" (p. 3).

Josh Friedman, an American journalist who covered the summit for New York Newsday, points out that UNCED was probably the most confusing international conference ever held. It was unlikely to be in the interest of any of the major power centers to have a clear coverage of UNCED because of the hidden agenda: the United States was only interested in a cosmetic or symbolic conference without any real obligations that would entail financial commitments on her part, the developing countries wanted to have cash and continue their own form of environmental abuse, and international organizations did not want to adopt any positions offensive to any major players. Friedman (1992) argues further that a lot of the information supplied to journalists was undecipherable, "political reporters did not understand the complexity of environmental problems, environmental reporters failed to see the political process underlying UNCED, and most reporters, generally used to being 'fed' information, did not receive comprehensible material" (p. 3).

Martin Lee (1992), of Fairness and Accuracy in Media, observes that numerous topics about reporting on the environment are lacking in the U.S. mainstream and electronic and print media: "environmental issues as seen from a Third World perspective, the link between poverty and environmental degradation, the role of the U.S. and her corporations as the most pernicious polluters in the world, the relation between the U.S. standard of living and the depletion of resources" (p. 6).

CONCLUSION

Our observation was that all four news agencies we analyzed had done a thorough, competent, and professional job of reporting on complex issues at the summit. They committed enormous resources to the event and produced more copy than almost any newspaper could reasonably find room for. A newspaper subscribing to any one of the agencies could have given its readers material from a variety of perspectives. Whether they chose to do so is a different question, and only an analysis of what actually appeared in the world's newspapers could throw light on how local gatekeepers affected the coverage.

We did find, however, that with the exception of IPS there was a disproportionate emphasis on conflict rather than on cooperation, and on the activities and views of a handful of rich nations and their leaders and of the issues most of interest to them, whereas poor countries—who stood to gain or lose most as a result of the deliberations—were relatively seldom heard. As Lee (1992) observes, the principal problem with reporting in the United States is sourcing, "that is to say reliance on one source introduces in one's report the bias that source represents. This amounts to environmental reporting taking place primarily from the perspective of the U.S. government or from that of the major corporations" (p. 5). This case study, limited as it is, indicates the importance of more—and more diverse—sources of news about global problems that only increased international understanding and action can begin to solve, and in particular the need to supplement these sources with people-to-people links that are coming to characterize the global civil society.

10

Multinationals of Solidarity: International Civil Society and the Killing of Street Children in Brazil *

Sonia Serra
Goldsmith's College &
Universidade Federal da Bahia

The transnationalization of capital and the globalization of communication and culture in "postmodern geographies" (Morley & Robins, 1989, p. 21) have been matters of concern for studies about cultural imperialism and the conglomeratization of the media. A less examined trend of this new era, in tandem with the "crisis" of the nation-state, is the role of supranational agencies and the transnational network of nongovernmental organizations (NGOs) in promoting the globalization of public issues and forms of international solidarity and citizenship. They represent important changes in the configuration of the public sphere, not yet duly researched, that must be considered for an up-to-date model of the development of social problems in the public arena.

One significant aspect of the process of "globalization," together with transitions to democracy in many countries and the rise of the "new social movements," is the increase in the number of international non-governmental organizations as well as the strengthening of the role of

*The author wishes to thank Annabelle Sreberny-Mohammadi, James Curran, and Sandra Braman for their helpful and stimulating comments on an earlier version of this paper and to acknowledge the financial support of the CNPq-Brasil.

transnational agencies in the public space. Some of these operate with large budgets, encouraged by neoliberal perspectives related to changes in the welfare state. The new communications and computer technologies are also new important elements in this picture, facilitating the production of information and interconnection between these organizations and other groups in society. But in a world in which politics and mass media are so closely intertwined their roles cannot be exaggerated.

The NGOs have been extremely important in producing and disseminating data about matters of social concern and quite successful in creating public agendas. However, it is argued here that the visibility of these issues, their public awareness and the formation of public opinion, still rely heavily on the publicity they acquire through mainstream mass media. Thus an understanding of the relationships between these transnational pressure groups and the media becomes an essential task in the debate about communication and democracy.

This chapter analyzes those tendencies involved in the emergence of an international civil society by describing the process by which the killing of street children in Brazil became a prominent issue on the political agenda at the domestic level and in the international sphere. It points out that the issue only really became salient in the Brazilian national press after the government and other established fora brought it to the policy agenda, thus confirming previous findings in the field. However, it also shows that it was the pressure exercised by transnational organizations (especially Amnesty International), in concert with national groups (around the National Movement of Street Boys and Girls, supported by many European agencies and UNICEF), that was crucial in pushing the government into action and challenging the terms of the public debate. This pressure was only effective after publicity was gained in the international and national news media.

THE INTERNATIONALIZATION OF THE PUBLIC SPHERE

In the 1980s, with the development of the mass media and the expansion of both state and corporate interests, the earlier analysis advanced by Habermas (1989) in the 1960s about the erosion of the bourgeois public sphere and the structural transformations of the conditions of public debate and the separation of state and society regained prominence in the field of political communication. Despite criticisms about the historical adequacy of Habermas's account, many authors have postulated the use of the concept of the "public sphere," either as an ideal-type "against which we can judge existing social arrangements" (Garnham, 1990, p. 109), or as a political goal, because the concept has "evocative power, providing us with concrete visions of the democratic society" (Dahlgren, 1991, p. 8).

Such visions usually involve the notion of a space between government and citizens, in which the latter can freely and equally debate public interest issues and influence policymaking. Several institutions in civil society can take part in this arena, in which the media are expected to perform a significant role in providing information, staging the struggle between competing interests or enabling the mobilization around common concerns, and helping the development of majority consensus through the formation of public opinion.

How useful can this concept be in this globalized world, in which the informed public debate no longer takes place in cafes and literary salons, but in which global discussions and chats are engaged through computer and television screens in the era of multichannels and instant world communications? As in earlier centuries, this public space still does not enable universal access on an equal basis because many individuals and nations can not fully join in these communication processes that are still marked by fragmentation and a certain degree of elitism in the way citizen participation in policymaking occurs.

Curran (1991b) argues that the concept of the public sphere "offers nevertheless a powerful and arresting vision of the role of the media in a democratic society and in this sense its historical status is irrelevant" (p. 83). He criticizes the West's liberal tradition of the role of the press in the public sphere that only viewed the media as channels between individuals and the state for, among other things, failing to take adequate account of the "way in which interests have become organized and collectivized" and the way the "media function in relation to modern systems of representation in liberal democracies" (1991a, p. 29). He proposes a model for the democratic organization of the media in the public sphere that should account for a better conception of the way "individual interests are safeguarded and advanced . . . partly through collective organizations like political parties and pressure groups, and at a strategic level through the construction and recomposition of alliances and coalitions" (p. 31). This should certainly provide for a better vision of the media "as a complex articulation of vertical, horizontal and diagonal channels of communication between individuals, groups and power structures" (p. 31). In this perspective, a core sector of public service media provides a national forum of debate and is surrounded by other types of commercial, professional, or civic media that guarantee that sectoral interests are voiced and that diversity and innovation can be fostered.

What is needed now is the application of this model to the wider society, at the global level, paying attention to the relationship between the media and the other institutions in the public sphere, to account for the way interests and representations have become internationalized. *Globalization* has undoubtedly been a key word in the debate of the late 1980s and early 1990s, although inequality and asymmetry remain major components of the global picture. What is significant in these debates, for our purposes here, is that "the role of communication and information have been finally and generally recognized as crucial elements in the new world order" (Sreberny-Mohammadi, 1991, p. 119).

The focus of this chapter is directed to one aspect that has been associated with this process: the increase in the number, scope, and role of intergovernmental bodies and international organizations and their communicative functions in constructing a global public sphere, alongside the global news media. The notion of a global public sphere is prefigured in recent theorizing about globalization. For Robertson (1992), "Globalization refers both to the compression of the world and the intensification of consciousness of the world as a whole" (p. 8). For McGrew (1992), it implies a "complex condition, one in which patterns of human interaction, interconnectedness and awareness are reconstituting the world as a single social space" (1992, p. 65). Since the Enlightenment, the idea of an "universal community of humankind" (McGrew, 1992, p. 62) has captured society's philosophical imagination. The prospect of an international society was strengthened with the establishment of the United Nations and has long held the attention of social scientists interested in international relations.

The aspiration for "global citizenship" and the notion of a supranational, global identity was further reinforced with the emergence of instant news media and visions of the "global village." But "like many other utopias, this one too foundered on the harsh realities of the postwar world, driven by cultural differences and conflicts, political and ideological antagonisms, and immense economic inequalities. The information and knowledge resources on which a global citizenship must be based . . . were never evenly distributed around the globe, either at the level of production of that information, or at the level of consumption" (Gurevitch, Levy, & Roeh, 1991, p. 196). This scenario of imbalance and "dependency" both fueled and frustrated the debate and struggle for a New World Information Order, captained by UNESCO in the 1970s.

More recently, the "crisis of the sovereignty of the nation-state"—a rather old problem for some countries, especially in the south—the rise of new social movements, and the development of new communication technologies, among other shifts brought about by the acceleration of the process of globalization, have led scholars in the field of communication studies to speculate about the development of an international public sphere and the transnationalization of civil participation in new terms, outside the frame of governments and media conglomerates. Nonetheless, little empirical research has yet been done on such themes. From a different perspective, however, the study of TV coverage of U.S./Soviet summits, conducted by Hallin and Mancini (1991) offered an interesting discussion about the role of the media in the "constitution of an international public sphere" (p. 249) and the "symbolic constitution of a global community" (p. 250).

Keane (1992) points out that the "decline of sovereignty" has profound implications for a democratic theory of the media because it demands a fundamental rethinking of the classical theory of "liberty of the press," which viewed communications systems only within the framework of the system of single nation states, and "it reminds us of the importance of the growing impact of supranational legal and political arrangements, and of the slow and delicate growth of an international civil society" (p. 30). For him, the development of an "international civil society," besides the possibilities offered by the new technologies and global communications media and the enforcement of international standards for rights of communication, depends essentially on efforts "to enrich *from below* the flows of information among communicating citizens, regardless of the nation states within which they live" (p. 28). To achieve this he emphasizes the importance, on the one hand, of forms of quality investigative journalism and, on the other hand, of public support for nongovernment associations, working to combat political censorship.

Frederick (1992a) also talks about the emergence of a global civil society, "that part of our collective lives that is neither market nor government but is so often inundated by them" as represented by the "worldwide movement of non-governmental organizations and citizen advocacy groups, uniting to challenge problems that . . . confound local—even national—solutions" (p. 219). He stresses the importance of "highly decentralized technologies—computers, fax machines, amateur radio, packet data satellites, VCRs, video cameras and the like" (p. 222), in the democratization of information flows to counter two fundamental problems: "increasing monopolization of global information and communication by transnational corporations; and the increasing disparities between the world's info-rich and info-poor populations" (p. 220). His argument is based on a few examples of the political impact of electronic networking.

Undoubtedly, the economic, technological, environmental, and cultural developments of the last decades are profoundly transforming the character of political action. If national decisions are constrained by the interests of transnational corporations and determined by international regulations and policies of intergovernmental institutions, like the IMF, the World Bank, the European Parliament, or the United Nations, only international mobilization can be effective in influencing public issues.

However, the case presented in this chapter gives more support to the view that "the main path to this goal is still by way of the means of public communication (the mass media) rather than technologically mediated interpersonal communication" (McQuail, 1992, p. 310). New technologies facilitate the mobilization of critical debate between informed private citizens at a global level, and specialized databases and news letters have become available. Yet government policymakers still rely on the media, especially quality newspapers, as sources of information about world affairs, thermometers of international public opinion, carriers of their messages to the general public, and means of communication between other elites.

THE GLOBAL RISE OF NGOS

The increase in the number, size, and scope of nongovernmental transnational organizations is indeed a significant aspect of the process of globalization, as pointed out by many authors (see, e.g., Archer, 1992; Luard, 1990; Willets, 1982). Seeking to protect sectional interests or promote larger causes, many different types of secular and religious NGOs have flourished in recent decades, covering diverse aspects of human life. The *Yearbook of International Organizations 1992/1993* lists around 15,000 international bodies, including religious orders and secular institutions (Union of International Associations, 1992).

Several organizations in the more industrialized countries of the North were initially formed to provide emergency aid, relief, and development aid to the countries in the South, and in many cases the humanitarian values and welfare concerns that inspired their emergence have been broadened and mixed up with more complex social, political, and economic problems. Later, others were established with more explicitly political objectives, for example, to mobilize for human rights, social justice, and ecological issues. Some operate with large budgets and have become "increasingly professional, politically astute, assertive and businesslike" (Golding, 1992, p. 516), whereas others, especially the ones that originated in Third World countries, are quite small and depend on their counterparts in the North to survive.

These NGOs have indeed become important actors in world politics. Of special importance here is their role in shaping public discourse and mobilizing public opinion at an international level, as well as their functions as fora of communication and production of meanings and their watchdog role, functions usually attributed to the press in the public sphere. Also significant is their relationship with formal media systems.

Especially during the 1980s, several international networks of nongovernmental organizations were formed to develop coordinated action to press for shifts in policies or raise new issues on the political agenda, while contributing to an ethics of international solidarity and citizenship. Their capacity to build international alliances and to get represented on intergovernmental bodies of high status, like the United Nations, increased their legitimacy. Their recent recognition by multilateral agencies like the World Bank has also increased their effectiveness, and the new technologies of communication have improved their ability to interact.

Certainly, the possibilities opened up by electronic networks and the spread of decentralized technologies, with great potential to empower groups in civil society and provide alternative channels for postmodern community communication at a transnational level, do stimulate our imagination and will not be dismissed. On the other hand, it must not obscure the fact that although communications media have failed democracy (Entman, 1989; Golding, 1990; Kellner, 1990), their centrality for contemporary public life is beyond doubt, and the pursuit for democratic policies for communication remains an essential requirement for the democratization of society (Curran, 1991a, 1991b; Keane, 1991).

Political responses to events are still related to the visibility they get in mass communication channels and the public concern thus created. Like governments and politicians, the social movements and the NGOs themselves are perfectly aware of this dependency of modern political activity on the media, and they struggle to reach broader publics and influence policymaking by pressing their agendas and meanings through public media. In this process they have to establish good relationships with the press and adjust or conform to their practices, routines, and newsworthiness criteria (Gitlin, 1980). Their success in so doing is related to the development of specific news management techniques (Ericson, Baranek, & Chan, 1989; Schlesinger, 1990) in the context of the unequal resources and positions of authority they have in society.

THE KILLING OF STREET CHILDREN
AND THE POLITICAL AGENDA

The analysis of the emergence of the killing of street children in Brazil as a prominent issue on the national political agenda and in the international scene, despite certain singularities, can provide a good example through which to discuss the role of transnational bodies and NGOs in the trend toward the globalization of civil society and the internationalization of the public sphere.

I show that the political impact of the issue was a consequence of international pressure, generated in large part by the extensive coverage the issue received in the international media. Other issues such as the campaign against the building of dams or logging in the Amazon or the demarcation of Indian areas in Brazil can also provide significant examples of the operation of the international public sphere, interactions among NGOs, intergovernmental bodies, and the media, as well as transnational corporations at the global level.

The capacity of the international movement of NGOs, in this case, to challenge the government and the powerful discourses and images prevalent in society and to influence the terms of the public debate was not just a consequence of their capacity to exchange information and provide fora for debates through technological, interpersonal, or community communication. It was, in fact, very much related to the ability of high status, established institutions, with legitimacy and resources, to publicize the issue via mainstream media and lobby parliaments and intergovernmental bodies.

In Brazil, the majority of the most influent NGOs were formed during the 1970s and 1980s, in the process of the organization of civil society to fight for the democratization of the country during the military regime. Their origins are linked to the Catholic Church—inspired by the Theology of Liberation—and engagement with grassroots organization, universities, and political parties of the left (Fernandes, 1988). Their existence is related on the one hand to the rise of social movements in the country and on the other hand to the support of the international community of nongovernmental organizations.

THE ISSUE OF THE KILLING OF STREET CHILDREN IN BRAZIL

The killing of the so-called street children in Brazil has shocked international public opinion in recent years. It has been the subject of several documentaries, news programs, press reports, and books and even of debates in foreign parliaments, becoming a matter of acute diplomatic embarrassment for the Brazilian government. In England, for instance, an all-party group was formed to campaign for the issue and urged the Prime Minister to press the Brazilian President in relation to the problem. The European Parliament has also passed motions condemning the killings and urging the Brazilian government to take measures to stop them.

The plight of poor Brazilian children and the violence against them has had international repercussions since at least the early 1980s, when Hector Babenco's prize-winning and prophetic film *Pixote* was first exhibited. In 1987, Fernando Ramos da Silva (or Pixote, as the main actor of the film became known) again captured the international stage when life copied art, and he, who had now become a petty thief, was deliberately shot dead by police officers. His death renewed attention to the issue of police violence, already denounced by the children and adolescents gathered in the National Movement of Street Boys and Girls.

The stories of other Brazilian children and adolescents, like "Brasileirinho," a 14-year-old boy involved with drug trafficking, who was shot dead by policemen in 1988, were published by newspapers and news magazines all over the world. Pictures of young children bearing fire arms in Rio slums and images of street children sniffing glue have since become commonplace in the global media.

The deliberate murder of these children and adolescents by vigilante or "extermination groups" escalated since 1987, and the involvement of businessmen, judges, and police officers with the death squads eventually became an issue on public and political agendas. The return of the activities of the death squads that specialized in killing "delinquents" was investigated by a special police committee from 1986 and was denounced by the Brazilian press and foreign newspapers. In 1988, members of the Catholic Church and organizations that worked with street children in the outskirts of Rio began to denounce the systematic killings of minors in the area.

Between 1988 and 1990, more than 4,600 violent deaths of children and adolescents were recorded in Brazil, especially in the slums and urban peripheries of large cities. Death squads and official police violence were responsible for a large number of these murders. The victims were poor, mostly male, Black, and aged between 15 to 17 years old, although many younger boys and girls were also assassinated. They were usually kidnapped and taken to distant places, where they were brutally tortured and then shot dead. Some had been involved with petty theft or drug trafficking. Photographs of their bullet-riddled bodies sometimes appeared in the front pages of popular newspapers, but the majority of these murders were routinely reported at the end of crime news pages.

In 1989, the murder of a Black 9-year-old boy, whose body was dumped in Ipanema, a wealthy area of Rio, after being strangled, caught the attention of human rights organizations for its unusual characteristics and motivated the first national survey on the assassination of children and adolescents in Brazil. A note left by the body read: "I killed you because you did not study and had no future. . . . The government can not allow the streets of the city to be invaded by kids." The results of this survey were made public during the Second Meeting of the Street Children Movement, in September 1989. However, up to 1990, there was little public awareness about the issue, and an ethnographic study found that the slaughter of minors by "extermination groups" had not provoked any public outrage in the country and was treated as a nonissue, even in the shantytowns where their families lived (Scheper-Hughes, 1992).

There is not enough space to give here a complete account of the conditions, events, and actors that contributed to the eventual prominence of this problem. This chapter focuses on the role of Amnesty International in prompting international media coverage, which represented a turning point in the way the issue developed in the political arena, both at the domestic and international levels.

First it is worth mentioning that the increase in the murders and their condemnation by the organizations around the street-children movement happened parallel to the successful campaign for children's rights, following the process of democratization in Brazil. This brought important shifts in the legislation and in the public image of the street children—once regarded as dangerous and disposable future criminals. All these positive changes were fostered by two global events sponsored by UNICEF: the International Year of the Child in 1979 and the Child Summit in 1990, which drew world attention to the problem of street children and to the issue of children's rights. Furthermore, at least in Brazil, it stimulated the production of scientific knowledge on the subject and provided a favorable environment for the denunciation of the violence against them.

Over the last decade, this intergovernmental body had a remarkable role in promoting public awareness about the violent conditions of the life and death of these children in Brazil and in gathering support for the struggle to grant citizenship rights to them. It has supported the groups working with street children, providing resources, technical advice, and legitimacy, and has sponsored many research projects and reports in the field. It has paid special attention to the media and promoted several seminars with journalists all over the country. In the early 1980s, the program "Alternative Services for Street Children Project," sponsored by UNICEF in collaboration with the Brazilian government, brought together technicians and an array of groups working with "abandoned" children, experimenting with new ways for dealing with them (Swift, 1991). In 1985, several nongovernmental organizations, many funded by foreign charities, launched the National Movement for Street Boys and Girls (MNMMR) seeking to create the conditions within society for the street children to express themselves and exercise their rights.

A large mobilization for children's rights followed, uniting the MNMMR with other institutions in civil society, with the support of the Catholic Church. The campaign was also supported by the media and an association of businessmen. The 1988 Constitution introduced principles of the International Convention on Children's Rights, even before this was formally approved by the UN. To regulate such principles, the new Statute for the Children and Adolescents was passed in 1990, replacing the former repressive legislation and state institutions. It was considered a model for every country in the world.

Besides the MNMMR and the Minor's Pastoral Services of the Catholic Church, several other NGOs, particularly IBASE (Brazilian Institute for Social and Economic Research), CEAP (Centre for the Coordination of Marginalized Peoples), and ASSEAF (an association of former inmates of boarding institutions), together with local human rights groups, worked to call attention, nationally and internationally, to the problem of the assassination of children and adolescents. Members of these NGOs visited Europe and also sent faxes and letters to international human rights organizations, especially Amnesty International, informing them of the killings.

Vigils, shows, street demonstrations, films, videos, and articles tried to sensitize the public and the media. The national meetings of the MNMMR, besides their organizational and political implications, staged highly emotional protests about the killings, in the presence of government officials, politicians, and representatives of international bodies such as the UN, OAS, UNICEF, and DCI (Defence for Children International), which attracted national and international press coverage. Books and reports of surveys that investigated the murders also got short periods of media attention (Dimenstein, 1991).

Later, government initiatives and Parliamentary Commissions of Inquiry, which resulted from the national pressure and international condemnation, especially after Amnesty International intervention, eventually brought the issue to the political agenda.

THE ROLE OF AMNESTY INTERNATIONAL

Amnesty International (AI) is the largest and best known of the human rights organizations in Britain, where it has nearly 300 local support groups. The International Secretariat in London has over 250 researchers. "The moral force of Amnesty is highly dependent on its being (seen to be) nonaligned with any government or partisan political interest. It is financed entirely by voluntary subscriptions and donations" (Burnell, 1991, p. 89).

The organization defines itself as "an international system of action networks . . . [and] a global web of interwoven and overlapping channels of communications" (Amnesty International, 1992a, p. 45). The postal service, telephone, telex, fax, electronic mail, and visits are used to link the International Secretariat and members, groups, and sections, vertically and horizontally. It combines diverse campaign techniques that include direct pressure on authorities and lobbying, but especially media and publicity are used to create pressure. As the organization points out it "owes its foundation to a newspaper article, and publicity remains one of the organization's most powerful tools for raising awareness about human rights issues" (Amnesty International, 1992a, p. 50).

Amnesty produces its own press, distributing a monthly newsletter by subscription, an annual report, and several other materials, which not only keep its membership informed, but are important sources for the mass media. It issues statements and news releases to international news agencies that are also sent to the sections for distribution to the national media in each country. The organization provides advice and guidelines for its groups and members on how to best approach the local media, issue news releases, and develop other efforts to create publicity, which demonstrates expert knowledge about news values and media strategies. Preliminary research conducted in Britain shows that Amnesty International is among the five most mentioned charities in the news media (Golding, 1992).

The denunciation of the deliberate killings of children by police violence or death squads began to appear in the annual reports of Amnesty International in the late 1980s. At first, these were just short paragraphs that reported "complaints alleging police violence against criminal suspects, including children" (Amnesty International, 1988, p. 98) and the increase in the murders attributed to the deathsquads. At that moment, rural violence was the priority concern in terms of the violation of human rights in Brazil, although the number of victims assassinated in land disputes was much lower, as the organizations in the defense of street children demonstrated.

The first survey to shed light on the killings was commissioned by the Defence for Children International (DCI), a United Nations consultative body based in Geneva, and conducted by a group of NGOs, coordinated by an association of former inmates of boarding institutions (ASSEAF) in 1988. It confirmed the assassination of 306 children and adolescents under 18 by death squads, between January 1987 and July 1988 in the municipalities of "Baixada Fluminense," a violent area in Rio (See CEAP, 1989). The second survey, carried out by the Brazilian Institute for Social and Economic Research (IBASE) with the support of the MNMMR and UNICEF, found that 1,397 children and adolescents under 18 had died violently in 16 cities researched, between January 1984 and July 1989, revealing that death squads could be related to many of these deaths (see MNMMR & IBASE, 1989)

Before 1990, the killing of street children was not recognized as an important issue by Amnesty International. But after producing a special report on torture and police violence in Brazil, the organization decided to launch a campaign. In May 1990, the international human rights organization visited the country, collected information, and acknowledged the fragility of the Brazilian movement in defense of street children and the indifference of public opinion and the authorities about the problem (Dimenstein, 1990). In June that year, Amnesty International published a report entitled *Beyond the Law: Torture and Extrajudicial Execution in Urban Brazil*, which called on the Brazilian government to stop widespread violations of human rights by civil and military police. Police brutality was the focus of the report. But on an item about death squads, it reproduced information of the study conducted by IBASE and published, in 1989, *Children and Adolescents in Brazil: the Silenced Life*, about the killings of children.

Before issuing the report, AI produced an international news release and scheduled a press conference in São Paulo for June 19. It received extensive coverage in the national press and was broadcast on prime-time television as well as being the subject of news items in the most important newspapers and news magazines abroad. Representatives of the organization met government officials, members of nongovernmental organizations, and the press. In a nationally televised speech President Collor promised: "We cannot and will not again be a country cited as violent in reports by Amnesty International. . . . We will not allow the 'new Brazil' to accept any form of disrespect for human rights" (Amnesty International, 1991a, p. 49).

In August, the president and other officials met Amnesty International representatives to discuss the organization's report. Contrary to his predecessors, who either ignored or tried to discredit the charges, Collor said he did not consider their work an interference in Brazil's internal affairs and promised he would study the organization's recommendations. Amnesty International subsequently sent 12 recommendations for safeguards against torture and other human rights violations (Amnesty International, 1991a).

This somehow reflected the new contours of Brazilian diplomacy in the field. The previously rigid emphasis on principles of nonintervention and national sovereignty were replaced by the acceptance of the idea of the universality of human rights issues and a more flexible, albeit critical, attitude in relation to the role of nongovernmental organizations and the importance of media publicity in international cooperation (Personal interviews with the Brazilian Ambassador and the Secretary of Human Rights of the Brazilian Embassy, in London, 1993).

In September, another survey carried out by IBASE and MNMMR, in consultation with the Centre for Violence Studies of the University of Sao Paulo (NEV/USP), was made public in an effort to keep the issue in debate, with new analyses (MNMMR/IBASE/NEV-USP, 1991). Amnesty International then issued another international news release, this time highlighting the assassination and torture of "hundreds of children in Brazil's cities" by death squads and on-duty police, citing the statistics collected by IBASE and reporting the organizations' contacts with the Brazilian government. It had considerable coverage in the international press as well as in the Brazilian media.

Amnesty's September newsletter also focused on the subject of the killings and cruelty against "poverty-stricken children and adolescents" (1990, p. 3). Amnesty's report containing the results of the survey was also reproduced in the Brazilian Press. Four hundred and twenty-four murders reported during 1989 in three regional newspapers in three Brazilian states, analyzed by the research, pointed out that at least one child was killed in Brazil each day.

On the same day that Amnesty's statement was issued, the Brazilian president called for full federal investigation of all the cases of killings of children featured in the statement. During the World Summit on Children at the United Nations, in late September, President Collor said in his speech that the Council for the Defence of Human Rights, attached to the Ministry of Justice, would be turned into an "instrument of permanent protection of the physical integrity of Brazilian Children," and that the Federal Government was already taking measures to see to it that "these shameful abuses against children are brought to a halt" (Rocha, 1991, p. 12).

Then, the British section of Amnesty International published an advertisement in the English press that said that Brazil had solved the problem of how to take the children off the streets: by killing them. It provoked an indignant reaction from the Brazilian government concerned with Brazil's international image. It was the Ministry of Foreign Relations, instead of the Ministry of Justice, who contacted the international human rights organization demanding an apology, which was issued by the general secretary of the organization, who nonetheless confirmed the denouncements (Fernandes, 1990).

After this incident with Amnesty International, the Brazilian government opened the dialogue with the MNMMR and other nongovernmental organizations. After much pressure from the organizations and the international condemnation reflected in the media coverage, by the end of the year it decided to bring the issue to the political agenda. A national commission with equal representation of government sectors and nongovernmental organizations dedicated to children's rights defense was set up and became a permanent working group, which outlined strategies and a National Plan of Prevention and Reduction of Violence Against Children. Other government initiatives also aimed to provoke impact followed.

At the international level, the Collor government, very pragmatically, adopted the strategy of recognizing the problem and demanding debt swoops or bargaining resources for related government projects. Like some representatives of national NGOs had done before, in early 1991, as previously announced in the Brazilian press, the Minister of the Child traveled around Europe to publicize the issue, providing the media with more information and calling for more international pressure over state governments to stop the killings, as well as trying to convert the international horror provoked by the dramatic slaughters in funds. The Minister visited Amnesty International and outlined a number of measures to combat the violence against children.

During 1991 and 1992, Amnesty International was still being briefed by organizations in Brazilian civil society, who were aware of the importance of international pressure and continued to press the Brazilian authorities and produce more reports about the killings of children and adolescents in Brazilian cities (e.g., Amnesty International, 1991b, 1992b, 1992c). The monthly newsletter and the annual reports also stressed the issue.

Before Amnesty International denounced this problem in June 1990, the efforts of the national movement of street children had drawn some attention to the murders in Brazil and in other countries. But the revelations by the international human rights organization, and the wide condemnation it provoked abroad, had a major effect in prompting government measures and influenced the public agenda, affecting the quality and quantity of the press coverage both nationally and internationally.[1]

AN INTERNATIONAL SCANDAL:
THE GROWTH OF THE ISSUE IN THE PRESS

In order to examine the nature of coverage of the murder of children and adolescents in Brazil in the international press, a sample of four leading newspapers of Europe and the United States—*El Pais, Le Monde*, the *Guardian*, and *The New York Times*—was selected. All of them are considered influential organs of the prestige press at an international level and give considerable importance to foreign affairs coverage. They all have correspondents in Brazil.

All news items about the killings of street children in Brazil found in the newspapers from January 1986 to December 1991 were analyzed in relation to the main event that generated the news and the authors and sources of the reports; letters to the editor were not included. In this phase of the coverage, 42 news reports about the murder of children and adolescents were found. The British newspaper, the *Guardian*, accounted for the highest number of items (36%), whereas the American *New York Times* had the lowest (7%).[2] The Spanish *El Pais* and the French *Le Monde* ran 31% and 26% of the stories.

What is significant in relation to these figures is that before Amnesty International distributed its press releases in 1990, only eight news items with references to the murders were located. After the

[1]The impact of Amnesty International's revelations in the international press on the Brazilian government can be attributed, to a certain extent, to the personality or the neo-liberal policies of the then-President Collor, who was very much concerned with his and the country's international image and gesture politics (Rocha, 1991). It can also be said that the reactions of Brazilian newspapers, government, and the general public to the international pressure reflect a mixture of awakening and shame through the horror of others, as well as a certain tradition of cultural dependency, very strong in the Brazilian society. This often translates into judging ourselves by foreigner's standards and valuing issues by the success they get abroad (Medina, 1991), as well as by a mixture of awakening and shame through the horror of others. Nonetheless, such individual or cultural singularities are in line with more global trends.

[2]This is an intriguing finding and needs better investigation because the total output of stories in the foreign coverage about Brazil in the U.S. paper is, as one would expect, usually much higher than in the British daily.

denunciations by the international human rights organization, and up to December 1991, the search in the newspapers studied found 34 stories that specifically reported the issue.

As early as August 1986, Jan Rocha, the *Guardian* correspondent, observed in a feature about the excessive use of murder by the police in Sao Paulo that one out of every three people killed was a minor, and street children were especially marked. In June 1988, the same paper had also published an article by Anthony Swift, a journalist who worked with international charities, that revealed that "justice committees" or death squads were responsible for a large number of deaths of street children in the northern city of Recife, who were involved in crime.

However, at the time, it was the criminal behavior of these youths, particularly their involvement with drug trafficking at a time when the "war on drugs" was high on the international agenda, that seemed to attract the most attention. The foreign or domestic press were not sensitive to the issue of the extra-legal killings of street children, despite the denunciations of such killings by members of the Minor's Pastoral of the Catholic Church and by local groups concerned with human rights or street children's welfare.

The first event to generate a feature calling attention to the denunciations made by the street children movement was the aforementioned murder of a Black 9-year-old boy in May 1989 in Ipanema. The police version related the murder as a settling of scores between drug dealers, but the local coordinators of the street children movement, who had been struggling to call attention to the killings of street children in Rio, promoted a seminar to discuss the issue and briefed journalists. They offered another version that suggested that the crime was part of a larger operation to "clean up" the streets, conducted by "extermination groups," possibly hired by shopkeepers and hotel owners. This motivated one story carried by *Le Monde*.

The second event staged by the national NGOs to attract international attention was the Second Meeting of the Street Children Movement in September 1989, when the results of the first national survey on the death squads' killings were released. Only the *Guardian* published a news report on the issue, delivered by the newspaper correspondent Jan Rocha. On the following day, *El Pais* carried a small news brief, dispatched by the Spanish news agency Efe, on the killings in Rio.

In the eight months that followed, before Amnesty International's press releases, only the British newspaper returned to the issue. The *Guardian* covered the launching of a toy manufacturers' foundation that, together with UNICEF, sponsored the production of a book by a Brazilian journalist to denounce the killings and ran two other stories. One, was about the creation of a special group of the police to hunt down criminals by vigilante groups in Sao Paulo, and another, was motivated by the repercussions in the tourism industry of a wave of crime and the extralegal killings of street children and poor adults in Rio.

The event that received the most coverage was undoubtedly Amnesty International's statement in September 1990 that prompted stories in all the newspapers in the sample. The report that examined the involvement of policemen in justice committees "dedicated to eliminate criminals or marginals" and the use of torture by policemen, "especially against black and poor people," precipitated an international media reaction. Alan Riding, the *New York Times'* correspondent wrote features on the problems of abandoned and destitute children in Brazil, the social stigma that they carried due to the involvement of a minority of these children in street crime, and the rising pressure on the police to get tough, at least as early as 1985. The paper also ran stories about urban violence in Brazil and the rise of vigilantism and official police violence. Even before the report by the United States human rights organization *Americas Watch*, published in December 1987, on the issue of the use of torture and killings by policemen in Brazil, the *New York Times* had already drawn attention to the involvement of policemen in death squads, either voluntarily or hired by shopkeepers and small businessmen. However, before Amnesty's International press release in September 1990, the paper had not reported on the issue of the killing of children and adolescents.

After the denunciations by the international human rights organization and up to December 1991, the search in the newspapers studied found 34 stories that dealt specifically with the extralegal killings of Brazilian children and adolescents. The event that received more coverage during the period was undoubtedly the Amnesty International statement in September 1990. The examination of the other events that made news on the issue also reveals the importance of the international pressure. Of the total number of stories, 31% were generated by activities or statements of international nongovernmental organizations, mainly Amnesty International; 24% by reports or statements by Brazilian authorities or government officials and agencies; and 19% by the efforts of national NGOs, involving the production of surveys, launching of books, and staging of manifestations and events. However, half of the items in this category were related to the announced kidnapping and later reappearance of the Rio Coordinator of the MNMMR and only the *Guardian* reported on the other activities of the national organizations. The remaining news items were motivated by other foreign reactions to the issue 14%, including statements by the Pope visiting Brazil, documentaries produced by British television and other international news, and, lastly, the slaughters themselves—12%.

Nonetheless, the analysis of the sources and participants named in the news reports shows that the national nongovernmental organizations (33%) outnumber official sources (25%) and international

NGOs (11%). Street children or their relatives were quoted in 16% of the stories, the media appeared as source for 6% of the news items, and ordinary people or celebrities accounted for 4%. The most prominent single actors in the foreign coverage were Amnesty International and the National Movement of Street Boys and Girls, especially represented by its Rio Coordinator. With the exception of *El Pais*, the figures in the content analysis show that in all dailies the national NGOs were given more voice than official national representatives. In general, at least in this case, the nonofficial sources were better represented in the Western press. Only one editorial was found in an issue during this period (in *El Pais*), and the majority of the items were news reports (40%) followed by features (36%) and news in brief (22%).

It is worth noting that although all the stories in the Guardian were by-lined by the paper's own correspondent (73%) or other members of the staff or stringers, the news agencies were responsible for 39% of the items in *El Pais* (the Spanish EFE), 46% of the news reports in *Le Monde*, and 33% in *The New York Times* (AFP, Reuters, or AP). Overall, the wires account for only 26% of the stories, and the foreign correspondents or special envoys were the authors of the majority of the items.

NATIONAL REPERCUSSIONS

Since the late 1970s, when the issue of urban violence first gained a political agenda in Brazil, the street children were at the center of this debate. According to many statements at the time, the "abandoned minor" emerged as the main problem to be dealt with, within the logic that "the pickpocket of today is the bandit of tomorrow" (Benevides, 1983, p. 47). They appeared in the press both as a threat to society and as victims of police violence and state neglect. At least as early as 1979, Brazilian journalists denounced the killing of "minors" by police and death squads. But the lists of disappeared children and adolescents published at that time had around a hundred names (Luppi, 1981).

Since the mid-1980s, as a result of economic recession, the number of children and adolescents forced onto the streets to make a living for themselves or their families greatly increased, whereas with the transition to democracy and the return to a civilian government, the study of their problems and the campaign for children's rights acquired more prominence and national media attention. At the same time, a minority of these youths recruited by drug dealers, especially in the slums and suburbs of Rio, or involved in street crime, acquired great visibility even in the foreign press. Their escalating murders by "unknown authors" were then daily routinely reported in the Brazilian press, on the inside pages of police news. In the last years of the decade, as already mentioned, the Catholic Church and NGOs drew attention to these killings, which were investigated by special commissions of the police and also denounced by concerned officials, politicians, and journalists.

The events that made news in the foreign press, as well as others not mentioned there, were first announced in Brazilian newspapers. Although not always recognized in the literature on structures of foreign news (see, e.g., Van Dijk, 1988), in many cases the national media seem to be the most important source for foreign correspondents, not only providing information, but also themes for coverage. In this case, the national press was also the most important source for surveys on the killings and an important element in the communication between the NGOs. However, up to the denunciation by Amnesty International, and the ensuing wave of foreign protest, the "extermination of the children" had not provoked public indignation and sustained prominent coverage in the national sphere.

The international scandal of the killing of the street children in Brazil had a major effect in promoting the issue onto the national political agenda and influencing state actions and policies and thus also the terms of the public debate. This obviously provoked important qualitative and quantitative changes in the content of news in the national press in terms of its placement, salience, and contours. The Parliamentary Commission of Inquiry, set up in the National Chamber of Deputies, spent eight months investigating the "extermination of children and adolescents" in Brazil and concluded in its final report that "it is true that the Brazilian press only moved this issue from the police pages to the political pages after the foreign press did so" (Câmara dos Deputados, 1992, p. 18).

The Brazilian press monitors the coverage of the most important newspapers and news magazines in the world and has correspondents abroad. The repercussions of the problem in the foreign media were reported in the papers, provoking different reactions and even indignant (e.g. *O Globo*, 1991) or favorable (e.g., *Jornal do Brasil*, 1991) editorials. But the changes in the placement of the problem in the national press were also obviously determined by the importance the issue got in the public debate, after the government and other institutions in the national public sphere also reacted to this. So the activities of the Parliamentary Commission of Inquiry (CPI) were daily reported as well as the reactions and measures of the government, which are part of the staff that make political news.

The installation of a Parliamentary Commission of Inquiry (CPI) to investigate violence against street children and links between the death squads and the police was first demanded during the second meeting of the MNMMR in September 1989, by the street children gathered in the capital of the Republic. They invaded the National Congress to demand the approval of a new legislation and denounce the violence against them. Following the occupation of Congress, Nelson Aguiar, the first head of the national children's welfare agency, after the military regime, and the author of the Statute bill, also called for the installation of a CPI to investigate the extermination of children, as demanded by the movement. At the same time, another congressman, the influence Senator Fernando Henrique Cardoso (elected President in 1994), announced he had started the collection of the 272 signatures needed for a Parliamentary Commission of Inquiry. In April 1990, it was formally requested by the deputy Benedita da Silva, a member of the Workers Party, after the organizations in the Brazilian civil society, with the support of international agencies, had been denouncing the problem and struggling to make it an issue in the public agenda and had even been able to get some space in the Brazilian press.

Nonetheless, the request for the CPI was only approved one year later, after the denouncements by Amnesty International were reproduced in the foreign press, documentaries produced by the British television were exhibited shocking foreign viewers and Brazilian newspapers (especially Dan Jordan's *The Child Killers of Brazil*), and the government had taken measures reacting to international pressure. However, it must be said that the foreign press, which condemned so vigorously the killings, completely ignored or played down this CPI investigation and other initiatives to solve the problem taken by the government or other organizations in Brazil.

CONCLUSION

The international civil society of nongovernmental organizations, together with intergovernmental bodies, are to help to develop an international public sphere and the globalization of citizenship. They provide global fora for critical-rational debate, voice public interests at an international level, and influence the world political agenda, besides checking on the governments of nation-states.

The "new communication technologies" offer significant possibilities to improve the level of information about public issues and the exchange of communication between social groups and civil societies to help create communities and movements that transcend national borders. However, the capacity of the mass media to reach broader publics and promote global awareness cannot be underestimated.

The example presented here shows how minority interests can get represented and promoted in the international public sphere, through the operation of an international civil society. This society links NGOs and small groups in less-developed countries with transnational organizations that have more legitimacy and power to press for the opening of spaces in the global media.

This chapter raises more questions than it supplies answers because its main purpose was to provide empirical grounds to incite the theoretical debate on the transnationalization of the public sphere and to spur further research. The relation between media agendas and policy agendas and the intermedia relations between the national and global levels need better theorizing before this idea of the international public sphere can be firmly conceptualized.

The concerns that presided this study differ somehow from the mainstream debate about the international role of the media in the new "globalized" but "not yet post-imperialist era" (Schiller, 1993, p. 97). They drew attention to the consequences of Western media reporting on national policymaking and public opinion and its dynamic effects and dependence on the national press in a developing country, highlighting the importance of new players in the international public sphere, in the context of the increasingly pervasive influences and tensions between the global economy and polity and nation-state sovereignty. Giddens (1990) identifies globalization as one of the most visible consequences of modernity. The "stretching" and intensification of social relations and activities across national territorial boundaries was facilitated by the existence of transnational social movements and networks, global systems of finance, trade, production, and communication. As a result, the destinies of communities and peoples are dependent on decisions and events happening many miles away, which seems to render unimportant distinctions between domestic and foreign domains of activity. However, it is important to qualify the conditions in which these interconnections take place.

In the actual "new world order" based on the dominance of the concepts and practices of the free market approach in the economy and of liberal democracy in the political sphere, intergovernmental organizations with more or less control by a few industrialized countries, such as the World Bank, the IMF, and the United Nations, narrowly determine the routes and closely watch the steps that most nations—willing or not—have to follow. There are concerns about the power of transnational corporate interests to which governments and media are linked or even subordinate to in influencing such policies, as well as worries about the conglomeratization and homogenization embedded in this process with the consequent reduction of available discourses. The transnationalization of problems related to poverty, the flows of drug trafficking and immigration, ecological threats, and human rights abuses have broadened the agenda of international cooperation and media scrutiny as issues for universal surveillance instead of national sovereignty.

Many nongovernmental organizations have consultative status in intergovernmental bodies like the United Nations and are organized in international networks seeking to influence policymaking at the global level. They are increasingly surpassing traditional forms of political representation, fueling democratic utopias and developing new ways of communicating, but they operate in the real world of interstate systems, markets, and mass media that are themselves subject to different pressures and mediation.

This leads to the conclusion that the international public sphere is not a monolithic unity, but rather involves a multiplicity of public spaces and contradictory discourses. The international fora that reflect East-West, North-South tensions and new demands becomes once again "an arena of competing interests fought out in the coarser forms of violent conflict" (Habermas, 1989, p. 132). Coexisting with religious, racial, and other sorts of power struggles, the awareness of the old poverty dilemmas and the new ecological threats contributes to the "relativising of structural conflicts of interest according to the standard of a universal interest" (Habermas, 1989, p. 235). It also delivers the promise of a new humanism, based on the ethics of solidarity and citizenship, within new contours of time and space, challenging the ambitions of efficiency and domination of international markets and nation-states.

This complex reality then cannot be encompassed by simply opposing globalization versus corporate transnationalization. In the case discussed here, the Western media undoubtedly gave more voice to nondominant interests in the Brazilian society and contributed to mobilizing public opinion and the national press, influencing policymaking and public debate at the national level.

Nonetheless, the arguments advanced by this illustration do not aim to dispute the "media imperialism" thesis (see, e.g., Herman & Chomsky, 1988). Further analysis on the way the story was constructed, the different explanatory frameworks used, and their relation to the several discourses in play is called for before any assessment can be made as to whether such coverage contributed to challenge or to reinforce stereotypical representations and to question or to maintain relations of domination between Western powers and a less developed country. This case could even raise a chilling hypothesis that the way some news outlets in the national and international press portrayed the Brazilian children and adolescents, especially the way some foreign newspapers and news agencies constructed and publicized the theme of Rio as a violent city in the late 1980s and early 1990s, helped to create a kind of "moral panic" (Cohen, 1972) that had dramatic real consequences. As a result of the prominence that issues of violence in Rio got in the international press, the number of tourists visiting the city dropped sharply, from 1.9 million in 1987 to 800,000 in 1991 (*Le Monde*, 1992; *El Pais*, 1990). This could have contributed to increasing the anger that the strategies of survival by street children provoked in some sectors of the Brazilian society.

This chapter tells a story of a different kind of conspiracy, of a reversing moral panic in which the media, sensitized by an international movement in defense of children's rights, played a significant role in publicizing the violence against poor children and adolescents in Brazil. This had important real consequences, influencing state policies, raising awareness, awakening solidarity, and favorably mobilizing public opinion at the international and domestic level.

By focusing on the role of an international NGO, this exploration of the transnational public sphere might have conveyed the wrong impression that it adheres to the view that the media are mere channels between society and policymakers (see Reese, 1991, for an overview of different trends in agenda-setting perspectives). On the contrary, the assumptions that guide this study suggest a more active role for the news organizations, which, although representing special public arenas, have not only to stage the negotiation between other contending forces in society, but to consider their own, sometimes conflicting, political, economic, and professional interests. It suggests the importance of examining the relationship between sources and the media in concrete processes developing in the broader setting of historically defined societies, besides news beats, and stresses the need to examine the notions of "primary definers" (Hall, Chritcher, Jefferson, Clarke, & Roberts, 1978) or "political entrepreneurs" (Schlesinger, 1990) in the new global context.

For the same reason, it has played down the vital and grave role of investigative journalism, which deserves better analysis and raises ethical considerations. Even before the survey by IBASE was conducted and Amnesty International releases were dispatched, some news magazines such as *Newsweek* or *L'Express* had already drawn international attention to the killing of street youths by vigilante groups or death squads, also revealed by national television programs and newspaper features.

In some cases the children portrayed in such stories were subsequently killed. Also the journalists who investigated the activities of the death squads in Brazil were subjected to all sorts of pressures including death threats that were sometimes realized, or they were forced to exile to escape such a destiny. The same happened to witnesses, relatives, judges, and ordinary people who campaign for children rights. This study indicates that there were important differences as well as similarities between the way various news outlets and individual journalists responded to the different interests, as well as significant tensions between the organizations in civil society that pressed to make violence against street children a matter of common concern. It clearly shows the significant role of the international press in mobilizing international involvement in what would once have been considered a "local" issue, suggesting the potential for human rights discourse to be a fulcrum for global public opinion.

11

A Little Village in a Big World: Young Squatters and the Limits of News

Paula Saukko
University of Illinois

Studies of the interaction between social movements and the news media have often been interested in the question of how negative or positive the coverage. The coverage of movements whose values deviate from what is considered "normal," that is, that do not coalesce with those of middle-class, middle-aged, White, moderate males, is often negative (Shoemaker, 1984). Thus, the media have either downplayed or distorted, for example, the 1960s student New Left (Gitlin, 1980), the antinuclear movement (Gamson & Modigliani, 1989), and Black protests (Diawara, 1990). Still, there are opposite examples, such as the positive coverage of some environmental groups (Linné, 1991; Lowe & Morrison, 1984) and squatters (Carle, 1991).

    Yet these studies do not typically pay much attention to what aspects of the movement are covered and what are not. In my study of a widely covered Finnish alternative[1] youth movement "Orange,"[2] which

---

[1]The term *alternative movements* is often used, at least in Europe, for movements creating new (alternative) meanings to a variety of issues, such as lifestyle and work (e.g., Rucht, 1990). Orange's activists described their movements as *alternative* in broad terms.

[2]The name *Orange* ("Oranssi" in Finnish) refers to the color. It was chosen

politicized topics ranging from national and local policies to global problems felt in the local, the boundaries or limits of news became unusually
visible. To trace these boundaries, I compared Orange's wide sphere of
attention to its narrow media image in two dimensions. First, I located the
focus of Orange and the news in the geographical continuum from the
local to the national and to the global. Second, I examined what scopes of
life, from the everyday to the "political" (narrowly defined), to which the
media and the movement pay attention.

In the media, Orange was mainly pictured as a squatters' movement protesting against local and national politics. But the activists were
not only seeking to oppose policies and to obtain a place to live, they
wanted to invent new physical, cultural, and social places for living and
spending leisure that in one of the activist's words constituted "a little village." This little village is also a response to the global trends of mass-
scale speculation that restructures cities, counseling techniques shaping
the self, environmental destruction, mass culture, and the dissolution of
traditional communities. Thus, the media coverage of Orange diverges
from the way the youth movement defined itself in two aspects:

1. The concerns of the movement encompass the local, national,
    and the global and therefore are not covered by the news
    media with their more restricted geographic focus. Although
    there have been numerous studies of bias in international
    news coverage, this study is among the first to isolate the
    media's relation to the nexus between the global and the local.
2. The movements' sphere of attention is wide also in terms of
    scope of life, paying attention both to the everyday and to
    political issues, whereas the news strictly focuses on the politi-
    cal, narrowly defined.

In the following, I first discuss how current globalization processes shatter the autonomy of the state, making old state-centered notions
of politics and democracy partially obsolete. Second, I examine how new
social movements inhabit and articulate the nexus between the global
and the local that is becoming a new crucial site of politics. Third, I argue
that the fact that the history and ideology of journalism are connected to
the state makes it hard for journalists to turn their attention to these new
global, local, and everyday dimensions of politics. Finally, I present how
all this is played out in my case study of Orange and the Finnish media.

---

because it was catchy, symbolized "friendship and wisdom," and did not have
any political connotations.

THE GLOBAL, THE LOCAL, AND THE IN-BETWEEN

One of the biggest challenges facing contemporary democracy is the globalization of economics, politics, and culture. Different parts of the world have been economically interdependent before, but the advanced telecommunications network has made it possible for transnational corporations to exercise control globally. Transnational corporations looking for investment opportunities with the most rapid profit turnover can quickly shift their production or financial assets from one place to another, changing constructed and natural environments and communities and causing a boom or collapse of local or even national economies (Castells, 1989; Harvey, 1989; Urry, 1990). International financial operations—that are invisible but have far-reaching consequences for individuals and regions—trade around 25 times as much each day in volume than is traded globally in goods (Daly, 1991).

The importance of international politics has also grown. International organizations, such as the European Union, attempt to pool resources to respond to these global forces, but they also make decisions that restrict the autonomy of their member states. In addition, worldwide culture industries plus large immigration waves have stirred up local and national cultures, making them at the same time both more homogenous and more heterogenous (e.g. Hall, 1991a, 1991b).

Crudely put, these developments can be understood in two opposite ways. The first tendency is to focus on the global and to be Orwellian about the transnational economy dictating the lives of millions who cannot affect the process (Castells, 1989; Harvey, 1993). The other option is to take a "bottom-up" view and celebrate the mushrooming of many local movements and groups resisting the global forces and see in them the seeds of a new global civil society (Hall, 1991b).

These new local movements are, in fact, umbilically connected to the global. They range from defensive projects, such as the Thatcherite nostalgia for the old imperialist England (Hall, 1991a); to environmental groups longing for a "holistic" unity between humans and nature (e.g., Eder, 1990; Eyerman & Jamison, 1989); to rastafarianism, a point of origin and protest to Blacks and also to young Whites all over the world (Gilroy, 1987). These movements respond to trends with global roots, such as the decay of certain regions and urban areas, environmental destruction, migration, and diaspora, and their ideas are also disseminated across borders by mass media.

Literature also increasingly explores the nexus—or the "in-between" as geographers Robert Sacks (1992) and Nicholas Entrikin (1991) have called it—in which the global is played out in the local and vice versa. Theories of chaos or complexity remind us that this relationship is not linear or one way; it cannot be described in terms of single cause and effect (Hayles, 1991). The global and the local form a complex web, in which a small change in some part can have unpredictable effects on the overall picture. The causes of a single occurrence can never be fully mapped out, but there is "order in chaos" and some of the multiple relations can be traced.

As a result of these developments, yet another set of distinctions is losing part of its explanatory power. It is often understood that the Orwellian scholars, known as political economists, talk about the economic and the political, whereas the more optimistic cultural studies people focusing on culture or the everyday address a separate scope of life. But as the state is losing its powers to global economic players (Braman, 1994; Held, 1990), and as the local and the everyday are becoming crucial sites in which these new forces are challenged, it becomes apparent that these spheres are also deeply intertwined.

SOCIAL MOVEMENTS: RENDERING DISPERSED POWER VISIBLE

What makes the study of new social movements interesting at this conjuncture is that they inhabit and articulate the nexus of the global and the local and operate in the economic, political, and the everyday. By new movements I mean those groups that have emerged since the 1960s and that differ from the old movements in that their interests and strategies are dispersed compared to the agenda of, for example, the workers' movement focusing on the state.

The strategies and gains of the old movements, however, are still often taken as a yardstick by which to measure the "political" impact of the new movements. For example, Rucht (1990) divides social movements into those that are "power oriented" and those that are "identity oriented," meaning by a *power orientation* the attempt to affect public policies. This attitude results in paradoxes, as for Rucht the struggle of the women's movement to change gender roles is not related to "power." There are two flaws in this standpoint. First, it falls prey to the feminist argument that defining some issues, such as domestic affairs, *private* (apolitical) is a highly political act that tries to "naturalize" (or at least render less important) the power relations in these areas of life. Second, the idea that only state policies are fully "political" is untenable in the contemporary world, in which the autonomy of the nation-state is seriously limited by the global forces and in which solutions to many new problems are sought at the local level.

Alberto Melucci (1989) has argued that *power* in contemporary societies manifests itself differently; it is ingrained in all levels and areas of life.[3] Thus, he sees current movements as agents that "render" this ubiquitous power "visible." According to Melucci, social movements are responses to new "systemic conflicts" that result from pressures on individual autonomy and the living environment caused by new forces, such as genetic technology, counseling, environmental destruction, and the arms race. Movements are not *apolitical*, but *prepolitical*, meaning that they politicize new, previously neglected issues and bring them to the policy agenda (see also Offe, 1987). They can also be *metapolitical*, articulating problems that cannot be resolved through state policies; sometimes state intervention in the minute detail of people's everyday life is the problem itself.

Melucci (1989) challenges the idea that the new social movements are "inefficient" because they have not substantially changed policies or had an effect on the international economic order. For Melucci, the often overlooked aspects of movements, such as their forms of organization, collective identities, lifestyle, dress, language, and the affective relations they promote all shatter the logic of complex systems (consumerism, time management, detached relationships, etc.). Many of these practices undermine capitalism's fundamental imperative to accelerate consumption and productivity, in fact, attacking the core of the global economy.

Yet Melucci (1989) leaves underexplored some issues that are of importance to my study. He refers to the geographical dimension mainly in relation to environmental and peace groups. But the global is not only present in these most obvious cases; it is also ingrained into the technologies that reach to the most intimate levels of our physical and emotional existence. The new medical and psychiatric inventions travel rapidly across space, but so do their counter-tendencies, such as women's attempts to redefine new reproductive technologies, ideologies of self-help groups, and alternative medicine. These ideas are shared by worldwide countercultures united by dress, music, eating habits, and ways of protesting; they are enhanced through tourism; through mass culture, such as news coverage of big demonstrations and Live Aid concerts (e.g., Crook, Pakulski, & Waters, 1992); and increasingly through electronic networks.

Finally, Melucci (1989) understands that the movements remain most of the time "latent," becoming "visible" or appearing in the media when their aims conflict with a public policy. I would argue that the "invisibility" of certain aspects of movements is not always the choice of movements, but is often due to the fact that the media ignore them, thus debilitating movements' ability to raise consciousness and discussion about these issues.

---

[3]Melucci has been influenced by Michel Foucault's (1979) notion that power is a ubiquitous and contradictory practice that takes place in all areas and levels of society.

Despite the fact that the gains of new movements have often been overlooked, in the end I would partially also agree with the more Orwellian vision that reminds us that the global economic forces moving money, goods, production units, and waste from one place of the world to another, changing people's everyday lives, remain largely untouched (Calhoun, 1993; Castells, 1989; Harvey, 1993). Not that these projects focus on wrong issues or areas, but they are weak and scattered. There are some budding projects and much utopian talk about effective networks that could counter global forces. But these examples are few and mostly in the making.

NEWS MEDIA—SIBLING OF THE LIBERAL STATE

The history of journalism as an institution and as a practice is bound to the liberal state putting journalism in a new situation as the power of the state is diminishing. According to Jürgen Habermas (1989), bourgeois literary and political pamphlets (that together with bourgeois economic newsletters were predecessors of contemporary news media) and other new forms of public discussion in salons and coffeehouses in the 18th century articulated the public discontent against European absolute monarchies, contributing to their fall and bringing about parliamentary democracy. One can ask how complete Habermas's historical picture is (Fraser, 1992), but it is evident that the birth of the press was related to the rise of the bourgeoisie and the liberal democratic state. Thus, due to historical and political reasons, the normative ideal of liberal press (encapsulated by Habermas) became that of a public forum that keeps an eye on and guides state decision making. This ideal dominates the self-understanding of professional journalists as well as much of journalism research also today.

Journalists often describe themselves as "critical of the state" and "being on the side of the citizens." Their most common self-critique is that they consider themselves to be too subservient to politicians. Schudson (1978) has argued that this "critical" attitude was exacerbated in the United States after Watergate and the Vietnam War, events that undermined the credibility of politicians. According to Aula (1991), the same kind of development took place in Finland later, after the resignation of the long-term authoritarian president Kekkonen in the early 1980s. The resignation and death of Kekkonen launched a self-criticism of journalism as it became public that the journalists close to him had hidden the fact that in the last years Kekkonen was seriously demented.

Journalism scholars also typically contrast actual media practices with the ideal of a public sphere in which citizens challenge state politics.

For example, media sociologists have criticized journalists for depending on official, often public, sources, thus ignoring citizens' initiatives and opinions (Altheide & Snow, 1992; Eliasoph, 1988; Meyers, 1992). Beat reporters' everyday interaction with beat sources like the police have ended up creating a common framework and language for both. In the case of crime, crime reporters interpret everything from the "law and order" perspective of the police (Ericson, Baranek, & Chan, 1989).

Yet, discussion of whether the media are for or against the state still reflects the same narrow vision of "politics" as does the research on social movements. This point has been made particularly by scholars studying popular culture or popular news (e.g., Fiske, 1992; for a Latin-American perspective, see Martin Barbero, 1993). They have argued that the popular press, focusing on crime and scandals and private affairs of celebrities, has been criticized because its gaudy and carnivalesque nature and focus on "private" matters does not fit the middle-class male culture, but is more faithful to the imagination of women and the working class.

Although it would be simplistic to argue that all news on family life, and so on, politicizes previously neglected issues, it becomes clear in the study on Orange that the media ignored the everyday life details of the movement. It might be easier to evoke issues such as emotions in the "entertainment" genre or to write human interest stories to "add color" to already prominent news issues (such as a feature story on a single mother attached to a piece of news on welfare policy). *Politicizing*, that is, challenging a relation of power in the everyday, might seem like a contradiction in terms.

Whereas the negligence of the everyday or the "private" both in politics and in "serious" journalism has been brought up by feminists (e.g., Fraser, 1992) and scholars focusing on popular culture, the idea that news often ignores the global dimensions of phenomena is not often touched on. There is vast literature on the bias in international news, but the idea that news misses the nexus between local everyday phenomena and the global (so much talked about in the social sciences today) passes largely unnoticed.

Finally, I argue that the ideal of objectivity makes journalism less receptive to new issues. Objectivity is, in fact, closely related to the ideal of "being critical"; both start from the assumption that the task of journalism is not to "understand" its sources, but to critically "examine" them. Thus, the objective journalist belongs to the same family of Enlightenment creatures as the normalizing psychiatrist (revealed by Foucault, 1979) or the positivist ethnographer (criticized by, e.g., Clifford & Marcus, 1986) who does not engage in a dialogue with his or her objects, but just "observes," "documents," and fits them to predefined schemes. This self-induced incapacity to listen impairs journalism's sensitivity to topics it is not used to reporting.

THE PUBLIC FACE OF SQUATTERS: PROTEST

I have traced the areas that journalism can and cannot talk about by comparing the private and public images[4] of the youth movement Orange. To map the private image of the movement I interviewed 17 of its activists and did some participant observation. The number of activists in Orange has varied, but maybe more than a thousand young have been involved in the movement during its existence; in 1993, 60 people lived in its houses. The youngest activists are in their early teens and the oldest in their early 30s; most come from middle-class families. The young ones go to school; many of the older ones were unemployed at the time of the interviews or went to vocational college. There are only a few university students in Orange, so it is not a student movement.

To trace the public image of the movement I analyzed over 100 news or feature stories on Orange between 1989 and 1993 (this example comes close to the total number of articles published in the print media in the Helsinki area).[5] Because Orange was covered by all major local and national media, my material varies; *Helsingin Sanomat*, a Helsinki-based major daily, published the largest number of stories on Orange. As I was also interested in the professional ideologies that explain the coverage of Orange, I interviewed a dozen journalists[6] who had covered the movement.

The birth of Orange is related to many global, national, and local developments in economics and politics at the turn of the decade. The end of the 1980s was a period of unforeseen economic boom in Finland. This was a result of many factors, such as an international upswing, the liberalization of financial markets in Finland, and "an unholy alliance" of social democrats and conservatives[7] in the government (resulting in a combination of economic liberalization and increasing government spending that accelerated the boom). The seeming abundance of money

---

[4]I have published a more detailed piece on the empirical study in Finnish (Saukko, 1993).

[5]Using the archives of the movement and its activists and Arhippa Ristimaki's preliminary list of articles published on Orange, I was able to locate most of the print news and features on the movement between 1989-1993. I also analyzed some TV and radio news and documentaries, but most audiovisual material proved to be impossible to locate due to its ephemeral nature.

[6]The journalists interviewed were mostly in their 30s (the coverage of a youth movement was assigned to young reporters, and they were most interested in it) and well educated. They were comprised equally of men and women.

[7]There are three big parties in Finland: the Social Democrats, the LIberals, and the Conservatives. It has not been a custom for the Social Democrats and the Conservatives to form the government as they represent the opposite ends in the left-right continuum.

resulted in the skyrocketing of prices, especially of real estate, always one of the favorite targets of investment of speculatory capital. Rents soared, which made it very hard to find a place to live for people who could not take advantage of the economic development, such as the young, students, pensioners, and people of low wages.

Thus, in January 1990, a group of young people for whom it was almost impossible to find a place to live by normal means decided to occupy an old empty wooden building owned by the Finnish Government Board of Real Estate. Orange did not inhabit the building right away, but rather organized an "occupation" as a media event to gain public sympathy to help lobby for the houses. This first occupation was covered, mostly favorably, by some media. But the real media success was the second occupation of an old soap factory ("Kookos" factory) in the heart of Helsinki in May 1990. Orange wanted to conserve the old industrial building and to convert it to a world house for the young. This would have been an international cultural meeting place; there were plans to run an international youth hostel and to provide space for bands and other artists to practice and for other movements to meet. The aim was also to open a casual cafe, in which the teenagers could get together and do things. The factory belonged to Finland's largest construction company, Haka, part of the social democratic corporate empire. The municipal council of Helsinki (also dominated by the social democrats and the conservatives) had given permission to Haka to tear it down and to construct its headquarters on the lot.

Although the dreams Orange tried to realize by occupying the houses span from the local and the national to the global, encompassing both the political and the cultural, the media mostly represented it as a protest against public policies. One target was national housing policy, which did not ensure a place to live for the young. Orange's occupation was a catchy topic as the difficult housing situation and the inadequacy of government policies were covered in the media almost daily. Thus, Orange's message fitted an already existing news agenda. During the occupation of the Kookos factory, Orange was represented as a more general protest against inefficient and corrupt politics. The occupation of Kookos was an especially juicy topic because the focus of its critique was the unholy left-right alliance, which had fueled the common sense mistrust of politics. Orange accused the big parties of political horse trade and ignorance of the needs of people without the power of money.

Even though Orange was at times articulated in the press from the typical "law and order" perspective (Ericson et al., 1989; Gitlin, 1980) as hooligans violating private property, its media treatment in general was surprisingly positive. This is explained by the historical conjuncture, the ability of the movement to deal with the media, and by the attitude of the journalists. The journalists whom I interviewed stated that they sympathized with Orange because it was "against the establishment." The journalists emphasized that they were on the side of the "little people" and saw that the basic flaw in journalism is that it often becomes the mouthpiece of official sources. The professional idea taking shape in the interviews was the classical liberal press ideal according to which journalism should function as a "critical watchdog" of the state and defend the interests of the citizens. Orange fitted this professional identity, providing the journalists an opportunity to highlight its characteristic.

The activists of Orange also identified themselves as a protest movement; they wanted to "mess up the plans" of the politicians because they were frustrated not to be able to acquire a place to live. In this respect the public and private image of the movement coincided almost one by one. In the end the coverage of Orange seems to be one of the rare occasions in which the media have lived up to the expectations of the "watchdog" ideology and allied with the citizens against strong political and economic interests. It underlines the argument of some scholars (Eliasoph, 1988; Meyers, 1992) that the professional routines, as such, do not inhibit the media from doing this.

Although the media only captured part of Orange's endeavors, the activists were happy with the positive coverage of the occupations as it helped them to attract new members and to attain their most immediate goal: the houses. The government rented Orange the first wooden building it occupied. The movement never got the Kookos factory (it did later acquire a smaller building for its youth cafe), but the permit to tear down the building was cancelled, and Haka never constructed its headquarters on the lot. As of now, the abandoned factory stands as a monument not only of the dashed grandiose dreams of the young, but also of the Finnish corporate empire, as Haka itself was swept away by the recession.

THE PRIVATE FACE OF SQUATTERS:
A LITTLE VILLAGE IN A BIG WORLD

The number of articles published on Orange drops considerably (to about one quarter in my example) after the movement gave up occupying houses and started to repair them and to run a youth cafe and a summer hostel in one of them. This shift is connected to the changes in the economic environment. The unusual boom was followed by a deep recession, which dropped the price of housing, thus making it possible for Orange to rent affordable houses. At the same time, housing disappeared from the news agenda, and growing unemployment (the figures soared from 3% to over 20%) became the prime topic of the news.

On the other hand, Orange's goal had gone beyond the simple political protest about the cost of housing from the very beginning. The dream of Orange was to create places that in the physical, social, and cultural dimensions fit visions of an alternative way of life.

Politics of Physical Place

Orange's struggle for place manifests itself at two levels: the young are after certain kinds of housing (an architectural issue), but they are also after certain areas of the city (an issue of urban design). The architectural goal was to obtain houses that would be on a human scale (such as the small wooden apartment buildings) and have a sense of history (like the old soap factory), but would not have been expensively or "gaudily" remodeled (the wooden houses were repaired by the activists themselves, recycling materials and conserving the old wood stoves). The urban design dream is reflected by the location of the first squatted house (and the two adjacent ones obtained later) in a picturesque old neighborhood close to the center that used to be run down and inhabited by the poor and had recently been gentrified.

However, as David Harvey (1989) explains, Orange's local politics of place relate to the larger global politics of space. According to Harvey, the fact that "speculatory" capital likes to invest in real estate has three consequences. First, it makes prices skyrocket. Second, it pushes poor people away from areas in which the price of land is expected to soar (such as in old working-class neighborhoods close to urban centers). Third, it tends to cause these areas to be destroyed or expensively remodeled, constructing gaudy "postmodern" architectural monuments, such as shopping centers or office buildings (like the planned Haka headquarters), or equally expensive housing projects for the middle class, often with a touch of "heritage."

Thus Orange's housing projects and its cafe are outposts resisting two things at two levels: First, they stand in opposition to local and national public housing policies that relocate the young and the poor to the huge, dull public housing projects with their bleak public youth houses at the far fringes of the city. Second, Orange's houses also stand against the larger global financial flows that can suddenly pour money into an area calling into existence all kinds of "development" projects that may buy out whole old neighborhoods, reconstructing in their place architectural inventions for the well-to-do. Furthermore, just as these projects not only represent the local, neither do they only represent the everyday. The global picture makes their connections to the global and the economic clear. On the other hand, the bad quality of public housing projects is no less a "political" issue than there being an insufficient quantity.

The last aspect of Orange's politics of physical setting—also intermingled with the global, local, economic, political, and the everyday—is their attempt to live "ecologically." The old, wooden houses with large yards were actually occupied with an eye to conserving the environment. The houses are mainly heated by wood or solar energy and repaired with secondhand materials. Waste is recycled. Ecology is also reflected in the activists' lifestyle; they live modestly, use secondhand clothes and furniture, and many are vegetarians. Some activists also seek a more spiritual relationship with nature and are attracted to New Age philosophies. But unlike many spiritual and lifestyle movements, Orange does not expect its activists to conform to any strict rules. Thus, meat eaters kept eating sausage in the common sauna (eating sausage in saunas is a Finnish tradition) as a counter-ritual to vegetarian practices.

Politics of Self and Community

One of the most important benefits for the activists was that Orange provided them with friends, a sense of community, and a place where you could be who you are and do what you want. Translated into theoretical terms, these ideas could be seen as attempts to create new cultural practices and meanings and social atmosphere.

Many of the activists interviewed had previously felt themselves "lonely" and "not able to relate to yuppie class-mates." Thus, Orange's housing projects and its youth cafe became places where the "different" could get together or where the difference could be created. As the houses were administered by the young themselves, they provided safe places for activities and ideas that could contradict adult middle-class values[8] (and would not be possible, for example, in a public youth house). In the houses the young created new meanings and practices of eating (vegetarian diet or the rasta diet with its religious connotations), dress (secondhand clothing, mixing punk, neo-hippie, and "alternative" styles), music and arts (there were many people making music, theater, and other kinds of arts), time (although "doing things" was stressed, rigid timetables and rushing were despised, for a stressed time-manager it felt like stepping into a slow-motion film), and human relations (the sense of a "little village").

An example of these practices is provided by the attempts of the young girls to give their own twists on sexuality by mocking the rigid

---

[8]Although Orange can be seen as young people's attempt to escape the surveying eyes of youth workers and other normalizing agencies, it did, naturally, have its own internal rules. For example, there was always an older activist to keep an eye on the younger ones in the youth cafe, aggressive behavior was not tolerated, and use of intoxicants was to some extent policed.

models offered by both the "no-no discourse" of different counselors and advisers (appearing in the media and at schools, etc.) and by the soft-porn femme-fatale image marketed by the "naughtier" teen magazines. For the cafe's internal diary, they had written a parody version of the women's magazine's "know who you are" quizzies. The right answer to the question, "Where would you go, if you wanted somebody immediately?", was not (romantic) Rome or Gambrini (a "naughty" disco) but Alepa, a discount grocery store.

As Melucci (1989) reminds us, these everyday activities cannot be dismissed as apolitical or everyday as they challenge some of the core logics of global capitalism, such as the acceleration of consumption and the productivity of labor (manifesting itself in the culture of "being busy"). In short, they are responses to the ubiquitous "technologies of the self" that appear at all geographical levels (from local youth houses to global mass media) and in every scope of life (in the surveillance at the workplace and at a marriage counselor), and that push people to conform to the system logic by advising them how to look, how to have sex, and what to do with one's life, and in which order.

Like the technologies, the counter-technologies also operate at multiple levels. Orange does not isolate itself from the big, bad world. On the contrary, its activists actively use global mass media, appropriating snippets from the contradictory flow of advertising, popular culture, and news sometimes to turn them against themselves—like interpreting the rasta/reggae culture in terms of anticonsumerism. Thus, Orange is part of the global counter-tendencies or "sensibilities" that promote an awareness of ecology and anti-rat-race lifestyles, similar dress, kinds of music, and similar protests (the practice of squatting is international). These resonances take also more concrete forms through the activists' informal and formal connections to foreigners and to other national and international organizations (the peace and environmental movements, Amnesty International, Greenpeace, pro-Third-World groups, and other green and left organizations).

Finally, even the activists' intimate and emotional longing for "belongingness" had structural roots as it is a response to the dissolution of old communities such as the workplace (to which the unemployed or self-employed did not have access), neighborhood, and family.

Journalism's Limited Notion of Public Sphere

The media, however, pretty much ignored these aspects of Orange. There were a few stories on the solar panels—they are, after all, one of the biggest experiments on solar energy in a residential site in Finland. But the articles focused on technological innovation as a way out of the environmental crisis, without paying attention to the movement's deeper critique of consumer culture and lifestyle. During the occupation of the soap factory some articles did touch on the issue of conserving the old industrial cityscape. But as Orange's actual architectural projects were not so monumental (the idea being not to be monumental), they were never understood to have anything to do with aesthetics or urban design.

Part of the reason the movement was not covered so widely after the squattings was that they did not try as often to get into the media. Yet, even though the press was invited to the closing of the first youth house and to the inauguration of the solar panels, the events did not attract journalists. The activists also hinted to some journalists that there were "culturally interesting things in the making" without much avail. Although the activists were in general happy with their media coverage, they were somewhat disappointed with the media's inability to present the full scope of their movement. Because the activists hoped their ecological, social, and cultural projects would make news in order to inspire other young people to do similar things, this was problematic because the inability of the media to publicize their projects made it difficult to create political discussions and formations around them.

The media's concentration on the squattings and negligence of other aspects of the movement also affected the activists' own self-understanding and motivation. Although some of the activists thought they did not need any more publicity, one of the leaders said that the problem was that "even our own people think that we aren't doing anything, when we aren't in the media." When I was conducting the interviews in the spring and summer of 1993, many people were tired of running the cafe and repairing the houses (a bigger job than they had expected) and felt "they were doing all this work" and were given "no credit" in the media. Yet this low did not kill the movement; when I visited Orange a year later, the movement seemed to have grown used to a more underground existence. Interestingly, Orange's occupation of a public youth house in the center of Helsinki that was supposed to be converted to other purposes "to save money" in late 1993 hardly made it to the news. Thus, it was not the occupations that attracted the media, but the fact that at that time Orange fitted an already existing news agenda that criticized the housing policy and the left-right coalition government. When the issue of the occupation was "just" that the young wanted a place to meet, it was not worth the attention.

Some of the journalists explained their lack of interest in Orange's everyday existence by stating bluntly that "squatting a house is news but repairing it is not." This attitude exemplifies not only the old argument that journalism is only interested in "conflicts," but also reflects the media's narrow definition of politics. They considered themselves to be on the side of the citizens against the state, yet their own world vision was so embedded in state politics that they did not understand the worries of the citizens that did not translate to state policies.

Finally, I argue that journalism's inability to capture these new areas of politics is also related to the ideal of being "critical" or "objective." Despite the fact that many of the young journalists interviewed did not believe in objectivity, it still seemed to guide their practice as they wanted to "scrutinize" and keep "at a critical distance" from their sources. This "detachment" makes journalism insular to topics that go outside the policy arena, whose language it understands and speaks, and whose problems it considers important, as it is the everyday habitat of journalists. It was the two feature writers—both women—who were the least preoccupied with being "critical" and, on the contrary, stated their goal is "to capture the language and the world view" of the people they interview, and who wrote two of the articles that focused on the countercultural aspects of the movement. We could speculate that this kind of "listening" journalism would better capture the worlds it is not used to exploring.

CONCLUSIONS

In conclusion, Orange's sphere of attention ranges geographically from the local, to the national, and to the global. It belongs to a larger "localization" response in the sense that it articulates and tries to find solutions to issues that are rooted in the larger complex global structures locally. It also operates in several spheres of life; its squattings were "political" critiques, in the narrow sense of the term, as they questioned public policies. Yet the issues that seem mundane or everyday are no less "political" than the attacks on housing policy. On the contrary, global pressures against identity, aesthetics, sense of time and space, the environment, and lifestyle might end up changing lives more profoundly than shortcomings in housing policy.

The public image of Orange was pretty much confined to the aspects that articulated "politics," understood in terms of issues related to local and national policy arenas. The practice of journalism seemed to come close to its stated liberal ideal, that is, it opened a public sphere in which citizens could air their discontent with state policies. In a way, Orange's coverage was one of the few occasions when journalism lived up to this ideal and actually rallied for the cause of citizens against the interests of the strong national, political, and economical elites.

However, this liberal journalistic ideal may have reached its limits in the contemporary globalizing and complex world. The global, inhabited by fast-acting transnationals, by a transnational culture industry that seduces people to change everything from personalities to cat food, and by diverse and mobile experts, is increasingly undermining the powers of the state. These strong global forces are being followed and at times countered by international organizations, migrant labor, and budding networks of nongovernmental organizations. Yet the current globally rooted problems are mostly fought where they are mostly felt, that is, in the local. Many movements like Orange try to find responses to global problems in the everyday, by creating new lifestyles, changing their consumption behavior, refusing to take part in the rat race, and taking over physical places with political force, not money, so as to enact their dreams and to contribute to global countercultural sensibilities.

Against this background, when journalism ignores the everyday aspects of Orange, it might be missing a small but crucial site in which an effort is made to challenge a web of many larger forces. The media's hesitation to cover these struggles and areas limits people's ability to understand, debate, and form larger (also global) political formations around them. This is a serious flaw if journalism wants to function as a public sphere that enhances democracy understood as the people's ability to affect the conditions of their lives in the contemporary world.

References

Adam, B. (1990). *Time and social theory*. Cambridge, England: Polity Press.

Adorno, T.W. (1990). Culture industry reconsidered. In J. C. Alexander & S. Seidman (Eds.), *Culture and society: Contemporary debates* (pp. 275-283). New York: Cambridge University Press. (Original work published 1944)

Ahmed, A., & Donnan, H. (Eds.). (1994). *Islam, globalization, and postmodernity*. London: Routledge.

Ajami, F. (1986). *The vanished Imam*. Ithaca, NY: Cornell University Press.

Albrow, M., & King, E. (Eds.). (1990). *Globalization, knowledge and society*. Newbury Park, CA: Sage.

Alexander, J. (1991). Bringing democracy back in: Universalistic solidarity and the civil sphere. In C. Lemert (Ed.), *Intellectuals and politics: Social theory in a changing world* (pp. 157-176). London: Sage.

Allen, J. (1992). Post-industrialism and post-Fordism. In S. Hall, D. Held, & T. McGrew (Eds.), *Modernity and its futures* (pp. 169-204). Cambridge, England: Polity.

Allende, I. (1987). *Of love and shadows*. London: Black Swan.

Altheide, D., & Snow, R. (1992). *Media worlds in the postjournalism era*. New York: Aldine de Gruyter.

Amnesty International. (1988). *Amnesty International report 1988.* London: Amnesty International Publications.

Amnesty International. (1990). *Beyond the law: Torture and extrajudicial execution in urban Brazil.* London: Amnesty International Publications.

Amnesty International. (1991a). *Amnesty International report 1991.* London: Amnesty International Publications.

Amnesty International. (1991b). *Torture of street children in police custody in Cuiaba.* London: Amnesty International Publications.

Amnesty International. (1992a). *Handbook.* London: Amnesty International Publications.

Amnesty International. (1992b). *Impunity and the law: The killing of street children in Rio de Janeiro State.* London: Amnesty International Publications.

Amnesty International. (1992c). *Extrajudicial execution of street children in Sergipe.* London: Amnesty International Publications.

Anderson, B. (1983). *Imagined communities: Reflections on the origin and spread of nationalism.* London: Verso.

Anderson, W. T. (1990). *Reality isn't what it used to be: Theatrical politics, ready-to-wear religion, global myths, primitive chic and other wonders of the postmodern world.* San Francisco: Harper.

Ang, I. (1990). Culture and communication: Towards an ethnographic critique of media consumption in the transnational media system. *European Journal of Communication, 5*(2-3), 239-260.

Appadurai, A. (1990). Disjuncture and difference in the global cultural economy. *Public Culture, 2*(2), 1-24.

Appadurai, A. (1993). Patriotism and its futures, *Public Culture, 5*(3), 411-430.

Arato, A. (1994). The rise, decline and reconstruction of the concept of civil society and directions for future research. *Mapping the Field of The Public, 1*(1-2), 45-56.

Archer, C. (1991). *International organizations.* London: Routledge.

Arendt, H. (1973). *The origins of totalitarianism.* New York: Harcourt Brace Jovanovich.

Arendt, H. (1975). *Crises of the republic.* New York: Harcourt Brace Jovanovich.

Aristotle. (1962). *Nicomachean ethics* (M. Ostwald, Trans.). New York: Macmillan. (Original work published 335-323 B.C.)

Aristotle. (1981). *The politics* (T. A. Sinclair, Trans., T. J. Saunders, Rev. Trans.). London: Penguin Books. (Original work published 335-323 B.C.)

Arnason, J. P. (1990). Nationalism, globalization and modernity. *Theory, Culture and Society, 7*, 207-236.

Aronson, S. H. (1986). The sociology of the telephone. In G. Gumpert & R. Cathcart (Eds.), *Inter/media: Interpersonal communication in a media world* (pp. 272-283). New York: Oxford University Press.

Aula, M. K. (1991). *Poliitikkojen ja toimittajien suhteet murroksessa?* [A turning point in the relations between politicians and journalists?] Helsinki: Yleisradio.

Bal, N. (1985). *De mens is wat hij doet, BRT-memoires* [One is what one does]. Leuven, Belgium: Kritak.

Balandier, G. (1985). *Le detour: Pourvoir et modernité* [The detour: Power and modernity]. Paris: Fayard.

Balandier, G. (1988). *Le désordre: Eloge du movement* [The disorder: In praise of movement]. Paris: Fayard.

Bar-Haim, G. (1989). Action and heroes: The meaning of Western pop information for East-European youth. *British Journal of Sociology, 40*(1), 22-45.

Barber, B. (1984). *Strong democracy.* Berkeley: University of California Press.

Barber, B.R. (1995). *Jihad vs. McWorld.* New York: Times Books.

Barthes, R. (1974). *S/Z.* New York: Hill and Wang.

Baudrillard, J. (1983). The ecstasy of communication. In H. Foster (Ed.), *Postmodern culture* (pp. 126-134). London: Pluto.

Bauman, Z. (1986). The left as the counter-culture of modernity. *Telos, 70*, 81-93.

Bauman, Z. (1990). Modernity and ambivalence. In M. Featherstone (Ed.), *Global culture: Nationalism, globalization and modernity* (pp. 143-171). London: Sage.

Bauman, Z. (1992). *Intimations of postmodernity.* London: Routledge.

Beck, U. (1992). *Risk society: Towards a new modernity.* London: Sage.

Beheydt, L. (1984). Taalbeheersing en taalzorg in de media [Command of and attention to language in the media]. *Ra-Tel, 14*(8-9), 8-12.

Beheydt, L. (1987). Taal in de media [Language in the media]. *Ra-Tel, 17*(6-7), 8-9.

Bendix, J., & Liebler, C. M. (1991). Environmental degradation in Brazilian Amazonia: Perspectives in U.S. news media. *Professional Geographer, 43*(4), 474-485.

Benevides, M. (1983). *Violencia, povo e policia* [Violence, people and police]. Sao Paulo: Brasiliense.

Benhabib, S. (1992). *Situating the self: Gender, community and post-modernisn in contemporary ethics.* New York: Routledge.

Bennett, T., Frith, S., Grossberg, L., Shepherd, J., & Turner, G. (1993). *Rock and popular music: Politics, policies, institutions.* New York: Routledge.

Berger, P., Berger, B., & Kellner, H. (1974). *The homeless mind.* New York: Vintage Books.

Bergesen, A. (Ed.). (1980). *Studies of the modern world-system.* New York: Academic Press.

Bernstein, B. (1971). *Class, codes and control. Vol. 1: Theoretical studies towards a sociology of language.* London: Routledge & Kegan Paul.

Bernstein, B. (1975). *Class, codes and control. Vol. 3: Towards a theory of educational transmission.* London: Routledge & Kegan Paul.

Beyer, P. (1994). *Religion and globalization.* London: Sage.

Biersack, A. (1989). Local knowledge, local history: Geertz and beyond. In L. Hunt (Ed.), *The new cultural history* (pp. 72-96). Berkeley: University of California Press.

Blumler, J. G. (1991). The new television marketplace: Imperatives, implications, issues. In J. Curran & M. Gurevitch (Eds.), *Mass media and society* (pp. 194-215). London: Edward Arnold.

Blumler, J. G. (1992). Public service broadcasting before the commercial deluge. In J. G. Blumler (Ed.), *Television and the public interest: Values in West European broadcasting* (pp. 7-21). London: Sage.

Boon, J. (1962). *Zo sprak Jan Boon: Toespraken tot een gemengd gehoor* [The words of Jan Boon: Speeches for a mixed audience]. Hasselt: Heideland.

Bourdieu, P. (1984). *Distinction: A social critique of the judgement of taste* (R. Nice, Trans.). London: Routledge & Kegan Paul.

Bowman, G. (1992). *Ethnicity, identity, fission: European community and the collapse of federation.* Paper presented to the Institute of Philosophy and Sociology Conference, East European Cultures after Communism: Traditional, Modernity, Post-modernity. Radziowijce, Poland.

Braman, S. (1990). Trade and information policy. *Media, Culture and Society, 12,* 361-385.

Braman, S. (1991). Contradictions in Brilliant Eyes. *Gazette: The International Journal of Communication Studies, 47*(3), 177-194.

Braman, S. (1994). The autopoietic state: Communication and democratic potential in the net. *Journal of the American Society for Information Science, 45*(6), 358-368.

Braman, S. (1995). Horizons of the state: Information policy and power. *Journal of Communication, 45*(4).

Brants, K., & Siune, K. (1992). Public broadcasting in a state of flux. In K. Brants & W. Truetzschler (Eds.), *Dynamics of media politics: Broadcast and electronic media in Western Europe* (pp. 101-115). London: Sage.

Brass, P. R. (1991). *Ethnicity and nationalism: Theory and comparison.* London: Sage.

Brazil. (1988). *Trade in services.* Report to the General Agreements on Tariffs and Trade (GATT).

Brecher, J. (1993). "The hierarchs" new world order—and ours. In J. Brecher, J. B. Childs, & J. Cutler (Eds.), *Global visions: Beyond the new world order* (pp. 3-12). Boston: South End Press.

Brecher, J., Childs, J. B., & Cutler, J. (Eds.). (1993). *Global visions: Beyond the new world order.* Boston: South End Press.

Brookes, S. K., Jordan, A. G., Kimber, R. H., & Richardson, J. J. (1976). The growth of the government as a political issue in Britain. *British Journal of Political Science, 6*(2), 245-255.

Brunn, S. D., & Leinbach, T. R. (Eds.). (1991). *Collapsing time and space.* Chicago: University of Chicago Press.

Buchanan, J. (1975). *The limits of liberty: Between anarchy and Leviathan.* Chicago: University of Chicago Press.

Buchanan, J., & Tullock, G. (1962). *The calculus of consent.* Ann Arbor: University of Michigan Press.

Burger, H. (1984). *Sprache der Massenmedien* [The language of the mass media]. Berlin: Aldine De Gruyter.

Burnell, P. L. (1991). *Charity, politics and the Third World.* London: Harvester Wheatsheaf.

Burnham, J. (1991). Of science and superstition: The media and biopolitics. In C. L. LeMay & E. E. Dennis (Eds.), *Media and the environment* (pp. 29-42). Washington, DC & Covelo, CA: The Freedom Forum Media Studies Center/Island Press.

Calderon, F. (1988). America Latina, identidad y tiempos mixtos: O como pensar la modernidad sin dejar de ser boliviano [Latin America, identity and mixed times: Or how to think about modernity without ceasing to be Bolivian]. In CLACSO (Ed.), *Imagenes desconocidas: La modernidad en la encrucijada postmoderna* (pp. 225-229). Buenos Aires: Ediciones CLACSO.

Calhoun, C. (1991). Indirect relationships and imagined communities: Large-scale social integration and the transformation of everyday life. In P. Bourdieu & J. S. Coleman (Eds.), *Social theory for a changing society* (pp. 95-120). Boulder, CO: Westview Press.

Calhoun, C. (Ed.). (1992). *Habermas and the public sphere.* Cambridge, MA: MIT Press.

Calhoun, C. (1993). Postmodernism as pseudohistory. *Theory, Culture and Society, 10,* 75-96.

Câmara dos Deputados. (1992). *Relatório da Commissâo Parlamentar de Inquérito que investigou o exterminio de Crianças e adolescentes* [Report of the Parliamentary Commission of Inquiry that investigated the extermination of children and adolescents]. Brasilia, Brazil: Congresso Nacional.

Carle, J. (1991). Husockupationer, sociala rorelser och mass media ouse [Occupations, social movements and mass media]. *Sociologisk Forskning, 3,* 42-64.

Carter, L. H. (1985). *Contemporary constitutional lawmaking: The Supreme Court and the art of politics.* New York: Pergamon Press.

Casetti, F., & Odin, R. (1990). De la paleo-á la néo-television: Approche semio-pragmatique [From paleo- to neo-television: A semio-pragmatic approach]. *Comunications, 51,* 9-26.

Castells, M. (1989). *The informational city.* Cambridge, MA: Basil Blackwell.

Centre for the Coordination of Marginalized People (CEAP). (1989). *The killings of children and adolescents in Brazil.* Rio de Janeiro: CEAP.

Chambers, I. (1985). *Urban rhythms, pop music, and popular culture.* New York: MacMillan.

Chambers, I. (1993). *Migrancy, culture, identity.* New York: Routledge.

Chang, J. (1991). *Wild swans: Three daughters of China.* London: Flamingo.

Chapple, S., & Garofalo, R. (1977). *Rock'n'roll is here to pay.* Chicago: Nelson Hall.

Charkiewicz, E., & Nijpels, M. (1993). *Dancing with futures: A mobile and flexible workshop/journal/thinkact group on . . . ecological and social transformations.* Amsterdam: WISE.

Chatwin, B. (1987). *The songlines.* New York: Viking.

Clark-Meads, J. (1992, February 8). 6 Euro firms band to expose talent. *Billboard,* p. 33.

Classen, C. (1993). *Worlds of sense: Exploring the senses in history and across cultures.* New York: Routledge.

Clastres, P. (1988). On ethnocide. *Art and Text, 28,* 51-58.

Clément, C. (1987). *Le goût du miel* [The taste of honey]. Paris: Grasset.

Clifford, J., & Marcus, G. (1986). *Writing culture: The poetics and politics of ethnography.* Berkeley: University of California Press.

Cloonan, M. (1991). *Censorship and popular music.* (Occassional Paper No.1). Liverpool: Institute of Popular Music University of Liverpool.

Cohen, J., & Arato, A. (1992). *Civil society and political theory.* Cambridge, MA: MIT Press.

Cohen, S. (1972). *Folk devils and moral panics: The creation of the mods and rockers.* London: MacGibbon & Kee.

Collier, A. (1992). Marxism and universalism: Group interests or a shared world? In R. Attfield & B. Wilkins (Eds.), *International justice and the third world* (pp. 77-92). London: Routledge.

Collins, R. (1989). The White Paper on broadcasting policy *Screen, 30*(1-2), 6-23.

Collins, R. (1990). *Television: Policy and culture.* London: Unwin Hyman.

Coman, M. (1993, June). *Le cas Rumain* [The Romanian case]. Paper presented to the symposium on La Transition en Roumanie: Communications et qualite de la vie [The transition in Romania: Communications and quality of life]. Bucharest, Romania.

Commission of the European Communities. (1987). *Green paper on the development of the Common Market for telecommunications services and equipment.* Brussels: European Commission, Com(87)290.

Commission of the European Communities. (1989). Council direct of 3 October 1989 on the coordination of certain provisions laid down by law, regulation or administrative action in member states concerning the pursuit of television broadcasting activities. *Official Journal of the European Communities, L198,* 23-30.

Commission of the European Communities. (1990a). *Commission directive on competition in the markets for telecommunications services.* Brussels: European Commission, 90/338/EEC.

Commission of the European Communities. (1990b). *Green paper on a common approach in the field of satellite communications in the European Community.* Brussels: European Commission, Com(90)490.

Commission of the European Communities. (1994, July 15). *Europe and the global information society, Bangemann Task Force Report to the European Council.* Cordis, Suppl. 2, 4-31.

Corbett, J. B. (1992). Rural and urban newspaper coverage of wildlife: Conflict, community and bureaucracy. *Journalism Quarterly, 69*(4), 929-938.

Cornea, A. (1990). Spatiu sacru [The sacred space]. *Revista 22, 26*(13), 15.

Cottle, S. (1993). Mediating the environment: Modalities of TV news. In A. Hansen (Ed.), *The mass media and environmental issues* (pp. 107-133). Leicester, UK: Leicester University Press.

Coulmas, F. (1992). *Language and economy.* Cambridge, MA: Blackwell.

Crapanzano, V. (1986). Hermes' dilemma: The masking of subversion in ethnographic description. In J. Clifford & G. E. Marcus (Eds.), *Writing culture: The poetics and politics of ethnography* (pp. 51-76). Berkeley: University of California Press.

Crook, S., Pakulski, J., & Walters, M. (Eds.). (1992). *Postmodernisation: Change in advanced society.* London: Sage.

Curran, J. (1991a). Mass media and democracy: A reappraisal. In J. Curran & M. Gurevitch (Eds.), *Mass media and society* (pp. 82-117). New York: Routledge.

Curran, J. (1991b). Rethinking the media as a public sphere. In P. Dahlgren & C. Sparks (Eds.), *Communication and citizenship* (pp. 27-57). New York: Routledge.

Dahlgren, P. (1991). Introduction. In P. Dahgren & C. Sparks (Eds.), *Communication and citizenship* (pp. 1-24). New York: Routledge.

Dahlgren, P., & Sparks, C. (Eds.). (1991). *Commumication and citizenship.* New York: Routledge.

Dahrendorf, R. (1994). The changing quality of citizenship. In B. van Steenbergern (Ed.), *The condition of citizenship* (pp. 10-19). London: Sage.

Dalby, S. (1994, July). *The trouble with geo-politics: Mapping the future of political geography and international relations.* Paper presented to the conference on Global Politics: Setting Agendas for the Year 2000, Nottingham, Trent.

Daly, M. (1991). Transitional economic bases: From the mass production society to the world of finance. In P. Daniels (Ed.), *Services and metropolitan development: International perspectives* (pp. 26-43). London: Routledge.

Daskalov, R. (1992, June). *Mass media and political journalism in the transition period: The case of Bulgaria.* Paper presented to the symposium, Mass Media in the Transformation of East-Central European Society, Bucharest, Romania.

Davis, M. (1992). *Beyond Blade Runner: Urban control—The ecology of fear.* Westfield: Open Magazine.

Dayan, D., & Katz, E. (1987). Performing media events. In J. Curran, A. Smith, & P. Wingate (Eds.), *Impacts and influences: Essays on media power in the twentieth century* (pp. 174-197). London: Methuen.

Dayan, D., & Katz, E. (1988). Articulating consensus: The ritual and rhetoric of media events. In J. C. Alexander (Ed.), *Durkheimian sociology* (pp. 161-186). New York: Cambridge University Press.

de Certeau, M. (1984). *The practice of everyday life* (S. Rendall, trans.). Berkeley: University of California Press.

Delors' grab-bag of solutions for Europe's unemployment. (1993, December. 10). *Christian Science Monitor*, p. 4.

Dennis, E.E. (1991). In context: Environmentalism in the system of news. In C. L. LeMay & E. E. Dennis (Eds.), *Media and the environment* (pp. 55-66). Washington, DC & Covelo, CA: The Freedom Forum Media Studies Center/Island Press.

Deprez, K. (1981). *Naar een eigen identiteit* [Towards an identity of its own]. Unpublished manuscript.

Deprez, K. (1989, October 29). Referentiekader voor het vlaamse Nederlands [A frame of reference for Flemish Netherlands]. *De Standaard.*

Deprez, K. (1991). Introduction. In K. Deprez (Ed.), *Language and intergroup relations in Flanders and Netherlands* (pp. 1-10). Dordrecht: Foris Publications.

Deprez, K. (1992, April 2). Bewust onzuiver Nederlans in Vlaanderen [Deliberate inaccurate Netherlandic in the Flemish community] *De Standaard.*

Desaulniers, J.P. (1985). Television and nationalism: From culture to communication. In P. Drummond & R. Patterson (Eds.), *Television in transition* (pp. 112-124). London: B.F.I. Publishing.

Deutsch, K.W. (1966). *Nationalism and social communication: An inquiry into the foundations of nationality.* Cambridge, MA: MIT Press.

Dewey, J. (1963). *Freedom and culture.* New York: Capricorn. (Original work published 1939)

Diawara, M. (1990). Black British cinema: Spectatorship and identity formation in "territories." *Public Culture, 3*(1), 33-47.

Dimenstein, G. (1990, September 6). Entidade viu descaso entre autoridades [Organization acknowledged neglect from authorities]. *Folha de São Paulo*, p. C3.

Dimenstein, G. (1991). *Brazil: War on children.* London: Lab.

Dixon, W.J. (1985). Change and persistence in the world system: An analysis of global trade concentration, 1955-1975. *International Studies Quarterly, 29*, 121-189.

Dobbelaere, K. (1991). Over godsdienst en de kerk in Vlaanderen in 2000 [Concerning religion and the church in the Flemish community in the year 2000]. *Onze Alma Mater, 45*(3), 205-229.

Donaldson, B.C. (1983). *Dutch: A linguistic history of Holland and Belgium.* Leiden: Martinus Nijhoff.

Dorfman, A., & Mattelart, A. (1975). *How to read Donald Duck: Imperialist ideology in the Disney comic.* New York: International General.

Downing, J. (1988). An alternative public sphere: The organization of the 1980s anti-nuclear press in West Germany and Britain. *Media, Culture and Society, 10*(2), 163-188.

Dunwoody, S., & Griffin, R. J. (1993). Journalistic strategies for reporting long-term environmental issues: A case study of three Superfund sites. In A. Hansen (Ed.), *The mass media and environmental issues* (pp. 22-50). Leicester: Leicester University Press.

Eder, K. (1990). The rise of counter-culture movements against modernity: Nature as a new field of class struggle. *Theory, Culture and Society, 7*, 21-47.

Ehrenreich, B. (1990, July-August). Laden with lard. *Z Magazine*, pp. 46-47.

Einsiedel, E., & Coughlan, E. (1993). The Canadian press and the environment: Reconstructing a social reality. In A. Hansen (Ed.), *The mass media and environmental issues* (pp. 134-149). Leicester: Leicester University Press.

Eliade, M. (1959). *The sacred and the profane: The nature of religion.* New York: Harper.

Elias, N. (1992). *Time: An essay.* Oxford, England: Blackwell.

Eliasoph, N. (1988). Routines and the making of oppositional news. *Critical Studies in Mass Communication, 5*, 313-334.

Elliott, P. (1982). Intellectual, the "information society" and the disappearance of the public sphere. *Media, Culture and Society, 4*(3), 243-253.

Entman, R. (1989). *Democracy without citizens.* New York: Oxford University Press.

Entrikin, J. N. (1991). *The betweenness of place: Towards a geography of modernity.* Baltimore: The Johns Hopkins University Press.

Enzensberger, H.M. (1974). *The consciousness industry: On literature, politics and the media.* New York: Seabury Press.

Enzensberger, H.M. (1992). *Mediocrity & delusion* (M. Chalmers, Trans.). New York: Verso.

Ericson, R., Baranek, P., & Chan, J. (1989). *Negotiating control: A study of news organizations.* Toronto: University of Toronto Press.

Eyerman, R., & Jamison, A. (1989). Environmental knowledge as an organizational weapon: The case of Greenpeace. *Social Science Information, 28*, 99-119.

Falk, R. (1987). *The promise of world order.* Philadelphia: The University of Pennsylvania Press.

Featherstone, M. (1990). Global culture: An introduction. In M. Featherstone (Ed.), *Global culture: Nationalism, globalization and modernity* (pp. 1-14). London: Sage.

Featherstone, M. (1991). *Consumer culture and postmodernism.* London: Sage.

Featherstone, M. (1993). Global and local culture. In J. Bird, B. Curtis, T. Putnam, G. Robertson, & L. Tickner (Eds.), *Mapping the futures: Local cultures, global change* (pp. 169-187). London: Routledge.

Featherstone, M., Hepworth, M., & Turner, B.S. (Eds.). (1991). *The body: Social processes and cultural theory.* London: Sage.

Ferguson, C. A. (1959). Diglossia. *World, 15,* 325-340.

Ferguson, H. (1992). *Religious transformation in Western society.* London: Routledge.

Fernandes, R. (1988). Sem fins lucrativos [Not for profit]. In L. Landim (Ed.), *Sem fins lucrativos: As organizacöes näo governmentais no Brasil* [Not for profit: The nongovernmental organizations in Brazil]. Rio de Janeiro: ISER.

Fernandes, R. (1990, November 14). O respeito que se exige: Para o ministro Rezek, o Brasil mudou mas o mundo não vê, guarda uma imagem superada do país [The respect that is demanded: For the Minister Rezek, Brazil has changed but the world does not see, it maintains an outdated image of the country]. *Isto É,* p. 4.

Feyaerts, G. (1982). *Radio in de jaren 80: Het progammabeleid op de openbare omroep* [Radio in de 1980s: The programming policy of PSB]. Unpublished doctoral dissertation, Katholieke Universiteit Leuven, Faculty of Social Science.

Finnegan, R. (1989). *The hidden musicians: Music making in an English town.* Cambridge, England: Cambridge University Press.

Fishman, J. A. (1972). *Language and nationalism: Two integrative essays.* Rowley, MA: Newbury House.

Fishman, J. A. (1977). Language and ethnicity. In H. Giles (Ed.), *Language, ethnicity and intergroup relations* (pp. 15-57). London: Academic Press.

Fiske, J. (1987). *Television culture.* London: Methuen.

Fiske, J. (1989). *Understanding popular culture.* Boston: Unwin Hyman.

Fiske, J. (1992). Popularity and the politics of information. In P. Dahlgren & C. Sparks (Eds.), *Journalism and popular culture.* London: Sage.

Forbes, J. (1993). Cross-boundary sub-states. In J. Brecher, J. B. Childs, & J. Cutler (Eds.), *Global visions: Beyond the new world order* (pp. 233-238). Boston: South End Press.

Forgacs, D. (1992). *Italian culture in the industrial era, 1880-1980.* New York: Manchester University Press.

Fornäs, J. (1993). "Play it yourself": Swedish music in movement. *Social Science Information, 32*(1), 39-65.

Foucault, M. (1979). *Discipline and punish: The birth of the prison.* New York: Vintage.

Foundation for American Communications. (1993). *The press and the environment.* Los Angeles: Author.

Francis, E. K. (1965). *Ethnos und demos sociologische beitrage zur volkstheorie* [Ethnos and demos as sociological contributions to the theory of nationalism]. Berlin: Buncker und Humblot.

Frankel, B. (1987). *The post-industrial utopians.* Oxford: Polity Press.

Fraser, N. (1986). Towards a discourse theory of solidarity. *Praxis, 5*(4), 425-429.

Fraser, N. (1992). Rethinking the public sphere: A contribution to the critique of actually existing democracy. In C. Calhoun (Ed.), *Habermas and the public sphere* (pp. 109-142). Cambridge, MA: MIT Press.

Frederick, H. (1992). Computer communications in cross-border coalition-building: North American NGO networking against NAFTA. *Gazette: The International Journal for Mass Communication Studies, 50,* 221-241.

Frei, G. (1985). Sköchn—Verzeichnis—oder die Verdrängung der Hochsprache beim Radio [Sköchn—inventory—or how standard language is superseded by radio]. In H. Padel (Ed.), *Des Schweizers Deutsch* [The German of the Swiss] (pp. 24-29). Bern: Hallwag Verlag.

Fricker, H. P. (1988). Zur Sprachwahl in Radio und Fernsehen: Von der Schwierigkeit, Publikums geschmack, Zeitgeist, Gestaltungsfreiraum der Programmschaffenden und bildungspolitische Forderungen miteinander in Einklang zu bringen [Language choice in radio and television: The problems of making audience taste, zeitgeist, production issues, and educational needs match]. In *Mundart-Hochsprache in Schule und Medien* [Low and standard language in schools and media] (pp. 28-35). Bern: EDK/SRK.

Friedman, J. (1988). Cultural logics of the global system: A sketch. *Theory, Culture and Society, 5*(2-3), 447-460.

Friedman, J. (1991). UNCED and the media. In *Proceedings: Environmental screening conference for UNCED* (pp. 2-3). New York: Third World Television Exchange. Washington, DC & Covelo, CA: The Freedom Forum Media Studies Center/Island Press.

Friedman, J. (1994). *Cultural identity and global process.* London: Sage.

Frith, S. (1987). Why do songs have words? In A. White (Ed.), *Lost in music: Culture, style and the musical event* (pp. 77-106). New York: Routledge.

Frontiers of finance: A survey. (1993, October 9). *The Economist,* pp. 1-22.

Fuga, A. (1992, June). *The nature of facts and alternatives in the Albanian mass media during the period of transition.* Paper presented to the symposium, Mass Media in the Transformation of East-Central European Society, Bucharest, Romania

Galtung, J. (1980). The non-territorial system. In *The true worlds: A transnational perspective* (pp. 305-40). New York: Free Press.

Galtung, J. (1993). The role of communication in rethinking European identity. *Media Development, 4,* 3-7.

Gamson, W., & Modigliani, A. (1989). Media discourse and public opinion on nuclear power: A constructionist approach. *American Journal of Sociology, 95*(1), 1-37.

Garnham, N. (1990). *Capitalism and communication.* London: Sage.

Garnham, N. (1992). The media and the public sphere. In C. Calhoun (Ed.), *Habermas and the public sphere* (pp. 359-376). Cambridge, MA: MIT Press.

Garnier, G. (1987). *Worldwide and local technologies.* [Exploratory Dossier 1, XII-617-87]. Brussels: European Commission FAST Programme.

Garofalo, R. (Ed.). (1992). *Rockin' the boat: Mass music and mass movements.* Boston: South End Press.

Geerts, G. (1974). Integratie en taalpolitiek [Integration and language policy]. *Kultuurleven, 41*(9), 940-943.

Geertz, C. (1973). After the revolution: The fate of nationalism in the new states. In *The interpretation of culture* (pp. 234-54). New York: Basic Books.

Geertz, C. (1983). *Local knowledge: Further essays in interpretive anthropology.* New York: Basic Books.

Gellner, E. (1983). *Nations and nationalism.* Oxford: Basil Blackwell.

George, S. (1992). *The debt boomerang: How Third World debt harms us all.* London: Pluto.

Gersh, D. (1992). Covering solid waste issues: Media shun crucial garbage, sludge issues for less critical global warming, water pollution coverage. *Editor and Publisher, 125*(35), 15-16.

Gibson-Graham, J. K. (1993). Waiting for the revolution: Or how to smash capitalism while working at home in your spare time. *Rethinking Marxism, 6*(2), 10-24.

Giddens, A. (1984). *The constitution of society.* Cambridge, England: Polity Press.

Giddens, A. (1990). *The consequences of modernity.* Stanford, CA: Stanford University Press.

Giddens, A. (1991). *Modernity and self-identity: Self and society in late modern age.* Cambridge, England: Polity Press.

Giddens, A. (1992). *The transformation of intimacy.* Cambridge, England: Polity Press.

Gilpin, R. (1987). *The political economy of international relations.* Princeton, NJ: Princeton University Press.

Gilroy, P. (1987). *There ain't no black in the Union Jack.* London: Hutchison.

Gilroy, P. (1993a). *The black Atlantic: Modernity and double consciousness.* London: Verso.

Gilroy, P. (1993b). *Small acts: Thoughts on the politics of black cultures.* Londres: Serpents Tail.

Giroux, H. (1992). *Border crossings: Cultural workers and the politics of education.* New York: Routledge, Chapman & Hall.

Gitlin, T. (1980). *The whole world is watching.* Berkeley: University of California Press.

Glasser, T. (1991). Communication and the cultivation of citizenship. *Communication, 12*(4), 235-248.

Golding, P. (1990). Political communication and citizenship: The media and democracy in an inegalitarian order. In M. Ferguson (Ed.), *Public communications: The new imperatives* (pp. 84-100). London: Sage.

Golding, P. (1992). Communicating capitalism: Resisting and restructuring state ideology—The case of Thatcherism. *Media, Culture and Society, 14*(4), 503-521.

Goodwin, A., & Gore, J. (1990). World beat and the cultural imperialism debate. *Socialist Review, 20*(3), 63-80.

Gordon, D. (1988). The global economy: New edifice or crumbling foundations? *New Left Review, 169*, 24-65.

Gore outlines data highway policy. (1994, January. 12). *New York Times*, p. C4.

Gramsci, A. (1971). *Prison notebooks.* New York: International Publishers.

Gray, J. (1989). *Limited government: A positive agenda.* London: Institute for Economic Affairs.

Gray, J. (1993). *Post-liberalism.* London: Routledge.

Greenberg, M. R., Sachsman, D. B., Sandman, P. M., & Salomone, K. L. (1989). Risk, drama and geography in coverage of environmental risk by network TV. *Journalism Quarterly, 66*(2), 267-276.

Grossberg, L. (1992). *We've got to get out of this place: Popular conservatism and postmodern culture.* New York: Routledge.

Gurevitch, M., Levy, M., & Roeh, I. (1991). The global newsroom. In P. Dahlgren & C. Sparks (Eds.), *Communication and citizenship* (pp. 196-216). London: Routledge.

Haas, W. (1988). Schweiz [Switzerland]. In U. Ammon, N. Dittmar, & K. J. Matteier (Eds.), *Sociolinguistics [Sociolinguistik]* (pp. 1365-1383). Berlin: Aldine De Gruyter.

Haas, W. (1990). Mundart und Standardsprache in der deutschen Schweiz [Dialect and standard language in German-speaking Switzerland]. In J. A. Van Leuvensteijn & J. B. Berns (Eds.), *Dialect and standard language in the English, Dutch, German and Norwegian language areas* (pp. 312-336). Amsterdam: Koninklijke Nederlandse Akademis van Wetenschappen.

Habermas, J. (1974). The public sphere: An encyclopedia article (1964). *New German Critique, 1*(3), 49-55.

Habermas, J. (1979). *Communication and the evolution of society* (T. McCarthy, Trans.). Boston: Beacon Press.

Habermas, J. (1984). *The theory of communicative action, Vol. 1: Reason and the rationalization of society* (T. McCarthy, Trans.). Boston: Beacon Press.

Habermas, J. (1987). *The theory of communicative action* (Vol. 2). (T. McCarthy, Trans.). Boston: Beacon Press.

Habermas, J. (1989). *The structural transformation of the public sphere: An inquiry into a category of bourgeois society* (T. Burger, Trans.). Cambridge, MA: MIT Press.

Habermas, J. (1990). *Moral consciousness and communicative action* (C. Lenhardt & S. W. Nicholsen, Trans.). Cambridge, MA: MIT Press.

Hall, S. (1991a). The local and the global: Globalization and ethnicity. In A. King (Ed.), *Culture, globalization and the world system* (pp. 19-40). Binghamton: State University of New York.

Hall, S. (1991b). Old and new identities, old and new ethnicities. In A. King (Ed.), *Culture, globalization and the world-system* (pp. 41-68). New York: Macmillan.

Hall, S. (1992). The question of cultural identity. In S. Hall, D. Held, & T. McGrew (Eds.), *Modernity and its futures* (pp. 274-316). Cambridge, England: Polity Press.

Hall, S., Critcher, C., Jefferson, T., Clarke, J., & Roberts, B. (1978). *Policing the crisis.* London: Macmillan.

Hallen, D. C., & Mancini, P. (1991). Summits and the constitution of an international public sphere: The Reagan-Gorbachev meetings as televised media events. *Communication, 12*(4), pp. 249-266.

Halliday, M.A.K. (1978). *Language as a social semiotic: The social interpretation of language and meaning.* London: Edward Arnold.

Hamelink, C. (1983). *Cultural autonomy in global communication.* New York: Longman.

Hamelink, C. (1991). Global communication: Plea for civil action. In B. V. Hofstein (Ed.), *Informatics in food and nutrition* (pp. 5-8). Stockholm, Sweden: Royal Academy of Sciences.

Hamelink, C. (1994). *The politics of world communication: A human rights perspective.* London: Sage.

Hamilton, A., Jay, J., & Madison, J. (1961). *The federalist* (J. E. Cooke, Ed.). Middletown, CT: Wesleyan University Press. (Original work published 1787)

Hannerz, U. (1991). Scenarios for peripheral cultures. In A. D. King (Ed.), *Cultures, globalization and the world system* (pp. 107-128). London: Macmillan.

Hannerz, U. (1992). *Cultural complexity: Studies in the social organization of meaning.* New York: Columbia University Press.

Hansen, A. (1991). The media and the social construction of the environment. *Media, Culture & Society, 13*(4), 443-458.

Hansen, A. (Ed.). (1993). *The mass media and environmental issues.* Leicester: Leicester University Press.

Harvey, D. (1989). *The condition of post-modernity.* Oxford: Basil Blackwell.

Harvey, D. (1993). From space to place and back again: Reflections on the condition of postmodernity. In J. Bird, B. Curtis, T. Putnam, G. Robertson, & L. Tickner (Eds.), *Mapping the futures: Local cultures, global change* (pp. 3-29). New York: Routledge.

Hassard J. (Ed.). (1990). *The sociology of time.* London: Macmillan.

Havel, V. (1993). *Summer meditations* (P. Wilson., Trans.). New York: Vintage Books.

Havens Center. (1994). *A proposal for a conference on global change and transnational democratic activism.* Unpublished manuscript, Havens Center, Sociology Department, University of Wisconsin-Madison.

Hawkins, A. (1993). Contested ground: International environmentalism and global climate change. In R. D. Lipschutz & K. Conca (Eds.), *The state and social power in global environmental politics* (pp. 221-245). New York: Columbia University Press.

Hayden, R. (1991, November). *Constitutional nationalism in Yugoslavia.* Paper presented to the 90th Annual Meeting of the American Anthropological Association, Chicago.

Hayek, F. A. von. (1945). The use of knowledge in society. *American Economic Review, 35,* 519-530.

Hayek, F. A. von. (1949). *Individualism and economic order.* London: Routledge.

Hayek, F. A. von. (1982). *Law, legislation and liberty, Vol. 2: The mirage of social justice.* London: Routledge.

Hayles, K. (1991). Introduction: Complex dynamics in literature and science. In K. Hayles (Ed.), *Chaos and order: Complex dynamics in literature and science* (pp. 1-33). Chicago: University of Chicago Press.

Heavy weather ahead for good ship Europe. (1993, December 13). *The European,* p. 8.

Hebdige, D. (1979). *Subculture: The meaning of style.* New York: Routledge/Methuen.

Hebdige, D. (1989). After the masses. In S. Hall & M. Jacques (Eds.), *New times: The changing face of politics in the 1990s* (pp. 76-93). London: Lawrence and Wishart.

Hegel, G. W. F. (1953). Reason in history (R. S. Hartman, trans.). New York: Macmillan. (Original work published 1837)

Hegel, G. W. F. (1974). The philosophy of right. In F. G. Weiss (Ed.), *Hegel: The essential writings* (pp. 253-283). New York: Harper & Row.(Original work published 1821)

Held, D. (1989). *Political theory and the modern state: Essays on state, power, and democracy.* Stanford, CA: Stanford University Press.

Held, D. (1990). The decline of the nation state. In S. Hall & M. Jacques (Eds.), *New times: The changing face of politics in the 1990s* (pp. 191-204). New York: Verso.

Held, D. (1991). Democracy and globalization. *Alternatives, 16*(2).

Hemmerechts, K. (1984). Van Arthur Boon over Bert Leysen naar Herman van Molle: Een halve eeuw germansteninbreng bij de omroep [From Arthur Boon to Bert Leysen to Herman van Molle: 50 years of Germanic scholarship in broadcasting]. *Onze Alma Mater, 38*(2), 129-140.

Herman, E., & Chomsky, N. (1988). *Manufacturing consent: The political economy of the mass media.* New York: Pantheon Books.

Hjarvard, S. (1993). Pan-European television news: Towards a European political public sphere? In P. Drummond, R. Paterson, & J. Willis (Eds.), *National identity and Europe* (pp. 71-94). London: British Film Institute.

Hobbes, T. (1991). *Leviathan* (R. Tuck, Ed.). Cambridge, England: Cambridge University Press. (Original work published 1651)

Hobsbawm, E.J. (1990). *Nations and nationalism since 1780.* Cambridge, England: Cambridge University Press.

Hobsbawm, E., & Ranger, T. (1983). *The invention of tradition.* Cambridge, England: Cambridge University Press.

Hohendahl, P. (1979). We are the world and its counterparts: Popular song as constitutional discourse. *Politics, Culture and Society, 3*(3), 315-341.

Howes, D. (1990). We are the world and its counterparts: Popular song as constitutional discourse. *International Journal of Politics, Culture and Society, 3*(3), 315-341.

Huber, P. (1987). *The geodesic network: 1987 report on competition in the telephone industry.* Washington, DC: US Department of Justice.

Hung, M., & Morencos, E. (1990, December 5). *World record sales 1969-1990.* London: London International Federation of the Phonographic Industry (IFPI), Press Information.

Hungerford, S. E., & Lemert, J. B. (1973). Covering the environment: A new Afghanistanism. *Journalism Quarterly, 50*(3), 475-481, 508.

Hurrell, A., & Kingsbury, C. (Eds.). (1992). *The international politics of the environment: Actors, interests, and institutions.* Oxford: Clarendon Press.

IFPI. (1989). *World sales of recordings 1988 and world sales trends 1981-1988.* London: IFPI.

IFPI. (1991, October 1). *World sales 1990.* London: IFPI.

IFPI. (1992, October 23). *World sales 1991.* London: IFPI.

IFPI. (1993a, June). *World sales 1992.* London: IFPI.

IFPI. (1993b). *Breaking down the sound barriers.* London: IFPI.

Ingold, J. L. (1985, July 1). Le triomphe des dialects: Quand les Suisses alémaniques boudent l'allemand et le français [The triumph of the dialects: When the German-Swiss ignore German and French]. *L'Hebdo.*

Inkeles, A. (1974). *Becoming modern.* Cambridge, MA: Harvard University Press.

Isaak, J. A. (1993). What's to be done? *Borderlines*, No. 29.

Jakubowicz, K. (1990). Musical chairs? The three public spheres of Poland. *Media, Culture and Society, 12*, 195-212.

Jakubowicz, K. (1992). Policy broadcasting act revisited. *Bulletin of the European Institute for the Media, 9*(4), 12-13.

Jameson, F. (1991). *Postmodernism, or the cultural logic of late capitalism.* Durham, NC: Duke University Press.

Jasay, A. de. (1990). *Market socialism* (Occasional Paper No. 84). London: Institute of Economic Affairs.

Jaspaert, K., & Van Belle, W. (1989). The evolution of the diglossic system in Flanders. In K. Deprez (Ed.), *Language and intergroup relations in Flanders and in the Netherlands* (pp. 67-82). Dordrecht: Floris Publications.

Jay, M. (Ed.). (1987). *An unmastered past: The autobiographical reflectiosn of Leo Lowenthal.* Berkeley: University of California Press.

Jensen, M. C., & Meckling, W. H. (1991). Specific and general knowledge, and organizational structure. In L. Werin & H. Wijkander (Eds.), *Main currents in contract economics.* Oxford, England: Basil Blackwell.

Johansson, P. O. (1991). *An introduction to modern welfare economics.* New York: Cambridge University Press.

Johnson, O. (1993, August). *Whose voice? Freedom of speech and the media in East Central Europe.* Paper presented to the Association for Education in Journalism and Mass Communication (AEJMC), Kansas City.

Kant, I. (1990). *Foundations of the metaphysics of morals and what is enlightenment?* (L. W. Beck, Trans.). New York: Macmillan. (Original work published 1784-85)

Kant, I. (1991). On the agreement between politics and morality according to the transcendental concept of public right. In H. Reiss (Ed.) & H.B. Nisbet (Trans.), *Kant: Political writings* (pp. 125-130). Cambridge, England: Cambridge University Press. (Original work published 1793-5)

Katz, E. (1986). *The new media and social segmentation.* Paper presented to the XI Congress of Sociology, New Delhi, India.

Katz, E., & Wedell, G. (1977). *Broadcasting in the Third World.* Cambridge, MA: Harvard University Press.

Keane, J. (1991). *The media and democracy.* Cambridge, England: Polity Press.

Keane, J. (1988). The modern democratic revolution. In T. Mastnak & R. Riha (Eds.), *The subject in democracy* (pp. 36-48). Ljubljana, Slovenia: Delavska enotnost, for Institut za marksisticne stuije ZRC SAZU.

Keane, J. (1991). The crisis of the sovereign state. In M. Raboy & B. Dagenais (Eds.), *Media, crisis and democracy* (pp. 17-33). London: Sage.

Keith, M., & Pile, S. (Eds.). (1994). *Place and the politics of identity.* New York: Routledge.

Kellas, J. G. (1991). *The politics of nationalism and identity.* New York: Routledge.

Kellner, D. (1990). *Television and the crisis of democracy.* Boulder, CO: Westview Press.

Kielbowicz, R. B., & Scherer, C. (1986). The role of the press in the dynamics of social movements. *Research in Social Movements, Conflicts and Change, 9,* 71-96.

King, A. (Ed.). (1991). *Culture, globalization and the world system.* London: Macmillan.

Kirby, A. (1989). A sense of place. *Critical Studies in Mass Communication, 6*(3), 322-326.

Kloppenburg, J. R. (1988). *First the seed: The political economy of plant biotechnology, 1492-2000.* Cambridge, England: Cambridge University Press.

Kobrak, F., & Luey, B. (Eds.). (1992). *The structure of international publishing in the 1990s.* New Brunswick, NJ: Transaction.

Krejci, J. (1978). Ethnic problems in Europe. In S. Giner & M. S. Arscher (Eds.), *Contemporary Europe, social structures and cultural patterns* (pp. 124-171). London: Routledge & Kegan Paul.

Kroker, A. (1992). *The possessed individual: Technology and the French postmodern.* New York: St. Martin's Press.

Kroker, A., & Cook, D. (1988). *The postmodern scene: Excremental culture and hyper-aesthetics.* London: Macmillan.

Kühn, P. C. (1980). Deutsche Sprache in der Schweiz. In *Lexikon der germanistischen Linguistik III* (pp. 531-536). Tubingen, Germany: Max Niemeyer Verlag.

Laclau, E. (1988). Politics and the limits of modernity. In T. Mastnak & R. Riha (Eds.), *The subject in democracy* (pp. 21-35). Ljubljana, Slovenia: Delavska enotnost, for Institut za marksisticne stuije ZRC SAZU.

Laing, D. (1992). "Sadeness," scorpions and single markets: National and transnational trends in European popular music. *Popular Music, 11*(2), 127-39.

Lash, S. (1990). *Sociology of post-modernism.* London: Routledge.

Lash, S., & Urry, J. (1987). *The end of organized capitalism.* Oxford: Polity Press.

Lash, S., & Urry, J. (1994). *Economies of signs and space.* London: Sage.

Latouche, S. (1986). *Faut-il refuser le developpement?* Paris: Presses Universitaires de France.

Leach, E. (1976). *Culture and communication: The logic by which symbols are connected.* Cambridge, England: Cambridge University Press.

Lean democracy. (1994, Summer). *DEMOS Quarterly.*

Lee, M. (1991). UNCED and the media. In *Proceedings: Environmental Screening Conference for UNCED* (pp. 5-6). New York: Third World Television Exchange.

Lefebvre, H. (1991). *Critique of everyday life* (J. Moore, Trans.). London & New York: Verso.

Lefort, C. (1981). *L'invention democratique: Les limites de la domination totalitaire* [The democratic invention: The limits of totalitarian domination]. Paris: Fayard.

Lefter, J. B. (1991). *Democratizarea mediilor* [The democratization of media]. *Agora, 3.*

Leibes, T., & Katz, E. (1993). *The export of meaning.* Cambridge, England: Polity Press.

Leitner, G. (1980). BBC English and Deutsche rundfunksprache: A comparative and historical analysis of the language of radio. *International Journal of the Sociology of Language, 26*, 75-100.

Leitner, G. (1983). The social background of the language of radio. In H. Davis & P. Walton (Eds.), *Language, image, media* (pp. 50-76). Oxford, England: Basil Blackwell.

Leitner, G. (1985). A diachronic study of broadcast communication. In G. Bentele & E. W. B. Hess-Lüttish (Eds.), *Zeichengebrauch in Massenmedien* (pp. 376-394). Tubingen: Max Niemeyer Verlag.

LeMay, C.L., & Dennis, E. E. (Eds.). (1991). *Media and the environment.* Washington, DC & Covelo, CA: The Freedom Forum Media Studies Center/Island Press.

Leong, W. (1989). The culture of the state: National tourism and the state manufacture of cultures. In P. Bruck & M. Raboy (Eds.), *Communication for and against democracy* (pp. 75-94). Montreal: Black Rose Books.

Lepsius, M. R. (1992). Beyond the nation-state. *Telos, 91,* 57-76.

Lerner, D. (1958). *The passing of traditional society: Modernizing the Middle East.* New York: Free Press.

Lerner, D., & Schramm, W. (Eds.). (1967). *Communication and change in the developing countries.* Honolulu: East-West Center Press.

Levi-Strauss, C. (1968). *Structural anthropology.* London: Allen Lane.

Lightman, I. (1992, May 16). NMPA: Global pub revenues jumped 20% over 12 months. *Billboard,* pp. 33, 85.

Linné, O. (1991). Journalistiset kaytannot ja ymparistouutiset [Journalistic routines and environmental news]. *Tiedotstutkimus* (Mass Communication Research), *14*(5), 31-40.

Lipietz, A. (1990). Pour un internationalisme modete (For a modest internationalism). In S. Mappa (Ed.), *Ambiotions et illusions de la cooperation Nord-Sud: Lome IV* [Ambitions and illusions about North-South cooperation: Lome IV]. Paris: Harmattan.

Lipschutz, R.D. (1992, Winter). Reconstructing world politics: The emergence of global civil society. *Millenium, 21,* 3.

Lipsitz, G. (1994). *Dangerous crossroads: Popular music, postmodernism and the poetics of place.* London: Verso.

Llewellyn, H. (1992, December 12). Latin American societies link goals. *Billboard,* pp. 39, 41.

Locke, J. (1960). *Two treatises of government.* New York: Cambridge University Press. (Original work published 1690)

Lodziak, C. (1986). *The power of television.* London: Pinter.

Lowe, P., & Morrison, D. (1984). Bad news or good news: Environmental politics and the mass media. *The Sociological Review, 32*(1), 75-90.

Luard, E. (1990). *The globalization of politics: The changed focus of political action in the modern world.* London: Macmillan.

Lukes, S. (1985). *Marxism and morality.* Oxford: Oxford University Press.

Lull, J. (1991). *China turned on.* London: Routledge.

Luppi, C. A. (1981). *Agora e na hora da nossa morte.* Sao Paulo: Brasil Debates.

Lyotard, J. (1984). *The postmodern condition* (G. Bennington & B. Massumi, Trans.). Minneapolis: University of Minnesota Press.

MacIntyre, A. (1966). *A short history of ethics.* New York: Macmillan.

MacIntyre, A. (1984). *After virtue.* Notre Dame: University of Notre Dame Press.

Macpherson, C. B. (1973). *Democratic theory: Essays in retrieval.* New York: Oxford University Press.

Malm, K. (1982). Phonograms and cultural policy in Sweden. In K. Blaukopf (Ed.), *The phonogram in cultural communication* (pp. 43-73). Vienna: Springer-Verlag.

Marcus, G. E. (1994). *Perilous states: Conversations on culture, politics, and nation.* Chicago: University of Chicago Press.

Marshall, T. H. (1950). *Citizenship and social class.* Cambridge, England: Cambridge University Press.

Martin Barbero, J. (1993). *Communication, culture and hegemony: From the media to mediations.* London: Sage.

Martinez, R. (1992). *The other side: Notes from the new L.A., Mexico City, and beyond.* New York: Vintage.

Marx, K. (1904). *A contribution to the critique of political economy.* Chicago: Charles H. Kerr.

Marx, K. (1978a). The German ideology. In R. C. Tucker (Ed.), *The Marx-Engels reader* (pp. 146-200). New York: W. W. Norton. (Original work published 1932)

Marx, K. (1978b). On the Jewish question. In R. C. Tucker (Ed.), *The Marx-Engels reader* (pp. 26-52). New York: W. W. Norton. (Original work published 1843)

Marx, K. (1978c). Grundrisse. In R. C. Tucker (Ed.), *The Marx-Engels reader* (pp. 221-293). New York: W. W. Norton. (Original work published 1939)

Marx, K. (1978d). Capital. In R. C. Tucker (Ed.), *The Marx-Engels reader* (pp. 294-442). New York: W. W. Norton. (Original work published 1867)

Marx, K., & Engels, F. (1935). The manifesto of the communist party. In *Selected works* (pp. 204-241). Moscow: Cooperative Publishing House of Foreign Workers in the USSR.

Massey, D. (1991). A global sense of place. *Marxism Today,* pp. 24-29.

Massey, D. (1993). Power-geometry and a progressive sense of place. In J. Bird, B. Curtis, T. Putnam, G. Robertson, & L. Tickner (Eds.), *Mapping the futures: Local cultures, global change* (pp. 59-69). London: Routledge.

Mattelart, A., & Cesta, Y. S. (1985). *Technology, culture and communication: A report to the French Minister of Research and Industry* (D. Buxton, Trans.). Amsterdam: North-Holland.

Mattelart, A., & Mattelart, M. (1992). *Rethinking media theory.* Minneapolis: University of Minnesota Press.

McClellan, S. (1992). Gearing up for green coverage. *Broadcasting, 122*(22), 14-16.

McCoy, M., & McCully, P. (1993). *The road from Rio: Am NGO action guide to environment and development.* Utrecht, The Netherlands: International Books/Wise.

McGrew, A. (1992). A global society. In S. Hall, D. Held, & T. McGrew (Eds.), *Modernity and its futures* (pp. 61-116). Cambridge, England: Polity Press.

McLuhan, M. (1964). *Understanding media: The extensions of man.* New York: New American Library.

McQuail, D. (1992). *Media performance, mass communication and the public interest.* London: Sage.

McQuail, D., de Mateo, R., & Tapper, H. (1992). A framework for analysis of media changes in Europe in the 1990s. In K. Siune & W. Truetzschler (Eds.), *Dynamics of media politics* (pp. 8-27). London: Sage.

McRae, K. D. (1983). *Conflict and compromise in multilingual societies: Switzerland.* Waterloo, Ontario: Wilfrid Laurier University Press.

Medina, C. (1991). The journalist as a cultural reader. In J. M. de Melo (Ed.), *Communication and democracy: Brazilian perspectives* (pp 195-206). Sao Paulo: ECA/USP.

Melucci, A. (1989). *Nomads of the present: Social movements and individual needs in contemporary society.* London: Hutchinson.

Mendes, C. (1992). Peasants speak: Chico Mendes—The defence of life. *Journal of Peasant Studies, 20*(a), 160-76.

Meyers, M. (1992). Reporters and beats: The making of oppositional news. *Critical Studies in Mass Communication, 9*(1), 75-90.

Meyrowitz, J. (1985). *No sense of place: The impact of electronic media on social behavior.* New York: Oxford University Press.

Meyrowitz, J. (1989). The generalized elsewhere. *Critical Studies in Mass Communication, 6*(3), 327-134.

Mill, J. S. (1974). *On liberty.* London: Penguin. (Original work published 1859)

Mires, F. (1989). La crisis del internacionalismo [The crisis of internationalism]. *Servicio Mensual de Informacioin y Documentacion, 113,* 17-20.

MNMMR & IBASE. (1989). *Crianças e adolescente no Brazil: A vida silenciada* [Children and adolescents in Brazil: The silenced life]. Rio de Janeiro: IBASE.

MNMMR/IBASE/NEV-USP. (1991). *Vidas em risco* [Lives at risk]. Rio de Janeiro: IBASE.

Modelski, G. (Ed.). (1979). *Transnational corporations and world order.* San Francisco: W.H. Freeman.

Mohanty, C. T. (1992). Feminist encounters: Locating the politics of experience. In M. Barrett & A. Phillipps (Eds.), *Destabilizing theory* (pp. 74-92). Cambridge, England: Polity Press.

Montesquieu, C. de S. (1989). *The spirit of laws* (A. M. Cohler, B. C. Miller, & H. S. Stone, Trans.). Cambridge, England: Cambridge University Press. (Original work published 1748)

Morgan, R. (1984). *Sisterhood is global: The international women's movement anthology.* New York: Anchor Press/Doubleday.

Morley, D. (1980). *The nationwide audience: Structure and decoding.* London: British Film Institute.

Morley, D. (1992). *Television audiences and cultural studies*. London: Routledge.

Morley, D. (1993). Active audience theory: Pendulums and pitfalls. *Journal of Communication, 43*(4), 13-19.

Morley, D., & Robins, K. (1989). Spaces of identity: Communications technologies and the reconfiguration of Europe. *Screen, 30*(4), 10-34.

Motamed-Nejad, K. (1979). The story-teller and mass media in Iran. In H. D. Fischer & S. R. Melnick (Eds.), *Entertainment: A cross-cultural examination* (pp. 43-61). New York: Hastings House.

Mouffe, C. (1988). Radical democracy: Modern or post-modern? (P. Hodenberger, Trans.). In T. Mastnak & R. Riha (Eds.), *The subject in democracy* (pp. 9-20). Ljubljana, Slovenia: Delavska enotnost, for Institut Za Marksisticne stuije ZRC SAZU.

Mowlana, H. (1994). Shapes of the future: International communication in the 21st century. *Journal of International Communication, 1*(1), 14-32.

Mowlana, H., & Wilson, L. (1990). *The passing of modernity*. New York: Longman.

Murdock, G. (1992). Citizens, consumers, and public culture. In M. Skovmand & K. C. Schroder (Eds.), *Media cultures* (pp. 17-41). London: Routledge.

Murdock, G. (1993). Communications and the constitution of society. *Media, Culture and Society, 15*(4), 521-572.

Music Business International. (1993). *Music Business International, 5*, 3.

Myerhoff, B. (1980). Re-membered lives. *Parabola, 5*(1), 74-78.

NACLA Report on the Americas. (1993a). Letters. *NACLA Report on the Americas, 27*(1), 2, 46.

NACLA Report on the Americas. (1993b). Letters. *NACLA Report on the Americas, 27*(2), 46-47.

NACLA Report on the Americas. (1993c). Letters. *NACLA Report on the Americas, 27*(3), 2, 45.

Negrine, R., & Papathanassopoulos, S. (1991). The internationalization of television. *European Journal of Communication, 6*(1), 9-33.

Negt, O., & Kluge, A. (1993). *Public sphere and experience: Analysis of the bourgeois and proletarian public sphere*. Minneapolis: University of Minnesota Press. (Original work published 1978)

Negus, K. (1992). *Producing pop: Culture and conflict in the popular music industry*. London: Edward Arnold.

Negus, K. (1993). Global harmonies and local discords: Transnational policies and practices in the European recording industry. *European Journal of Communication, 8*(3), 295-316.

North and South hold environment hostage. (1992, June 3). *The Seattle Times*, p. A3.

Nozick, R. (1974). *Anarchy, state and utopia*. New York: Basic Books.

Nussbaum, M. (1992). Human functioning and social justice. *Political Theory, 20*(2), 202-246.

Oakeshoot, M. (1975). *Hobbes on civil associations*. Oxford, England: Basil Blackwell.

Offe, C. (1984). *Contradictions of the welfare state.* London: Hutchinson.

Offe, C. (1987). Challenging the boundaries of institutional politics: Social movements since the 1960s. In C. S. Maier (Ed.), *Changing boundaries of the political: Essays on the evolving balance between state and society, public and private in Europe* (pp. 63-106). Cambridge, England: Cambridge University Press.

Ohmae, K. (1990). *The borderless world: Power and strategy in the interlinked economy.* London: Collins.

Ong, W. J. (1977). *Interfaces of the word.* Ithaca, NY: Cornell University Press.

Ong, W. J. (1982). *Orality and literacy: The technologizing of the word.* New York: Methuen.

On Thinking the Black Public Sphere. (1994). *Public Culture, 7,* 1.

Oxford Encyclopedic Dictionary. (1991). (J.M. Hawkins & R. Allen, eds.). Oxford: Oxford University Press.

Pap, L. (1990). The language situation in Switzerland. *Lingua, 80*(2), 109-148.

Pataki, J. (1992, July 24). Political battle in Hungary over broadcasting dismissals. *RFE/RL Research Report, 1*(30), 26.

Patterson, O. (1991). *Freedom in the making of western culture.* New York: Basic Books.

Paul, I., & Savio, R. (1993). *Global human security: A new political framework for North-South relations.* Rome: Inter Press Service.

Pearce, R. D., & Singh, S. (1992). *Globalizing research and development.* New York: St. Martin's Press.

Peeters, D. (1962). *Zo was Jan Boon* [This was Jan Boon]. Antwerpen, Belgium: Aristenonds Rockoxhus.

Pekacz, J. (1994). Did rock smash the wall? The role of rock in political transition. *Popular Music, 13*(1), 41-49.

Pepper, R., & Brotman, S. (1987). Restricted monopolies or regulated competitors? The case of the Bell Operating Companies. *Journal of Communication, 37*(1), 64-72.

Peters, J. D. (1993). Distrust of representation: Habermas on the public sphere. *Media, Culture and Society, 15*(3), 541-71.

Peterson, M.J. (1992, Winter). Transnational activity, international society, and world politics. *Millenium, 21,* 3.

Petesch, P. L. (1992). *North-South environmental strategies, costs, and bargains.* Washington, DC: Overseas Development Council.

Petras, J. (1993). Cultural imperialism in the late 20th century. *Journal of Contemporary Asia, 23*(3), 139-148.

Pickering, M. (1987). The past as a source of aspiration: Popular song and social change. In M. Pickering & T. Green (Eds.), *Everyday culture: Popular song and the vernacular milieu* (pp. 37-67). Milton Keynes, UK: Open University.

Pieterse, J.N. (1994). Fundamentalist discourses: Enemy images. *Women Against Fundamentalism, 5,* 2-6.

Plant, R. (1974). *Community and ideology: An essay in applied social philosophy.* London: Routledge and Kegan Paul.

Pool, I. de S. (1990). *Technologies without boundaries.* Cambridge, MA: Harvard University Press.

Pool, I. de S., Inose, H., Taksaki, N., & Hurwitz, R. (1984). *Communications flow: A census in the United States and Japan.* Tokyo: University of Tokyo Press.

Porter, V. (1993a). The consumer and transfrontier television. *Consumer Policy Review, 3*(3), 132-8.

Porter, V. (1993b). The freedom of expression and public service broadcasting. *Journal of Media Law and Practice, 14*(2), 46-50.

Portes, A. (1976). On the sociology of national development: Theories and issues. *American Journal of Sociology, 82*(1), 55-85.

Poster, M. (1984). *Foucault, Marxism and history: Mode of production versus mode of information.* Cambridge, England: Polity Press.

Poster, M. (1990). *The mode of information: Poststructuralism and social context.* Chicago: University of Chicago Press.

Punter, O. (1971). *Societe Suisse de radiodiffusion et television 1931-1970* [Swiss Radio and Television Institute, 1931-1970]. Lausanne: Presses Centrales.

Radojkovic, M. (1992, June). *Prehistoric stage of media in the postcommunist countries.* Paper presented to the symposium Mass Media in the Transformation of East-Central European Society, Bucharest, Romania.

Rahman, M.A. (1993). *People's self-development: Perspectives on participatory action research.* London: Zed Books.

Rakow, L. F. (1991, May). *Technology and social change: The telephone in the history of a community.* Paper presented to the International Communication Association, Chicago.

Ramseier, M. (1988). *Mundart und Standardsprache im Radio der deutschen un rätoromanischen Schweiz* [Dialect and standard language on Radio DRS]. Aarau, Switzerland: Sauerländer Verlag.

Rawls, J. (1971). *A theory of justice.* Cambridge, MA: Harvard University Press.

Rawls, J. (1993). *Political liberalism.* New York: Columbia University Press.

Reese, S. D. (1991). Setting the media's agenda: A power balance perspective. In J. A. Anderson (Ed.), *Communication yearbook* (Vol. 14, pp. 309-340). Newbury Park, CA: Sage.

Reingold, H. (1994). *The virtual community.* London: Minerva.

Richardson, K., & Corner, J. (1986). Reading reception: Mediation and transparency in viewer's accounts of a TV program. *Media, Culture and Society, 8*(4), 337-341.

Richstad, J., & Anderson, J. (Eds.). (1981). *Crisis in international news.* New York: Columbia University Press.

Rifkin, J. (1987). *Time wars: The primary conflict in human history.* New York: Simon and Schuster.

Ris, R. (1979). Dialekte und Einheitsprache in der deutschen Schweiz [Dialect and standard language in German Switzerland]. *International Journal of the Sociology of Languages, 21,* 41-61.

Robbins, B. (Ed.). (1993). *The phantom public sphere.* Minneapolis: University of Minnesota Press.

Robertson, R. (1990). Mapping the global condition: Globalization as the central concept. In M. Featherstone (Ed.), *Global culture: Nationalism, globalization and modernity* (pp. 15-30). London: Sage.

Robertson, R. (1992). *Globalization: Social theory and global culture.* London: Sage.

Robins, K. (1991). Tradition and heritage: National culture in its global context. In J. Corner & S. Harvey (Eds.), *Enterprise and heritage: Crosscurrents of national culture* (pp. 21-44). London: Routledge.

Robinson, D., Buck, E., & Cuthbert, M. (1991). *Music at the margins: Popular music and global culture diversity.* London: Sage.

Rocha, J. (1991). Introduction. In G. Dimenstein (Ed.), *Brazil: War on children* (pp. 1-15). London: Lab.

Rogers, E. M. (1976). Communication and development: The passing of the dominant paradigm. *Communication Research, 3*(2), 61-80.

Rogers, E.M. (1983). *Diffusion of innovations* (3rd ed.). New York: The Free Press.

Rorty, R. (1983). Postmodernist bourgeois liberalism. *The Journal of Philosophy, 80*(1), 585-598.

Rorty, R. (1989). *Contingency, irony, and solidarity.* Cambridge, England: Cambridge University Press.

Rorty, R. (1994). The grandeur and twilight of radical universalism. *Thesis Eleven, 37,* 119-127.

Rosenau, J. N. (1984). A pre-theory revisited? World politics in an era of cascading interdependence. *International Studies Quarterly, 28*(3), 245-306.

Rosenau, J. N. (1990). *Turbulence in world politics.* Princeton, NJ: Princeton University Press.

Rucht, D. (1990). Strategies and action repertoires of new movements. In R. Dalton & M. Kuechler (Eds.), *Challenging the political order: New social and political movements in Western democracies.* Cambridge, England: Polity Press.

Rutkowski, A. (1994). Signature block used on e-mail posted to public lists on net during 1994.

Rutten, P. (1991). Local popular music on the national and international markets. *Cultural Studies, 5*(3), 294-305.

Sacks, R. (1992). *Place, modernity and the consumer's world.* Baltimore: The Johns Hopkins University Press.

Said, E. (1995, February 1). Orientalism revisited. *Times Literary Supplement.*

Sakamoto, Y. (1991). The global context of democratization. *Alternatives, 16,* 119-128.

Saukko, P. (1993). Identiteetin rajankayntia: Oranssi-liike journalismin ja aktivistien tulkinnoissa [Negotiating boundaries of identity: The Orange movement as interpreted by journalism and its activists]. *Tiedotustutkimus* [Mass Communication Research], *16*(3), 3-16.

Saxer, U. (1989). Kommunikationsprobleme in der Mehrsprachigen Schweiz [Communication problems in multilingual Switzerland]. In *Proceedings of the seminar Regionalsprache und Massenkommunikation* [Regional language and mass communication]. Bern: UNESCO.

Scannell, P. (1992). Public service broadcasting and modern public life. In P. Scannell, P. Schlesinger, & C. Sparks (Eds.), *Culture and power* (pp. 317-348). London: Sage.

Scheper-Hughes, N. (1992). *Death without weeping: The violence of everyday life in Brazil.* Berkeley: University of California Press.

Schiller, H. (1991). Not yet the post-industrialist era. *Critical Studies in Mass Communication, 8*(1), 13-28.

Schiller, H. (1993). Not yet the post-imperialist era. In C. Roach (Ed.), *Communication and culture in war and peace* (pp. 97-116). Newbury Park, CA: Sage.

Schlapfer, R., Gutzwiller, J., & Schmid, B. (1991). *Das Spannungsfeld zwischen Mundart und Standarsprache in der Deutschen Schweiz Spracheinstellung einiger deutsch und Welshschweizer: Eine Auswertung Rekrutenprüfungen 1985* [The area of tension between dialect and standard language in German-Switzerland: Language attitudes of some German- and Welsh-Swiss—Results of research among military recruits]. Aarau, Switzerland: Sauerländer Verlag.

Schlesinger, P. (1990). Rethinking the sociology of journalism: Source strategies and the limits of media-centrism. In M. Ferguson (Ed.), *Public communication* (pp. 61-82). London: Sage.

Schlesinger, P. (1991). *Media, state and nation: Political violence and collective identities.* London: Sage.

Schoenfeld, A. C., Meier, R. F., & Griffin, R. J. (1979). Constructing a social problem: The press and the environment. *Social Problems, 27*(1), 38-61.

Schudson, M. (1978). *Discovering the news: A social history of American newspapers.* New York: Basic Books.

Seagal, D. (1993). Tales from the cutting-room floor. *Harper's,* pp. 50-58.

Sepstrup, P. (1991). *Transnationalization of television in Western Europe.* London: John Libbey.

Servaes, J. (1992). Europe 1992: The audiovisual challenge. *Gazette, 49*(1-2), 75-97.

Shankman, P. (1984). The thick and the thin: On the interpretive theoretical program of Clifford Geertz. *Current Anthropology, 25,* 261-279.

Shinar, D. (1987). *Palestinian voices: Communication and nation-building in the West Bank.* Boulder, CO: Lynne Riemer.

Shinar, D., Olsthoorn, J., & Yalden, C. (1990). *Dis-membering and remembering: An improved conceptual framework for the analysis of communications in socio-cultural change.* Montreal: Concordia University Press.

Shiva, V. (1993). The greening of the global reach. In J. Brecher, J. B. Childs, & J. Cutler (Eds.), *Global vision: Beyond the new world order* (pp. 53-60). Boston: South End Press.

Shoemaker, P. (1984). Media treatment of deviant political groups. *Journalism Quarterly, 61*(1), 66-75.

Sieber, P., & Sitta, H. (1986). *Mundart und Standardsprache als Probleme der Schule* [Dialect and standard language as a problem for schools]. Aarau, Switzerland: Sauerländer Verlag.

Silverstone, R., & Hirsch, E. (1992). *Consuming technologies: Media and information in domestic spaces* (pp. 15-32). New York: Routledge.

Singh, K. J. (1979). Gandhi and Mao as mass communicators. *Journal of Communication, 29*(3), 94-101.

Sklair, L. (1991). *Sociology of the global system.* New York: Harvester Wheatleaf.

Smith, A. (1983). Ethnic identity and nationalism. *History Today, 33,* 47-50.

Smith, A. (1989). Public interest and telecommunications. In P. R. Newberg (Ed.), *New directions in telecommunications policy* (pp. 334-358). Durham, NC: Duke University Press.

Smith, A. (1990). Towards a global culture? *Theory, Culture and Society, 7*(2-3), 171-193.

Smith, A. (1992). Nationalism and the historians. In A. D. Smith (Ed.), *Ethnicity and nationalism* (pp. 58-80). Leiden, The Netherlands: E. J. Brill.

Sonderegger, S. (1985). Die Entwicklung des Verhéltnisses von Standardsprache und Mundarten in der deutschen Schweiz [The evolution of the relation between standard language and dialects in German Switzerland]. In W. Besch, O. Reichmann, & S. Sonderegger (Eds.), *Sprachgeschichte: Ein Handbuch zue Geschichteder Deutschen Sprache und Ihre Erforschung* [Language history: A handbook for the history of the German language and its study] (pp. 1873-1939). Berlin: De Gruyter.

Spybey, T. (1992). *Social change, development and dependency.* Cambridge: Polity Press.

Sreberny-Mohammadi, A. (1991). The global and the local in international communications. In J. Curran & M. Gurevitch (Eds.), *Mass media and society* (pp. 118-138). London: Edward Arnold.

Sreberny-Mohammadi, A. (1994a). *Women, media and development in a global context.* Paris: UNESCO.

Sreberny-Mohammadi, A. (1994b). Women talking politics. In *Broadcasting standards council research working paper IX: Perspectives of women in television* (pp. 60-80). London: Broadcasting Standards Council.

Sreberny-Mohammadi, A., & Mohammadi, A. (1994). *Small media, big revolution: Culture, communication and the Iranian revolution.* Minneapolis: University of Minnesota Press.

Steenbergen, B., van (1992, July). *Towards a global ecological citizen: Citizenship and nature, a pair apart?* Paper presented to the symposium on Recent Developments in Environmental Sociology, Woudschoten, Netherlands.

Stefanik, N. (1993). Sustainable dialogue/sustainable development. In J. Brecher, J. B. Childs, & J. Cutler (Eds.), *Global visions: Beyond the new world order* (pp. 263-272). Boston: South End Press.

Stocking, H., & Leonard, J. P. (1990, November/December). The greening of the press. *Columbia Journalism Review,* 37-44.

Stokes, M. (1991, November). *The arabesque debate.* Paper presented to the Institute of Popular Music, Liverpool University, Liverpool, England.

Strauss, L. (1973). The problem of political philosophy. In *What is Political Philosophy?* (pp. 9-27). Westport, CT: Greenwood Press.

Street, J. (1986). *Rebel rock, politics and popular music.* Oxford: Blackwell.

Streeter, T. (1990). Beyond freedom of speech and the public interest: The relevance of critical legal studies to communication policy. *Journal of Communication, 4*(2), 43-63.

Stroop, J. P. A. (1991, November). *Welk Nederlands na 1992?* [Whither Netherlands after 1992?]. Paper presented to the conference Het Nederlands na 1992 [The Netherlands after 1992]. Amsterdam.

Stroop, J. P. A. (1992). *Weg standaardtaal: De nieuwe koers van het Nederlands* [Standard language out: The new course for the Netherlands]. *Onze Taal, 61*(9), 179-182.

Swift, A. (1991). *Brazil: The fight for childhood in the city.* Florence: UNICEF.

Tagg, P. (1990). Music in mass media studies. In K. Roe & U. Carlsson (Eds.), *Popular music research* (pp. 103-114). Gothenburg, Sweden: Nordicom.

Tagg, P., & Clarida, R. (n.d.). *Ten little tunes.* Unpublished manuscript.

Taussig, M. (1993). *Mimesis and alterity: A particular history of the senses.* New York: Routledge.

Taylor, C. (1989a). *Sources of the self.* Cambridge, MA: Harvard University Press.

Taylor, C. (1989b). Cross-purposes: The liberal-communitarian debate. In Rosenblum (Ed.), *Liberalism and the moral life* (pp. 159-182). Cambridge, MA: Harvard University Press.

Taylor, C. (1993). The motivation behind a procedural ethic. In R. Beiner & W. J. Booth (Eds.), *Kant and political philosophy* (pp. 337-360). New Haven, CT: Yale University Press.

Tehranian, M. (1979). Iran: Communication, alienation, revolution. *InterMedia, 7*(2), March, 6-12.

Temple, D. (1988). On economicide. *Interculture, 98,* 36-47.

Thompson, J. (1993). The theory of the public sphere. *Theory, Culture and Society, 10*(3), 173-189.

Thompson, J.B. (1994). Social theory and the media. In D. Crowley & D. Mitchell (Eds.), *Communication theory today.* London: Polity Press.

Thompson, J.B. (1995). *The media and modernity.* London: Policy Press.

Tocqueville, A. de. (1945). *Democracy in America* (Vol. 1 & 2, P. Bradley, Ed.). New York: Alfred A. Knopf. (Original work published 1834-1840)

Tomlinson, J. (1991). *Cultural imperialism.* Baltimore: The Johns Hopkins University Press.

Tomlinson, J. (1995). Homogenisation and globalisation. *History of European Ideas, 20*(4-6), 891-897.

Totok, W. (1992, August). Rolul mediilor de informare [The role of information media]. *Revista, 22,* 7-13.

Touraine, A. (1992). *Critique de la modernite* [Critique of modernity]. Paris: Fayard.

Transnationals Information Exchange. (1993, December). Car and society conference. *TIE Bulletin,* p. 1.

Tuan, Y. (1977). *Space and place: The perspective of experience.* Minneapolis: University of Minnesota Press.

Tudoran, D. (1992, August). Viata politica romaneasca: Mass media in perioda de tranzitie [The Romanian political life: Mass media in the transition period]. *Revista, 22,* 7-13.

Turner, B. (1994). *Orientalism, post-modernism and globalism.* London: Routledge.

Turner, V. (1964). Betwixt and between: The liminal period in "rites de passage." In J. Helm (Ed.), *Proceedings of the American Ethnological Society for 1964* (pp. 4-20). Seattle: American Ethnological Society.

Turner, V. (1968). Myth and symbol. In *International Encyclopedia of Social Sciences, X,* 576-582.

Turner, V. (1969). *The ritual process.* New York: Aldine de Gruyter.

Turner, V. (1977). Process, system and symbol: A new anthropological synthesis. *Daedalus, 106*(3), 61-80.

Turner, V. (1986). *The anthropology of performance.* New York: P.A.J.

Ugboajah, F. U. (1974). *Mass communication in African traditional societies.* Paper presented to the IBI Regional Seminar, Ibadan, Nigeria.

Uncle Sam's super-highway. (1994, January 13). *Financial Times,* 13.

Unger, R. M. (1983). *The critical legal studies movement.* Cambridge, MA: Harvard University Press.

Union of International Associations. (1992). *Yearbook of international organizations, 1992/93.* München: K. G. Saur.

Urry, J. (1990). The end of organized capitalism. In S. Hall & M. Jacques (Eds.), *New times: The changing face of politics in the 1990s* (pp. 94-102). New York: Verso.

The Uses. . . . (1991). *The Economist.*

U.S. Congress. (1994). Proposed telecommunications infrastructure bill, S. 1822. Washington, DC: Government Printing Office.

U.S. Information Agency. (1993). *USIA World, 11*(4). Washington, DC: Author.

van Gennep, A. (1960). *The rise of passage.* London: Routledge and Kegan Paul.

Van den Bulck, H. (1995). Media, taal en identiteit: Media afhankelijkheid en het belang van de eigen taal in de identiteit van kleine taalge-meenschappen in Europe. Het Vlaamse Voorbeeld [Media dependency and the importance of an indigenous language for the identity of minor language communities in Europe. The Flemish instance.] In P. Rutten & M. Hamers-Regimbal (Eds.), *Sommatie 92: Internationalisering in massa-communicatie en culturele identiteit [Internationalisation in mass communication and cultural identity]* (pp. 111-126). Nijmegen: Instituut voor Toegepaste Sociale Wetenschappen.

van Dijk, T. (1988). *News analysis: Case studies in international and national news in the press.* Hillsdale, NJ: Erlbaum.

Van Elderen, P. (1986). Pop and government policy in the Netherlands. In S. Frith (Ed.), *World music, politics and social change.* Manchester: Manchester University Press.

Van Poecke, L. (1996). Media, culture and identity formation in the light of post-modern invisible socialisation. *Communicatie.*

Van Poecke, L., & Van den Bulck, H. (1993). National language, identity and culture in the light of the increasing globalization of media culture. *Communicare, 12*(1), 5-23.

Vargas, E. (1992). *UNCED and the media—Proceedings: Environmental Screening Conference for UNCED.* New York: Third World Television Exchange.

Venturelli, S. (1993). The imagined transnational public sphere in the European Community's broadcast philosophy: Implications for democracy. *European Journal of Communication, 8*(4), 491-518.

Virilio, P. (1986). *Speed and politics: An essay on dromology* (M. Polizzotti, Trans.). New York: Semiotext(e).

Walker, R. B. J. (1991). On the spatiotemporal conditions of democratic practices. *Alternatives, 16,* 243-62.

Walker, R. B. J. (1993). *Inside/outside: International relations as political theory.* Cambridge, England: Cambridge University Press.

Wallerstein, I. (1974). *The modern world system.* New York: Academic Press.

Wallerstein, I. (1979). *The capitalist world-economy.* New York: Cambridge University Press.

Wallerstein, I. (1984). *The politics of the world-economy: The states, the movements, and the civilizations.* New York: Cambridge University Press.

Wallerstein, I. (1990). Culture as the ideological battleground of the modern world-system. In M. Featherstone (Ed.), *Global culture* (pp. 31-55). London: Sage.

Wallerstein, I. (1991). *Geopolitics and geoculture.* Cambridge, England: Cambridge University Press.

Wallerstein, I. (1992). Culture as the ideological battleground of the modern world-system. In M. Featherstone (Ed.), *Global culture: Nationalism, globalization and modernity* (pp. 31-57). London: Sage.

Wallis, R., & Malm, K. (1992). *Musical activity and media policy.* New York: Routledge.

Wallis, R., & Malm, K. (1984). *Big sounds from small peoples.* London: Constable.

Walsh, R. (1992). Psychology and human survival: Psychological approaches to contemporary global threats. In S. Staub & P. Green (Eds.), *Psychology and social responsibility: Facing global challenges* (pp. 59-85). New York: New York University Press.

Walters, R. G. (1980). Signs of the times: Clifford Geertz and historians. *Social Research, 47*(3), 537-56.

Walzer, M. (1992). The civil society argument. In C. Mouffe (Ed.), *Dimensions of radical democracy* (pp. 89-107). London: Verso.

Wang, G., & Dissanayake, W. (1984). *Continuity and change in communication systems.* Norwood, NJ: Ablex.

Wasser, F. (1995). Is Hollywood America? The transnationalization of the American film industry, *Critical Studies in Mass Communication, 12*(4), 423-437.

Waterman, P. (1988). The new internationalisms: A more real thing than big, big Coke? *Review, 11*(3), 289-328.

Waterman, P. (1989). For the liberation of internationalism: A long march through the literatures. *Alternatives, 14*(1), 5-47.

Waterman, P. (1992). *International labour communication by computer: The Fifth International?* (Working Paper #129). The Hague: Institute of Social Studies

Waterman, P. (1993). *Globalization, civil society, solidarity: The politics and ethics of a world both real and universal.* The Hague: Institute of Social Studies.

Weber, M. (1930). *The Protestant ethic and the spirit of capitalism* (T. Parsons, Trans.). London: Allen & Unwin.

Weber, M. (1946). *From Max Weber: Essays in sociology* (H. H. Gerth & C. Wright Mills, Trans.). New York: Oxford University Press.

White, S.A., Nair, K.S., & Ashcroft, J. (Eds.). (1994). *Participatory communication: Working for change and development.* Thousand Oaks, CA: Sage.

Wicke, P. (1991, July). *The role of popular music in world changes.* Paper presented to the International Association for the Study of Popular Music, Berlin.

Wicke, P. (1992a). The times they are a-changing: Rock music and political change in East Germany. In R. Garofalo (Ed.), *Rockin' the boat: Mass music and mass movements* (pp. 81-92). Boston: South End Press.

Wicke, P. (1992b). The role of rock music in the political disintegration of East Germany. In J. Lull (Ed.), *Popular music and communication* (2nd ed., pp. 196-206). Beverly Hills: Sage.

Wilkins, L., & Patterson, P. (1987). Risk analysis and the construction of news. *Journal of Communication, 37*(3), 80-92.

Wilkins, L., & Patterson, P. (1990). Risky business: Covering slow-onset hazards and rapidly developing news. *Political Communication and Persuasion, 7*(1), 11-24.

Willetts, P. (Ed.). (1982). *Pressure groups in the global system.* London: Frances Pinter.

Willis, P. (1978). *Profane culture.* New York: Routledge.

Willis, P. (1990). *Common cultures: Symbolic work at play in the everyday cultures of the young.* Milton Keynes, UK: Open University Press.

Wilson, T. (1993). *Watching television: Hermeneutics, reception and popular culture.* Cambridge, England: Polity Press.

With time waning, Europeans reject U.S. movie compromise. (1993, December 14). *New York Times*, p. 1.

Wober, J. M. (1990). Language and television. In H. Giles & W. P. Robinson (Eds.), *Handbook of language and social psychology* (pp. 561-582). Chichester, UK: Wiley.

Worsley, P. (1984). *The three worlds: Culture and world development.* Chicago: The University of Chicago Press.

Wouters, C. (1990). *Van minnen en sterven: Informalisering van omgangsvormen rond seks en dood* [About courting and dying: Informalization of manners regarding sex and death]. Amsterdam: Bert Bakker.

Young, I. M. (1990). The ideal of community and the politics of difference. In L. Nicholson (Ed.), *Feminism and postmodernism* (pp. 300-323). London: Routledge.

Zolberg, A. R. (1980). Strategic interactions and the formation of modern states: France and England. *International Social Science Journal, 32*, 687-716.

Zolberg, A. R. (1991). Bounded states in a global market: The uses of international labor migrations. In P. Bourdieu & J. S. Coleman (Eds.), *Social theory for a changing society* (pp. 301-324). Boulder, CO: Westview Press.

Author Index

Subject Index

al and real life, 72
mediation of, 69-76; *see also*
Global experience

F

Familiarity, with world political
leaders, 72
"Father knows best" policy, of
Flemish and German-Swiss
Public Service Broadcasting, 165
Finland
political parties in, 250n; *see
also* Orange youth movement
Flemish community(ies)
ethnolinguistic identities in, 158-
161
modernity/national project in,
170-171
national identity in, formation of,
161, 161n
postmodernity and, 173-174
Public Service Broadcasting
language policy for, 165-67
self-identification of, 161-162
Forests
as environmental issue in Rio
de Janeiro, 202
as topic at Rio Earth Summit, 214
Framing, description of, 171
Freedom
to breach rules, 173-174
for ethnos/demos, 129
mystification of, 139-140
source of, 113-114
Funding, as topic at Rio Earth
Summit, 215

G

GATT; *see* General Agreement on
Tariffs and Trade
GDR; *see* German Democratic
Republic
GEF; *see* Global Environmental
Facility

General Agreement on Tariffs and
Trade (GATT), 32, 107, 130
German Democratic Republic (GDR)
changes and music in, 189-190
German-Swiss, description of, 158n
German-Swiss community(ies)
ethnolinguistic identities in, 158-
161
linguistic identity in, 162
modernity/national project in,
170-171
postmodernity and, 173-174
Public Service Broadcasting
language policy for, 167-169
self-identification in, 162-163
Global
redefining of, 41, 41n
terminology of, 1, 4
Global alternatives
complex, 49-50
Global awareness, local lifestyle
and, 74-76
Global capitalist, 55; *see also*
Earth citizen
Global challenges, 245
Global civil society, 54-55, 198
Global cultural ecumene, national
policy making in, 16-17
Global culture
from cultural globalization to,
51-53
media charisma and, 141-149
Global Environmental Facility
(GEF), 202
Global experience, modernity and,
63-65, 85-87
awareness/lifestyle, 74-76
globalization of place, 65-69
globalized communities, 76-85
mass-mediated communities,
79-85
mediation of experience, 69-76
mode of media awareness, 71-74
risks, 77-79